OBODA-DUBČEK-ČERN

THE PRAGUE SPRING

FREEDOM HOUSE

Freedom House is an independent organization that places human freedom in the broad context of individual rights and global politics. Freedom House believes that civil rights at home and advocacy of human rights abroad depend upon American power, its prestige, and its human values.

In international affairs, these values concentrate our attention on violations of human rights by tyrants on the right as well as the left of the political spectrum. At home, our values stress the need to provide all citizens equality of opportunity, not only in law but in daily civic and private performance.

Freedom House has a very active program that includes bimonthly and annual publications, public advocacy, press conferences, lecture series, and research of political rights and civil liberties in every country.

PERSPECTIVES ON FREEDOM

This publication is one in a series of Perspectives on Freedom. The separate publications differ in topic, in the method of examination, in length, but each is intended to illuminate some aspect of freedom endangered. The series represents one aspect of the extensive program of Freedom House. The views expressed are those of the authors and not necessarily those of the Board of Freedom House.

THE PRAGUE SPRING: A MIXED LEGACY

Edited by Jiri Pehe

Perspectives on Freedom
No. 10

First published in 1988.

Cover design by Emerson Wajdowicz Studios, N.Y.C.

Library of Congress Cataloging-in-Publication Data

The Prague Spring.

(Perspectives on freedom ; no. 10)
Includes index.
1. Czechoslovakia—History—Intervention, 1968– —
Personal narratives. 2. Czechoslovakia—Politics and
government—1945– . I. Pehe, Jiri. II. Series.
DB2232.P74   1988   943.7'04   88–16261
ISBN 0–932088–27–9 (alk. paper)
ISBN 0–932088–28–7 (pbk. : alk. paper)

Distributed by arrangement with:

UPA, Inc.
4720 Boston Way
Lanham, MD 20706

3 Henrietta Street
London, WC2E 8LU England

Contents

Acknowledgments

The editor of this book wishes to thank James Finn for his invaluable comments, judgment, suggestions and editorial guidance; Mark Wolkenfeld for his contribution to, and unyielding concern for, the style of the book and for his editorial assistance; Linda Stevenson for her editorial suggestions; and Lillian Tung and Luz Vega for their good will and humor while bringing this book to life.

Introduction

ON 21 AUGUST 1968, Soviet-led armies invaded Czechoslovakia and ended the period of liberalization that came to be known as the Prague Spring and "socialism with a human face." In 1988—the 20th anniversary of the Prague Spring—the Soviet Union itself experiences an invasion: an invasion led by the ideas of the Prague Spring. What the Red army sought to destroy in Czechoslovakia twenty years ago is now conquering the Soviet Union. History has completed one of its paradoxical cycles.

The Czechs have a tradition of being in the middle of major paradoxes of history. In the 1420s they became the first Protestant nation in Europe—only to be invaded by forces representing the ruling Catholic doctrine of the times. One hundred years later, some of *their* ideas, incorporated in the teachings of the Reformation, invaded parts of Europe, and Christianity was to never be the same. Another one hundred years later, when parts of Europe had become Protestant, Czech Protestant nobles were defeated by Catholic Hapsburgs, and the nation was forcibly re-Catholicized. Though the Hussite revolution was one of the last historical events in which the Czechs *physically* fought against invaders, it also started the small nation's tradition of using *ideas* as a force capable of changing dogmas and bringing down empires. The Prague Spring falls within this tradition.

The ideas and lessons of the Prague Spring fall into two categories. The first is connected to the hopes of reform Communists that "democratic socialism" (communism) is possible. The ideas of "socialism with a human face," allege reformists, were never really tested because they were suppressed prematurely by force. That these ideas have now reached the Soviet Union may show at last, they say, that communism is capable of developing from rigid totalitarianism to a new, higher form of "socialist democracy." The second category of ideas is that of people who see the importance of 1968 not in the hope for "socialism with a human face," which they perceive as just another utopia, but in the effects that were originally unintended, or at least not fully foreseen, by the reform-minded Communist leaders. These unintended effects consist in the quick rise of a number of independent movements and ideologies which—if left unchecked—would eventually *disintegrate* the Communist system and lay the foundations of a new civic culture, and ultimately, a Western-style democracy. The Communist system cannot be really reformed, allege the protagonists of this school of thought. It is a totalitarian structure in which the elite's monopolies of economic, political and ideological power both support and permeate each other. In that sense the totalitarian system is a fragile structure. Once the central control and the repression that supports it are relaxed, the totalitarian structure begins to crumble, and this process of disintegration is not likely—and should not be allowed by independent movements—to stop at a certain point.

The Prague Spring combined both of these basic directions of thought, although during 1968 they presented themselves in a number of hues. Political choices were often overshadowed by other elements. For the Prague Spring was much more than just a political movement. It was an eruption of intellectual energy in a profoundly Western nation that had been "abducted" to the East. In a sense, the Prague Spring was an intellectual attempt at a *return* to Europe and, ultimately, to the West. It is not an accident that various attempts of East Europeans to extricate themselves from the Soviet dominance have taken place in the three Central European nations—Hungary, Czechoslovakia and Poland—whose cultural and intellectual heritage is predominantly Western. The revolts have not been aimed merely against communism, they were also aimed against the Byzantine character of values imposed on the region by the Soviet dominance.

While it is not clear whether, or how fast, the 1968 developments would have resulted in a return to a Western-style democracy, the Soviet Union could not have tolerated even the Westernized version of communism. Such communism was too unstable, too close to a Western-type socialism and, as such, it represented a threat to the very foundations of totalitarian power across the Soviet empire. It also represented an escape from the Byzantine cultural code of the empire, and ultimately from the empire itself. However unrealistic the ideas of the Prague Spring may appear to the minds of political analysts today—however doomed to be crushed from within or without—the ideas, on the whole, did not

2

represent anything more than a spontaneous *experiment in freedom*. However, given the structure of totalitarian power, that is exactly why the Soviet Union had to crush such an experiment.

The totalitarian system cannot co-exist with any degree of freedom for long. Yet, the elite may be—and various leaders have been—tempted to introduce elements of freedom into the system, hoping that while they will be able to control the process, such a move will improve the system's economic performance. However, one of the lessons of the Prague Spring is that the ruling elite in a totalitarian system may not know exactly what the permissible degree of freedom is, and for how long it can be allowed to exist in the system before the "reform" reaches the point of "no return."

For many people, the Prague Spring was a learning period which they entered with the belief that a reformed, more humane and democratic version of communism is the best they can hope for, especially because the Soviet Union would never allow a return of real democracy. For many in 1968 Czechoslovakia, as well as for many in 1981 Poland, the omnipresent, watchful eye of the Soviets put limits on their behavior. Today the ball of reform is in the center of the empire, and the ideas of the Prague Spring are acquiring a new meaning.

There are of course many differences between Czechoslovakia in 1968 and the Soviet Union of today, but there are also at least as many similarities. The main similarity is that the Communist leadership finds it necessary to initiate reforms in order to save the country from economic and political disaster. However, as the example of the Prague Spring shows, the democratization process tends to snowball and is difficult to stop, as people drawn into the reform process gradually give it a broader meaning than the leadership had intended.

The main difference between Czechoslovakia and the Soviet Union is that there is no outside power waiting at the Soviet border to stop the democratization process *if* it snowballs and the slogan of democratization grows into one asking for democracy. Such a development may appear unlikely due to another major difference between Czechoslovakia and the Soviet Union—the latter is a country with almost no democratic traditions. However, the composition of the Soviet populace, its educational level, and, yes, its level of sophistication, are now much higher than they were twenty years ago when the Soviet Union invaded Czechoslovakia. The Soviet Union has gradually been losing its character of the traditional Communist society dominated by proletarian leaders who are shielded by the pseudo-proletarian ideology. The slow but steady progress in the economy and education, and the increased exposure of the Soviet people to Western media and influences, have transformed the Soviet Union into a country in which—within and without the Party—an entire class of nonideological professionals is waiting for its chance. This class of better educated people may also understand better than their proletarian predecessors that mere democratization, without real democracy, may not be enough.

Today many people within the Soviet empire see communism as an utterly corrupt system that should be done away with. Reforms initiated by the leadership are welcome. However, many people welcome them only because the changes create social space for pushing for more than just another, though "improved," version of communism. Can the ruling elite succeed in stopping the snowballing effect before such a snowballing effect starts to disintegrate the Communist system itself? This is an untested area because, in the past, the Soviets have always stepped in and helped the embattled East European leaderships. Even in Poland in 1981, where the suppression of Solidarity was seemingly achieved solely by Polish authorities, the Polish army could not have succeeded without the moral and material support of the Soviets, and the threat of a military intervention.

The legacy of the Prague Spring is mixed: we could, in fact, speak quite accurately of the legacy of ideas and the legacy of defeat. While the legacy of ideas is now felt in the Soviet Union, Czechoslovakia remains under the spell of that other legacy. The last twenty years in Czechoslovakia have been marked by harsh oppression and by ideological and economic return to Stalinist methods. Not unlike the forcible re-Catholicization of the country in the seventeenth century, the forcible re-Stalinization of Czechoslovakia that followed the Soviet invasion of 1968 led to a "dark age."

The Czechs have turned away from public matters to privacy. Their passivity has become not only a means of survival but also of sabotaging the economic, political and ideological efforts of the neo-Stalinist regime. As a result, both the system and the nation have suffered, each in its own way. Communist rulers have presided over an unprecedented economic, environmental, moral and cultural decline that has cost the Communist system an almost complete loss of legitimacy. The nation has suffered a loss of identity; its traditional civic culture has almost vanished. Twenty years after 1968, Czechoslovakia is ruled by a group of men who are despised by their nation; the nation reveres few values, including patriotism. Cynicism is prevalent within the leadership as well as the nation.

4

The humiliation following the defeat in 1968 is still very much present in the minds of the 1968 generation. Almost 400,000 people lost their jobs during the purges that followed the invasion. Many others were asked to recant their 1968 "errors" and did so out of fear for the well-being of their families or their careers, and lost self-respect. During the past twenty years, the country has become a show-case of the destructive powers of neo-Stalinism. Before World War II Czechoslovakia belonged among the ten nations with the highest standard of living in the world. Today, the country is unable to compete in the world markets. Its factories resemble museums of prewar technology; the economy is in decline. A flourishing democracy at the time when its neighbor in the West was being swept by Nazi totalitarianism, and its neighbor in the East was already under the rule of Communist totalitarianism, Czechoslovakia is now one of the most repressive regimes in the world.

Czechoslovakia has been a laboratory of all major historical forces of this century. As other Central European nations, the Czechs and Slovaks experienced a period of upsurge in nationalist feelings at the beginning of the century and eventually gained independence from the Austro-Hungarian empire. The country transformed itself into a model democracy, only to be overrun by Nazi totalitarianism. After becoming a democracy again, the country fell under the control of a totalitarian empire of the East in 1948. Czechoslovakia's attempt at the "democratization" of the Communist system resulted in the second occupation of the country within one century. Seemingly, Czechoslovakia cannot escape the effects of ideological and power designs originating outside its borders, in countries of great historical ambitions.

Yet, there is hope. While the generation of 1968 has lived with the legacy of defeat and humiliation, it has not forgotten the glory of the Prague Spring, and through it the glory of the days when Czechoslovakia was a free democratic country. As the ideas of the Prague Spring are coming back to life in the Soviet Union, the silenced generation of Czechs appears to show more courage and is accompanied by a younger generation of people with few or no memories of 1968. Destructive as the period of neo-Stalinism in Czechoslovakia has been, it has not succeeded in completely eradicating democratic traditions of the nation. A number of independent activities that have sprung up in the past few years, as well as the revival of interest in public matters, show that the Czechs are beginning to believe once again that their own political and civic activities have meaning, that they may be able to become masters of their own fate.

The reflections by writers gathered in this book on Czechoslovakia in 1968 and the twenty years that have followed assume a special meaning, especially in light of the Soviet events. They become reflections on the Soviet system and the Communist system in general. The essays describe not only the Czechoslovak reality but what a neo-Stalinist, anti-reform period may look like in the Soviet Union if the current attempt at change is stopped by force.

Among authors represented in this book are some of the chief players in the 1968 Czechoslovak drama. Others experienced the drama in exile, and have written on Czechoslovak events extensively. The book is not intended to cover the entire spectrum of change that occurred in Czechoslovakia in 1968, or all the aspects of the situation in the following twenty years. Rather, the authors reflect on topics they find important, or which they think have not been sufficiently addressed in the large number of articles and books that have been written on the Prague Spring. In the view of some of the authors, "socialism with a human face" remains a viable model for future Communist developments; others have reevaluated their views; and some have never believed in any version of Communism.

Whatever one may think about the various currents of ideas produced during the Prague Spring, and about their ability to transform or destroy the Communist system, these ideas must be grappled with as they are now again emerging in the Communist world. At a recent Freedom House symposium, the exiled Soviet writer Vassily Aksyonov said: "I knew personally some of those people who are now active participants in the glasnost process. I remember 1968, the time of invasion of Czechoslovakia, and these people were awfully irked by the action taken by Brezhnev's leadership. They felt insulted, actually insulted. They are Dubceks actually. They are fascinated with the idea of socialism with a human face. The great difference is that it has sprung up in the center of the empire." Even for those of us who are not great admirers of "Dubceks," Aksyonov's statement provides certain hope: First, a country ruled by "Dubceks" may be, at least temporarily, willing to tolerate independent ideas and their protagonists, who in turn may eventually form a real opposition. Second, the ideas and practice of socialism (communism) with a human face, however utopian and doomed in advance they may appear, fare much better than any kind of Stalinism, especially when experienced by people *inside* Communist states.

Mikhail Gorbachev, though no democrat, is not a traditional "blue collar" Communist. He seems to think that socialism with a human face—a "democratic" version of a one-Party system—is possible, and with its

help, the improvement of the economic performance of the Communist system. He seems to be aware of the ideas of the Prague Spring,
although he has not yet acknowledged openly that the Prague Spring is
a major source of his inspiration. It remains to be seen whether he is
falling for a trap that may help to destroy the system he is trying to
save, or whether the system will prove to be unchangeable and bury the
current reformers.

As at several times in their history, the Czechs—overpowered and on
the brink of a seeming assimilation by a powerful neighbor—watch their
ideas at work. Though the final results of the reform process in the Soviet
Union cannot be predicted, it is certain that the Soviet Union will become
a different country from what it was before Mikhail Gorbachev's rise
to power. The tremors of that change will change Czechoslovakia too.
Paradoxically, those tremors are the aftershocks of Czechoslovakia's Prague
Spring.

JIRI PEHE

Encounters with History
or *Une éducation sentimentale* 1938-1968

Jan Vladislav

1.

WE EACH HAVE encounters with history, because we are part of it. But most of the time we are unaware of this fact and find ourselves in a position akin to that of Molière's M. Jourdain, who spoke prose without knowing it. All the greater his surprise, therefore, when he discovered this to be the case. At that point he started to put on airs, but it did nothing to improve his prose.

The modern world was equally surprised when it discovered that it was capable of making history. In places, its vanity swelled out of all proportion, just like that of M. Jourdain. Nor does the discovery seem to have done anything to improve people's understanding of history. Far too many statesmen, journalists and, particularly, propagandists believe that they can know in advance what will be recorded as history, and in what direction their version of history will go. This false certainty prevents them from perceiving the real future as it creeps up noiselessly or actually crouches nearby unobserved. But the future can and often does creep out of quite neglected corners of history that we have not previously noticed.

After all, history is not a set of facts which can be arranged like pictures or sculptures in a museum, or that can be explored one by one like the castles of the Loire. It is not a *donnée,* nor a thing, nor a trail blazed in advance. It is much more like a set of possible trails, a collection of ideas about how things used to be—or better still: a number of working hypotheses. They are hypotheses, though they differ from working hypotheses in physics, say, in that they can be neither proved nor disproved. Not even those experiments carried out on society in accordance with theories—experiments that smack of vivisection—provide any proof.

Whatever their results, there is no way they can be checked. Since their conditions cannot be recreated even approximately, such experiments just disappear forever in the well of history.

What is even more astonishing is how, in the most important respect—in practice—people forget that history is fundamentally a hypothesis. Working hypotheses—no matter which—are not merely used as a source of moral precepts, they are even used as the basis for practical instructions on how to change history, though time and again such practices have proved false and it has been demonstrated that

History isn't made
by those who ponder on it
or those who ignore it. History
doesn't blaze new trails, but just keeps doggedly on,
detesting easy stages; it goes neither straight
forward nor straight back, but is always changing track
and its route isn't found in any timetable.
History neither justifies
nor blames.
History is not intimate,
because it is external.
History distributes
neither caress nor whiplash
History teaches nothing
of concern to us.
And to realize this
makes it neither truer nor more just.

Eugenio Montale's skepticism would seem to be justified, particularly in today's world which deliberately expounds history with confidence in order to go about transforming it with all the more self-assurance. In this respect, our century looks just like an enormous stage-set for a series of often bloody historical spectacles which seek to *implement in natura* the true, and definitive version of history.

One of these historical plays has been running in serialized form in the countries of Central and Eastern Europe. To those members of the audience who watch it from outside—from the circle seats and boxes of the so-called Free World—the play could well appear interesting, even fascinating. As spectators they can indulge their various loves and hates with impunity.

Quite likely, the play's self-appointed directors—those who have convinced themselves that they know what it means and how it will end—

find it both fascinating and absorbing. However, as far as everyone else is concerned—actors with minor parts and, above all, the anonymous and defenseless individuals with walk-on parts—the history of that part of the world looks quite different. Many of them joined the play under a misapprehension or by mistake, or against their will, and with every passing day almost all of them become ever more aware, even if only in a vague and unarticulated way, of the growing gulf between the lines they are supposed to say and the reality they must experience.

The self-appointed directors are oblivious of this gulf—inevitably so, since they themselves are not on stage and look at the play through the eyes of their script, which they take to be life itself. They blame any deviations or omissions from the script on reality's wanton interference with their ideal. But the actors and those with small parts have to bear this gulf in mind with every step they take because their lives are at stake. Hence their prospects are fundamentally and, it would seem, irreconcilably different from the directors, which also explains why the two sides can scarcely reach any understanding even with the best will in the world.

It is precisely this "increased difficulty" of communication that is one of the principal themes of the Central and Eastern European historical drama in question. The theme is not a new one nor is it one confined to this particular area of the world. It crops up naturally in every society, but there are few places where it assumes such a specific form or plays such an important role as here, and in few places has it received such attention on the part of writers. How many books, essays, plays and so on, return again and again to the problem of communication between the word and the world, between thought and power?!

My earlier reference to "the best will in the world" was not a mere rhetorical device by any means. Good will is an attribute for which we would seek in vain among the self-appointed directors. The only time they display anything remotely resembling good will is when they severely feel the pinch, and then it is no more than a tactical maneuver designed to salvage as much as possible of their unchanging and remorseless script. And when all else fails, such directors save their own scripts by scribbling all over the writings of others. Take the case of Jaroslav Seifert, for instance, whose *oeuvre* in the closing decades of his life had much in common with that of the later works of Eugenio Montale, even though the two poets were unknown to each other.

In Seifert's collection *Halley's Comet* published in an extended version in 1969, pride of place is given to the long poem "Prazsky hrad" (Prague Castle), completed in July 1968. Its title is rather deceptive, though, for

11

it is not another one of Seifert's typical celebrations of Prague and its skyline. The piece is also concerned with the poet's own encounters with history. Although it is not a polemical poem, Seifert's vision of our history is naturally too personal, and hence too nonconformist, for it to coincide with the official script. So the self-appointed directors of our history had recourse to their tried and tested method for correcting reality: in the subsequent edition of *Halley's Comet* published in 1970 as part of Volume 7 of the poet's collected works, they simply ordered the deletion of three stanzas which not merely constitute the core of the poet's personal encounter with history, but also his ardent appeal for the future. In Seifert's poem, this appeal rings out from within the crowd in the courtyard of Prague Castle:

> But how I wished amid that din to
> yell out several faltering words.
> a prayer that some hand should wipe away
> the fear residing in those waiting eyes,
> for I so want to believe the time has come at last
> to call murder by its proper name of
> Murder!

> Knavery, albeit crowned with laurels
> would be knavery once more,
> lies once more lies as in days of yore.
> And brandished pistols would no more open
> innocent doors.

> But I wanted too much
> in this century and in this land
> where the illusory tree in bloom
> so quickly turns to sand.

The last lines of this censored passage of Seifert's poem "Prague Castle" sum up not just the experience of one generation but of our history throughout this century. And in their final bitterness, they are not far removed from the skeptical views on history that Montale expressed about the same time.

Montale is not only skeptical about history and its didactic role. Though a poet, he has his doubts about the power ascribed to poetry. On receiving the Nobel Prize in 1975, he declared with characteristic wit that poetry was actually something superfluous, whose sole virtue lay in never having harmed anyone so far. It was first and foremost an expression of the sort of modesty which would not come amiss in other pursuits, such as science and, above all, politics, although neither of these can claim never to have harmed anyone. But it was not merely an expression of modesty. It was a warning lest we ascribe too great a power to words, which are the raw material of poetry (and history, for that matter), power by which we are wont to be enslaved. Another poet and Nobel prizewinner, Czeslaw Milosz, also highlighted this danger when he described certain East European regimes as *logocracies*: states ruled by the *unbridled word*.

Montale's statement about poetry's superfluousness has to be accepted with reservation and in light of his skepticism about history's didactic role. If he truly had no regard for poetry it is unlikely that he would have spent his whole life writing it. And if he had absolutely no trust in history it is unlikely that he would have pondered on it in his verse. And in this respect one can also apply to him something that Seifert once wrote:

But I know, of course, all too well
that the poet must tell more
than hides within the roar of words.
That more is poetry.
Else he could not with the lever of verse
prise a bud from out its honeyed cup
or make a chill
    run down our spine
when he is stripping bare the truth.

2.

We each have encounters with history because it is part of our lives. And each of us has encountered it at least once face to face, as it were, even if these were not necessarily historic occasions. History often prefers to reveal itself to us in less conspicuous ways, such as in the form of a woman that I once caught sight of in the Excelsior Cafe in Prague shortly after an air-raid towards the end of the war—apparently crazed, with unkempt hair, harried features and an absent expression. (The cafe stood just opposite the National Museum on a site now occupied by the Parliament building.) That blankly staring woman in disarray, dressed in whatever clothes had come to hand, sat by the door on the edge of her chair with a chopper at her feet. Most likely, she was waiting for one of the lorries which in those days would take people to all parts of Bohemia and even as far afield as Moravia. There was a ban at that time on private rail travel over seventy kilometers (if I remember rightly) though people travelled all the same—to their homes, their families, their friends, or for provisions. Thus they would wait in the Excelsior and elsewhere, either by prior arrangement or "on spec" for one of those lorries powered by wood gas which used to take passengers going their way for a consideration. That distraught woman with a chopper at her feet epitomized the end of the war.

But people's encounters with history do not inevitably assume such a visual, poignant or irrational form. I recall, for instance, a young lad in a village on the eastern slopes of the White Carpathians with his ear pressed one morning to an ancient wireless, unable and unwilling to believe the news he is hearing. It was a news bulletin, though I doubt that is what they would have called it in those days. What the lad heard was a detailed report of the occupation of Prague by the German army. It was the morning of 15 March 1939 and he was alone at the time, having just come home from the railway station from which he travelled to school each day. All trains had been cancelled that morning. It is hard to say what impression the news had on that youngster with his ear glued to the radio-receiver. Not only had his childhood come to an end, but all of a sudden he realized with absurd though unwavering certainty that it was also the end of a particular world.

It was the same certainty, the certainty of an ineluctable and irredeemable end, that the same man was to feel twenty-nine years later as he heard from from a new, modern Japanese-made transistor the first announcement that the Prague underground transmitter was going off the air and taking leave of its listeners and freedom—not complete freedom, but freedom of some kind, at least. The short broadcast ended with the national anthem, that rather sentimental song that had crackled through the loudspeaker of the old wireless back in March 1939. In August 1968, that farewell broadcast, complete with the National Anthem, was to be repeated on several subsequent days! The immediate effect was heart-rending, but it gradually became almost tragicomic. Nonetheless, those were days of an exultant encounter with history. People can say what they like about the Czechs and their alleged unwillingness to fight, but those were also days of *grandeur*. And those who did not experience them cannot have the faintest idea.

Distant observers have the least idea of what these events meant. Some of those who took part in the events in Paris of May 1968 might just have experienced something similar: those who realized, either vaguely or with clarity, that maybe the time had arrived for a revolution of a new kind, one that did not seek power. For surely the forgotten and unsung revolution that occurred in Prague after the "entry of the fraternal troops" (the official euphemism) was something of the sort. It was a revolution experienced by thousands or even tens of thousands, particularly in Prague, a revolution that no one mentions, because in the eyes of politicians and historians the only true and authentic revolutions are those which involve a change of *power* and the establishment of a new regime which then asserts itself as a new fact of history. But what if the time has truly come for new revolutions, in other words, changes which are not impelled by naked power, as was the case with earlier revolutions which turned out so badly, in the long run if not immediately?

There followed further encounters with history, more than one of them ambiguous and cautionary, such as when our diminutive listener of March 1939 was to observe with his own eyes the end of the occupation, six years later. His experience of May 1945 was not always edifying, by any means. In the course of those few days, he witnessed examples not just of unprecedented sacrifice but also senseless acts of folly and mad behavior, including his own, the memory of which was to make him shudder in the later years. For the first time in his life he saw heroes, as well as his first corpses. And of course he also saw his first malingerers, men who time and again made themselves out to be hardened fighters but who would take to their heels at the sight of a solitary armored car in the distance beyond the rickety barricade across the street called *Na sekyrce*, or even a lorry with the last poor wretches in German uniform desperately trying to escape to the West.

In the end, it was one of these jumpy "heroes" who was to assume the role of executioner for a Soviet officer who ordered the shooting of several German civilians in retaliation for sniper fire from neighboring villas. It was 10 May, and the "hero" shot them in a ditch at *Borislavka* with a revolver that he had obtained from a pal on the barricade in exchange for a few packs of cigarettes. As he observed these events, our chance eye-witness was suddenly seized by a vague feeling that the terrible power that was only just collapsing was not going to disappear for good. Germs of it were lurking here and there in human breasts, just waiting for the chance to return. And the chance was soon to present itself in many cases.

These scenes too come under the heading of encounters with history. In all respects, May 1945 was first and foremost a revolution, in the sense of *a change of heart and mind.* Our eyewitness was to discover that most of his friends who, in conversation just a month earlier, had been not just full of hope at the idea of liberation but also apprehension about the form of the expected freedom, suddenly seemed to have forgotten their erstwhile fears for good, and all the more enthusiastically welcomed the new regime lock, stock and barrel, dazzled by the vision of their own participation in it. Three or four years later, they were to taste its bitterness for themselves, some of them down to the last drop.

There was another encounter with history, another small piece of glass to add to the kaleidoscope whose images occasionally assume a comical aspect. The comical encounter came in the summer of 1968, by which time the shattered boy of March 1938 and the skeptical young man of May 1945 had become a forty-five-year old man with no great illusions left. This was probably why he clung so tenaciously to the few that remained, such as the idea that truth is more likely to be found on the side of those *without* power. It was probably the same reason why, even then, in June 1968, he could not rid himself of his skepticism about what was going on, though now and then he would have qualms about it which he preferred to keep to himself. It was one night when his mind was on such matters that his thoughts were interrupted by the telephone's ring. It was a friend and distant neighbor urgently calling him to come over and see him. In those turbulent times this was nothing out of the ordinary and so, in spite of his skepticism, he did as he was bade. The phenomenon later to be called the Prague Spring was still continuing into the clear, dewy nights of early summer. "Come over in your car," his friend had told him, and he obeyed without demur. He neither expressed surprise nor asked any questions; such happenings were not altogether uncommon at that time.

They met in a broad street, unusual for its rows of plane trees. Their striped bark shone in the moonlight and recalled Cézanne and his Aix-en-Provence. All the scene lacked was a tower and a belfry. Although the friend's news was dramatic it did not astonish our eye-witness. It actually came as a relief. It was something definite at last, even if it was the news they had feared the most. In short, his friend told him that there were well-grounded fears that a Soviet invasion would take place in the next few days with some support from the local population, chiefly certain sections of the police and armed forces, and various Party officials. The information was entirely classified but verified, his friend assured him, which was why something had to be done to prevent its happening. And the first steps were already being taken. But it needed the help of more people, particularly in order to keep watch at night or make regular tours of inspection of certain areas of the city so as to keep an eye on things and report findings to a particular phone number. Our man wrote the number down and even dialed it in his disbelief: it worked. It was apparently a direct line to certain units of the army and police who were determined to prevent any invasion.

In the face of his friend's conviction and practical proposals, all doubt seemed misplaced. Besides, his friend's news sounded quite probable, and timely action might indeed prevent a palace revolution that could provide a pretext for invasion. He, therefore, did not give the matter any lengthy thought and promised his friend he would keep regular watch at the time specified. There were others rendering a similar service at different hours and in different places. Thus it came about that our man spent about a week driving around a particular neighborhood between midnight and two in the morning. But apart from observing courting couples, drunks and people hurrying home from meetings, he noticed nothing out of the ordinary. Then one evening he received another call from his friend, this time cancelling the operation. He discovered why the following day, when his friend explained that it had all been a mistake, or rather a well-intentioned and well-planned operation thought up by an acquaintance of his who was undoubtedly a brilliant mathematician but also, apparently, a bit mad. The perpetrator had just been taken into mental hospital after having succeeding in mobilizing several hundred people, including members of the armed forces and police...

That was in June. Not quite two months later, our man was awakened around two A.M. by telephone. It was the same voice again, the same friend: "They're here. I know you're not going to believe me now, but open your window and hear for yourself." Then he rang off. Our man also put the phone down and went to open the window. The room was instantly flooded with a roar that merged with the terrifying, though long forgotten, dream from which he had been awakened. The house he lived in was on the Western side of the city in the direction of the airport. There could be no doubt. And shortly afterwards came the sound of a higher pitched roar along with the clank of iron on stone. Half an hour later he was to see the tanks with his own eyes. They were rolling towards the city center. The mad mathematician had been right, but just a little premature.

It has been the fate of many people to be endowed with such pre-mature clarity of vision, as were many of the intellectuals of the 1940s and 50s. In those days, of course, they did not end up in the mental hospital but went straight to prison, unless, that is, they were tortured to death or went to the gallows. Their stories, their encounters with history, are an important part of that hidden face of our history which re-mains largely unknown both in the home country and abroad, a history that still remains to be written. One moral of all those stories would be that each of these encounters with history also challenges us to make a choice.

Let us be frank: every such encounter is a shock. Each time it is a terrifying experience, but it is also a salutary one. What is terrifying is the extent of human *powerlessness*, what is salutary is realizing the scope of unbridled *power*. Why such a shock should cause some people to make one choice and others a different one, why, after such an encounter with history, some should seek to identify with whoever is in power while others are suspicious of all regimes, teacher History does not tell us. When it comes to such a choice, where does it actually occur and why does it take the form it does? There are questions I ask in vain.

I once knew a devout rabbi who lost his faith for good during his time in a concentration camp. I know many others, who, on the contrary, found God in prison. And like all of us, I know of one man who was sentenced to life imprisonment by a regime which he had served unquestioningly. When he was subsequently released he did everything he could to win power for himself and, blinded forever by the enormous scope for action that it offered, he went on to send others to the same prison cells he had left not long before. I am afraid that Eugenio Montale is right after all when he says that history teaches us nothing that concerns us, and even when we realize this fact, it does nothing to make history more true or more just...

Translated by A.G. Brain

Recalling Days of the Invasion

Frantisek Janouch

THE TWENTIETH ANNIVERSARY of the Prague Spring and of the Soviet invasion cannot be passed in silence. Even more so because, amidst the ever louder, harsher and more frequent condemnations of the Brezhnev regime coming from the Kremlin today, the Soviet Union still does not speak about that invasion. The invasion threw a Central European nation into a long-lasting crisis whose end is not yet in sight, despite the Kremlin-inspired perestroika and glasnost.

It is our duty to keep recalling the nocturnal intervention of an army of a half-million in a peacefully sleeping country, an intervention that violated international law, the Charter of the U.N., and the provisions of the Warsaw Pact. We must continue to recall the invasion everywhere and on every occasion until a remedy is introduced.

Instead of general reflections and appeals, I have decided to publish several pages of recollections of dramatic events of August and September 1968. Perhaps in this way I can communicate our shock and powerlessness.

A Sunday afternoon

A countdown to the launch of the military invasion has started and has continued mercilessly: fifty-eight hours were left to the beginning of the tragedy. It was then that I took a friend, Frantisek Kriegel*—he was deadly tired and exhausted—for a walk in the woods south of Prague.

---

* Frantisek Kriegel, a physician by profession and member of the CP Politburo in 1968, was among the members of the leadership who were abducted to Moscow on 21 August. He was the only member of the leadership who refused to sign Moscow protocols renouncing reforms.

It was a beautiful summer afternoon: the sun shone and the forest had a pleasant smell. We rested on felled trees and talked about the future and about the possibility of occupation. Kriegel was very worried. He considered the situation serious. However, he excluded the possibility of a military intervention and occupation. The situation in Czechoslovakia, he thought, was completely different from that of Hungary in 1956. The international climate had changed considerably. He was thinking aloud about steps that Big Brother might take: an economic blockade; attempts at a coup d'etat; pushing its own people into the leadership.

Kriegel also talked about how strange a historical period we were experiencing and about the responsibility he felt for the fate of our republic. In the evening we returned to Prague. We stopped in my apartment for a cup of tea. Kriegel used the occasion to borrow a book.

"I have trouble sleeping lately and would like to have something interesting to read." I gave him Koestler's *Darkness at Noon* which I had recently brought from Switzerland. He returned the book in several days —days during which we had grown much older and wiser.

"It wasn't the best reading for the night before August 21st," said Kriegel. "When the KGB arrested me and moved me from one place to another, scenes from Koestler's book were constantly on my mind..."

The answer

It was a hot summer. We all felt inner anxiety. And we all wanted to do something...something to make sure that our worst fears would not come true. On 1 August I wrote to my friend, an important Western physicist. I wrote how I feared for the fate of my country, its sovereignty, and the future of the big experiment we had started in January.

"I would prefer to be wrong but I am afraid that our country was and is in immediate danger of a military intervention..."

I asked my friend to consider steps that Western intellectuals could take to avert such danger...His answer arrived on 21 August 1968. The mail was still being delivered on that day, at least in our district. My friend wrote:

"I received your letter on the day the newspapers announced that the danger of invasion has passed. It was a great relief for me because I was not sure that the voice of Western scientists could help in any way. Let's appreciate that now such a voice is not necessary. Dubcek was very crafty. I wish that the present situation lasts and that you avoid Polish transformations..."

As I read my friend's letter I heard the shots and thunder of tanks in the city.

Ten days later in Vienna, we embraced each other, I and my friend Weisskopf. His eyes were full of tears. So were mine.

The awakening

The telephone woke me up shortly before one A.M.

"We are being occupied," announced a familiar female voice, sounding empty and strange. "Listen to the radio and then come."

I hung up. My entire body was shaking. Through the open window, the cold air of the night was flowing into the room. Streets were still calm and silent. Prague was sleeping peacefully. The news which I had just received was so absurd and unbelievable that it could not be true: it must have been a nightmare. Desperately, I waited to wake up.

But the awakening was not coming, so I began ringing my friends, waking them up. It was an unpleasant duty, but nothing better occurred to me at that moment.

Then I set off for the city, which was still peacefully sleeping: only in its center taxis were driving around blowing their horns. I too pressed the horn of my car. In the empty streets it sounded unusually loud.

"What are we going to do?" asked a gas-pump attendant, tears in his eyes. "Our government should ask the United Nations for help!"

Large transport planes began to thunder over the city, above which dark, heavy clouds were hovering. From that heavy sky rain began to fall and to sprinkle the streets. And with heavy hearts we shed tears, tears of helplessness and hatred. Why this? Why?

It was already half past three. Our beautiful city began to wake up. But it had had no way of knowing what awaited it after the awakening: a return to a deep past, perhaps to medieval times, to the times of Tartar invasions. I felt anxiety when I realized what was awaiting my city. I felt sorry for the unrepeatable spring and summer which had just ended. And I felt sick at the thought of foreign mercenaries and tanks coming to crush the Spring under their feet, under their treads.

Three men

I was in the apartment of Dr. Kriegel. The invasion did not catch up with him at home: he was at the meeting of the Secretariat of the Central Committee of the Communist Party. Though the occupation armies were already in the city, the street *Na smetance* was still calm and empty.

At six in the morning someone rang the doorbell. Three men in raincoats were standing at the doorstep.

"Is Dr. Kriegel at home?"

21

"Who are you and what do you want?" I asked, instead of answering their question.

One of the men showed me a state security I.D.

"Dr. Kriegel is not at home. Do you want to arrest him?"

"We have a message for him," he answered, not very convincingly.

I tried to find out their intentions: "The occupants are already in the streets of the city. Are you with them or with Dubcek?"

The answer, again, was quite ambiguous: "The situation is very complicated..." Then one of the men asked whether he could use the phone.

"This is 'crow.' I am calling from the apartment of Dr. Kriegel. The order could not be executed. The end." He hung up and left with the other two.

My body began shaking again—for the second time during that fateful night. So this is what the tanks with the red stars brought us. I felt as if I was thrown back in time to the fifties. Only with one difference: now I fully understood what was going on.

Lenin Avenue

It is one of the most modern avenues in Prague. It has been finished recently and named Lenin Avenue. It connects the airport with the big round square—the Square of the October Revolution.

On 21 August, at half past four, a friend from Dejvice called: "The Russian tanks are already on Lenin Avenue. I can see them from my window." I was not able to answer. Words stuck in my throat and tears came to my eyes. I was remembering 9 May 1945, when, also early in the morning, another friend from Dejvice had called me: "Soviet tanks are already here. I can see them from my window."

Twenty-three years ago that call marked the end of hopelessness; today the call was its beginning. Between these two calls—an entire epoch.

On one of the walls outside, a sign summarizing our feelings appeared: *Your fathers were liberators—you are aggressors!*

In the afternoon I was at Lenin Avenue: new asphalt was destroyed by the treads of tanks. At the Square of the October Revolution, tanks were distributing "ideas." How big and heavy such ideas must be if the occupants needed tanks and an army of half a million soldiers armed to the teeth to distribute them.

The emotion

Around an armored vehicle, a discussion stuttered: linguistic problems were extensive. Russian was not our common language.

I joined the discussion. A moment later, a swarthy first lieutenant with a mustache became nervous. I knew fairly well not only his language but also his country. He, however, knew desperately little about the country to which he had come last night. He tried to find a way out of the discussion: "This is what you, intelligentsia, say, but what about the working class?" he asked, exactly in the spirit of political lessons from times long past.

An old worker, who had followed our discussion attentively, suddenly turned to me and said:

"Translate this to him. Do you see my hands?" (I did not have to translate that. He shoved his old, overworked hands right under the officer's nose). "We, workers, are saying the same thing, and we absolutely identify with the comrade intellectual here. Why do you meddle in our affairs?" In order not to leave any doubts in the officer's mind, he embraced me. The officer grew perplexed, and my eyes—for how many a time that day—again filled with tears.

This story makes me feel somehow awkward. However, the story happened exactly that way, book-like. It was 21 August, five o'clock in the afternoon. Italy Street. Several hundred meters farther down, from the building of Czechoslovak radio, shooting could be heard.

The flag

Porici, the first afternoon of the occupation: a demonstration was approaching from the direction of Republic Square. Several hundred marching young people sang, almost inaudibly, the national anthem. Two boys and two girls who were marching in the front row carried between them a bloodied Czechoslovak flag. People with clenched fists and tears in their eyes were standing at the sides of the street. The occupiers, resting on their tanks in front of the *Rude pravo* building, grew attentive and nervous.

An armored vehicle was coming from the Tesnov train-station. Its gun was aiming at the slow procession. The groups of onlookers grew tense. The demonstrators were not scared, however, and they did not slow down. Only the words of the national anthem grew louder.

The armored vehicle slowed down, and then—before the bloodied flag— veered to a side and stopped. The procession proceeded without hindrance.

The Moscow newspaper, *Pravda,* undoubtedly used this case as an example of the political maturity and discipline of the occupiers. However, no Soviet journalist would dare to describe what was possible to read in the faces of the Russian soldiers.

Moscow time

It was fifteen past nine, the evening of the third day of the occupation. The streets of Prague were dark, deserted and gloomy.

I was driving fast, taking home a female acquaintance. At ten P.M. the ban on outdoor activities was to go into effect—a *komendantskij cas*, as it was called by the Russians. During past days the occupants showed how seriously they observed the undeclared state of emergency. There were forty-five minutes until the beginning of the ban when we came to the Palacky Bridge. The bridge entrance was barricaded by tanks and armored vehicles. A soldier with a machine gun indicated that we had to turn back. I stopped the car and asked him to call his commander. The commander came. He was a small man with a child-like face.

"*Komendantskij cas!*" he said resolutely.

"From ten o'clock," I objected.

The officer glanced at his watch:

"It is already quarter past eleven."

Suddenly I felt superior to the tanks and the machine guns around us. "Don't you know that in Prague we have Prague time, not Moscow time? There is a two hour difference between the two, dear!"

He grew nervous and looked at his watch. "Anyway, that means that it is already a quarter past ten..."

"You should learn how to count to two before you will take command of these toys..." I responded and looked around.

"Don't be offensive!"

"You offend yourself when you don't know how to subtract two!"

The officer again glanced at the watch. Then he realized his mistake and shouted: "Vana, move one tank, we'll let this car go."

Then he looked at us and almost apologetically said: "I will let you go, but I am not certain how you'll manage at the other side of the bridge."

I waved my hand and went ahead. The idea of sleeping in the middle of the Palacky Bridge, barricaded by tanks on both ends, was not appealing.

I felt as sorry for this old, proud and cultural city, into which these Vanas came to "normalize" the situation, as I felt sorry for the young officer with the badge of the *Komsomol*—a pawn in this cynical super-power game. This was our city, and until 21 August I had considered these boys our brothers.

On a wall several blocks down the street was scrawled a popular wisdom: *Cain and Abel were also brothers.*

Silence

A line of Czech cars formed on the road in front of the railway crossing. An army jeep with several Soviet officers was among the cars. The train was not in sight. One of the officers studied a map. Then he got out of the car and asked one of the drivers the distance to Tabor.

"*Neponimaju* (I don't understand)," was the answer.

The officer did not give up and turned to another driver, who answered he did not know. The third one did not even bother to answer. He only pointed to a road sign whose big letters read: **Moscow 1,800 KM.**

Tanks

The trip toward the Austrian border took unusually long. The roads were full of Russian military transports. Tired and dusty Russian soldiers were sitting on armored vehicles, disinterested in what was going on around them.

Tanks rumbled around and the earth shook. The already bad roads were being further destroyed by tank treads. The air was full of dust, fumes and the hopelessness of a defenseless and humiliated country.

Finally, I crossed the Austrian border. Behind the border there was peace and silence. Peace could be smelled in the air. Not far from the border a police car appeared with a blue warning light on the roof. An army jeep followed. And then, a heavy carrier which—to spare the road of destruction—carried a clean tank. The scene was repeated twenty minutes later. Austria fortified its border with two tanks. I pictured the hundreds of Soviet tanks in the streets of Prague and the hundreds that I had met on the way to the border.

Perhaps nothing else could better manifest the powerlessness of small nations when confronted with the arrogance of big ones. And nothing could better demonstrate the absurdity of small nations maintaining their armies than the sight of these two Austrian tanks and carriers.

Panic

People were waiting in line at the West German Consulate in Vienna. "Please pay attention," shouted an angry pale young man in jeans. "Czech cars with Russian drivers roam around Vienna and abduct Czechoslovaks back to Czechoslovakia." The atmosphere in the room grew tense; people gathered around the young man to learn more about what he was warning them against.

I joined the discussion and expressed my doubts: "In my opinion, it is not logical. They would have to close the border first. I also don't see how they could get the people across the border without problems. It does not sound plausible."

I felt that my answer somehow relieved people of their anxiety and tension. So many alarming rumors traveled around that people were thankful for a mere attempt to refute some of the news. Later, however, I myself began to feel uncertainty. I remembered how two days before the invasion I tried to persuade my friend that the occupation of Czechoslovakia by the Soviet army would have been an absurd and illogical step, and that therefore it was not plausible.

An escape

I met him somewhere in Austria. He was depressed. He spent part of his youth in the Teresin ghetto and, his mother had perished in one of the German extermination camps. The powerlessness and hopelessness of the past days were still very much alive in his memory. The uncertainty and insecurity of the future were a burden to him.

"My grandfather escaped from Russian pogroms by fleeing from Berdicevo to Kisinev. My father fled in fear of Russian pogroms from Kisinev to Prague. And now I, for a change, once again in fear of Russian pogroms, have escaped from Prague to Austria. I would like to know when, where, and from whom, my children will be running away..."

Words and Tanks: The Revival, The Struggle, The Agony and Defeat (1968-1969)

Jiri Hochman

ONE NIGHT IN EARLY March 1968, the editors of a Prague daily newspaper took the daring decision to bypass the censors and publish a news story revealing thievery and nepotism in high Party places. The printers gladly cooperated. Under the existing system of press control their support was indispensable. Together, they carried through the idea—an unheard of act since the suppression of an independent press in Czechoslovakia twenty years before.

The newspaper was *Prace,* the official daily morning newspaper of the trade unions. The story that by-passed the censors was about the defection of a general in the Czechoslovak army who had been under investigation for wholesale black market trade stolen in grass seeds. What made the story even more sensitive was the fact that the general was a protege of the recently deposed first secretary of the ruling Communist party, who was still holding on as head of state.

The publishing of the story had an immediate, electrifying effect on all the other media in the capital and, slightly later, on those in the rest of the Czech lands. Even Slovakia, with its different conditions and priorities, did not lag behind for long.

In a few days, the agents of censorship who had for years been working in shifts around the clock on each newspaper, radio and television station quietly walked away. This collapse of censorship was in itself a phenomenon which still needs to be thoroughly examined as a part of the whole development of the Prague Spring. Censorship had been legalized in Czechoslovakia only two years earlier; and its official abolition took place four months after *Prace* breached the censorship barriers.

Journalists were not the first in the long struggle for reforms. However,

27

they still defended them months after the Soviet invasion when other groups had already given in.

It deserves to be emphasized that journalism in Czechoslovakia at that time did not function under "glasnost" as it has been practiced in the Soviet Union since 1985. In the USSR "glasnost" allows a measured relaxation of censorship. In Czechoslovakia, at least for nine out of the fourteen months of the whole drama, journalists had removed censorship altogether.

This essay will attempt to encapsulate the role of journalism and journalists in the Czechoslovak reform movement of 1968 and 1969—their revival, their struggle, their agony and defeat. It is a story of a short-lived freedom of the press in the hostile environment of the Leninist political system.

The first salvo of the Czech "artillery of the press" was fired in early March 1968. There were over 4,300 members of the Union of Czechoslovak Journalists, essentially a licensing agency in line with the Soviet political model implemented in Czechoslovakia.[1] When the last (fifth) Congress of the Union had been held in October 1967, no other information about the membership was released. More detailed figures became available in 1968. By June of that year, after three months of considerably relaxed conditions for admission, the Union's membership rose to 4,900 members. About 2,500 of them worked in Prague; another 1,000 worked in other parts of Bohemia and Moravia, namely in regional centers like Brno, Ostrava, Plzen and Hradec Kralove. The rest were members from Slovakia. An undisclosed number of Slovaks also worked in the central media in the capital.[2]

The Union of Journalists

A recent unofficial inquiry into the situation of the Union at the time of the reform movement showed that between 55 to 60 percent of the Union's members were Communists. In the central media, however, the latter category made up almost 80 percent, and almost 100 percent among senior editorial ranks. Twenty-five percent of the Union's members were women. The membership also included over 600 retirees, and some 200 media bureaucrats at various levels, including the officials working in many press departments of the central administration.[3]

Several officials from the press subdivision in the Ideological Department of the Party Central Committee (C.C.) apparatus were also members of the Union. This department was the higher instrument of media control, instructing the journalists what and how to write, and the censors what to prevent being published. That even several officials from the so-called Central Publication Administration, the censorship authority, were also members of the Union of Journalists was hardly surprising under the general circumstances. They did work in the media, didn't they?

The Union was a strictly controlled "transmission handle" of the Party policy-making bodies, the Presidium (Politburo), the Secretariat, and the C.C. apparatus. Its activities were limited largely to formal licensing of journalists and to rendering petty services to members in good standing.

At its Fifth Congress in October 1967, when the process of the gradual decay of the post-1948 political system had already reached an advanced stage, the Union still gave the impression of an entirely docile body. There were no indications that a few months later the mass of its members would wholeheartedly throw themselves into the reform movement. The delegates of the Congress passively voted an officially sponsored resolution which included the approval of the seizure of the writers' weekly, *Literarni noviny*, by a group of henchmen hired by the Party Secretariat. No voices were raised to demand a relaxation of censorship or to propose an act of solidarity with the ten editors of *Literarni noviny* who had been sacked a few months earlier.

All that, however, did not reflect either the real mood or the real opinions of the mass of journalists, including a fair proportion of the delegates attending the Congress. Even the Union's general secretary, Adolf Hradecky, whose unrewarding task consisted in following the Party's orders to steer the Congress along its humiliating course, had had a split personality for quite some time. In 1966, he had launched and since then edited, the new Union's weekly, *Reporter*, which, along with a few other publications of its type, played an important role in making way for fresh ideas.[4]

The weight of fear

The explanation of the behavior of the journalists' Congress can best be found in the general behavior of the rest of the society at that time. The principal stabilizing factor in any Communist society is fear. No successful reform movement in an established Communist system can be set in motion before important parts of the society overcome that fear. The second basic prerequisite is a divided leadership of the ruling Party, with some of the top bureaucrats being interested, for whatever reasons, in some, even very limited, changes. That occurred in Czechoslovakia in the fall of 1967 and the winter and spring of 1968.

Overcoming fear, however, is essential. It requires a certain period of relative relaxation of political and ideological restraints. In different countries of the Soviet bloc, different amounts of time have been needed to shake off this fear, produced by the rulers' previous brutalities and intolerance. The Soviet Union is undergoing its Prague Spring now, but the absence of experience with that society's behavior under comparable conditions makes it impossible to guess how long the Soviet society (and its journalists) may need before they start acting independently.

In Czechoslovakia, an uneven, occasionally interrupted process of relative moderation in internal political and ideological controls had been going on for over five years before 1968. It was taking place in a situation generally characterized by the failure of the regime to admit honestly the crimes committed during the first several years after the takeover of 1948, and to try effectively to redress them as much as possible. The situation was also characterized by the apparent incompetence of the rulers in managing the nation's affairs, particularly the economy.

During those years, scientists, writers and others pushed step by step the limits of the permissible in various fields of intellectual activity, well beyond those customary in a Leninist-type system. Frequently using indirect and implicit ways, historians and economists, philosophers and writers gradually exposed the absurdity of the system. The journalists played their role too: Much of the above activity was reflected in the media. Interviews and reviews carried the opinions of the intellectual elite to the general society. Journalists specializing in economics, in cultural affairs and in science were in the forefront of this endeavor. Since the early 1960s, when sociology was more or less rehabilitated as a science, even the state of the society started to be publicly discussed. A modest part of hidden public opinion was thus cautiously brought forth. On the other hand, independent political journalism still could not exist. For that, it was necessary to remove the censorship, and that was impossible without an open revolt.

It has to be understood that journalists were more vulnerable to the regime's intimidation than the rest of the intellectual front. First, it was easy to replace them; the Party does not need a good press, it needs an obedient press. Secondly, journalists lacked the relative independence of writers and other artists, and of many scientists. The pressure of the regime, acting through the chief editors and their deputies, through censorship and a constant flow of directives, was more immediate than in other sectors. For the journalists, an untimely revolt was tantamount to complete professional suicide. The writers' rebellion in June 1967 was obviously too early for them. The regime still seemed to be too strong and solid. That appearance changed when the division in the leadership became known in December 1967, and when it manifested itself by the removal of Antonin Novotny from the position of the Party's first secretary. Then the breakthrough came at the earliest opportunity.

The fact that most of those who launched and then carried through the journalistic revolt against the Communist regime were themselves members of the Communist party was only of secondary significance. Most of the rebellious writers and scientists were Communists, too. In Czechoslovakia, and especially in the Czech lands, the Communist party enjoyed the undeserved support of large segments of the intellectual strata since the 1930s. Political choices presented themselves in distorted and oversimplified ways throughout the whole period between the Great Depression and the rise and fall of Naziism in Germany. These attitudes, caused by abnormal situations, continued to affect the Czech political scene in the 1945-1948 period, when it was probably still not too late to prevent the coming enslavement by the Soviets. Most reform-minded journalists active in 1968 and 1969 were products of those times. Only a few, however, were truly converted to the Oriental political philosophy of Leninism, so alien to Central European traditions. "Practicing, but not believing," in the words of a Polish writer, was probably the prevailing state, especially since the introduction of the Soviet Byzantine political style in the early 1950s. For most of this generation, the implementation of the Soviet system was a historical accident in the middle of which they were trapped, together with their former political opponents and the whole society.[5]

They were striving to discern a line between socialism, which was still their creed, and the oligarchic political system which they detested. That was still their essential frame of mind when, with the breakdown of censorship in the first days of March 1968, the events started to unravel the system.

The coming of spring

As H. Gordon Skilling observes in his monumental work on the Prague Spring, *Czechoslovakia's Interrupted Revolution*, "the journalists emerged as active exponents of reform and as a powerful force without which the Prague Spring can hardly be imagined."[6] Foreshadowing this reversal were meetings of Party cells in various media outlets. At these meetings, rank-and-file members were formally informed, in the usual incomplete way, about the recent C.C. session and the election of the new first secretary, Alexander Dubcek.

The heated discussions which followed the fragmentary information in many of these meetings signaled the changing political climate. There had been virtually no discussions of a substantive nature in local cells of intellectual Party organizations since 1956, when the apparatchiki had silenced the previous movement for the de-Stalinization of the system.

31

In most cases, throughout those years, Party meetings ended without any discussion, and were reduced to an empty ritual before a passive, silent audience.

Among the meetings held in the Party cells of the central media in Prague, the stormiest took place, surprisingly, in the editorial organization of the Party's chief newspaper, *Rude pravo,* on 9 January 1968. Lasting for almost eight hours, this meeting adopted a resolution with two demands: First, that the organization be given full, and not piecemeal information about the proceedings of the last C.C. session. And second, that this information *be published.* Of over eighty editors present, only one voted against: the chief editor, O. Svestka, a member of the C.C. and later a leading pro-Soviet protagonist in the events which soon followed. There were no abstentions.

Twelve years earlier, the ideological boss Hendrych called the same group of people, in the same room, "savage petty-bourgeois elements." This time, he was not there, and Svestka was completely isolated. Even a handful of editors who would later betray their country and desert to the Russians in the post-occupation period, like Jan Fojtík, voted against Svestka that night.

In spite of the superficially subdued mood and business-as-usual appearance of the media in the weeks before the breakthrough, it was possible to feel that this was a lull before a storm. It did not take long for the storm to arrive.

The main importance of the actual removal of censorship in March was that newspapers and other periodicals, as well radio and television, could start to serve as media for the expression of reemerging public opinion. Sales of all periodicals began to rise immediately, and on radio and television programs, news and commentary drew the biggest response. Only a short time before that they had been commonly scorned for their formalism and lack of real content.

Journalists were also quick to move to take control of their organization, the Union of Journalists. Its leadership was changed by the end of March, and the most immediate demand was for complete independence of the Union from the Party and the State organs. In Prague, a city organization of journalists constituted itself, becoming the leading force in the Union. An extraordinary congress of the latter was soon convened to formulate other demands of the media workers: First, the adoption of a constitutional amendment explicitly prohibiting censorship. Second, equal access to information for all media—implicitly a demand to end the system of special treatment for Party publications. The Union also decided to federalize its structure, creating a Czech and a Slovak union with a joint board. The journalists were the first organized group to carry out such a measure.

Some editorial collectives were moving faster than others along the course of the "rehabilitation of Czechoslovak journalism," as it was termed in the main document adopted by the Congress. That rate of change depended largely upon the outcome of the struggle for the removal of the media bureaucrats appointed by the old regime. In some cases, like that of *Rude pravo* or the Czechoslovak News Agency (CTK), these old appointees were firmly entrenched and protected by the conservatives in high Party positions. This situation reflected the complexity of the relations between the press and the new Party leadership.

Dubcek and the press
Whether the new leadership was willing to launch any reforms at all, and, if so, how much real sense they would make, were valid questions, especially in the first weeks following the fall of Novotny. Apart from the change in the position of the first secretary, no signs of any other motion were discernible in the general behavior of the regime. Although a new "action program" of the Party was known to be under preparation, none expected that it would propose meaningful changes. The fact that the first draft of this program was so smoothly approved by the old Presidium on 19 February showed that the skepticism was well justified.[7]

The events of March changed the picture profoundly. In the first place, the pressure of the reemerged public opinion made further personnel changes inevitable. Secondly, the original draft of the "action program" had to be revised to meet, at least formally, some of the most obvious public expectations. These adjustments were approved by the C.C. plenum in early April.

To the journalists, the half-hearted character of the personnel changes and of the "action program" were quite obvious. It showed the paradox of a situation in which the new policy depended upon the approval of the old Central Committee. Clearly, more pressure was needed to affect more thorough changes as a precaution against a conservative backlash. As long as the existing political structure was in place, the key issue was an early extraordinary Party Congress that could elect a different Central Committee. The next obvious step was to change the electoral law for local and national elections, and to hold the elections as soon as possible. At the same time, however, it was politically necessary to support the moderate reformers in the new leadership for the same reason. The framework of the system remained unchanged, and the top Party organs remained the centers of power. Thus the journalists, like the reform-minded public, were caught in a dilemma which characterized the situation until April 1969.

Fear that the conservative majority of the C.C. and its many exponents in the Party apparatus had made only reluctant concessions and waited for any opportunity to reverse the development, proved fully justified in May and June. The reactionary forces became much more visible and active during those weeks. There were several explanations for this. For one, they were alarmed by the openness of public discussions to which they were not accustomed and for which they were poorly prepared. Secondly, they were able to figure out at that time that their political careers would be finished after the next Party Congress if the delegates were freely chosen; in June, the Congress was convened for 9 September. Finally, they felt encouraged by the growing Soviet criticism of Czechoslovak reforms, echoed by other bloc countries.

In this polarization of forces during May and June, the media—while consistently supportive of the reforms—became more critical of their slow pace and vague contents. The May plenum of the C.C., as well as some public speeches of members of the leadership (including Dubcek), seemed to give substance to the fears that the reforms might be stopped altogether, eventually by force. All that led to a certain radicalization of editorial opinion and to actions such as the manifesto *Two Thousand Words*, published on 27 June 1968.[8] Journalists actively participated in this campaign, the aim of which was to mobilize public opinion against the danger threatening the achievements of the last several weeks. As further developments showed, this behavior was perfectly justified.

It must also be noted that the contention between the forces defending the reforms and those opposing them was following a moderate course. The journalists, while overwhelmingly pro-reform, never refused to let the conservatives express their point of view. Moreover, for reasons which resulted from the internal and external circumstances, no one called for a complete removal of the political system in which the Communist party held the dominant position. It was probably apparent to all, left and right, that if the reforms were to result in genuine democratization, its outcome would have to be an open electoral contest. Nevertheless, these alternatives were carefully avoided in the media.

I recall a discussion among the editors of the *Reporter* weekly at the end of June or beginning July 1968 where it was realistically concluded that the reforms were bound to be limited, at least in their first stage, to just changing the totalitarian system of the past to an authoritarian system. After such a switch, the Party leadership would continue to tolerate freedom of the press and a certain independence of public opinion at large. The society, on the other hand, would have to tolerate the existing political framework. Most of us thought that the Russians might accept that much. Only the late Stanislav Budin, who was then chief editor, and who knew more than the rest of us combined, was skeptical about that.

Press freedom and the Soviet factor

That so many were so slow to realize that even the limited changes accomplished in April were in fact entirely unacceptable to the Soviets, was mainly the result of a rather traditional Czech lack of interest in Russian and Soviet affairs. Few among the reformers, including the journalists, were really aware of the meaning of the internal developments in the USSR since the fall of Khrushchev. It was not sufficiently clear to most of us, specifically in the first feverish weeks after the collapse of censorship, that the reformist trend in Prague was running against a decisively anti-reformist trend in Moscow. The absence of serious concerns among the reformers about Soviet reactions was based on illusions which had originated during the Khrushchev era. In 1968, they no longer had substantiation.

It was equally characteristic that only a few had a clear idea about the real state of relations between Prague and Moscow. The fact that there had been no Soviet troops permanently stationed in Czechoslovakia between 1945 and 1968 led many to believe that the spectacular subordination of the state's policies to Soviet interests might have been, to a large extent, quite voluntary on the side of the leaders, most of whom were old-style Comintern types.

Whether it was true or not, a story circulated in Prague in the spring of 1968 that Dubcek had to go to Dresden in March to learn from Brezhnev about the real state of Czechoslovak relations with Moscow. Novotny allegedly had not told Dubcek about that. Five years later, Josef Smrkovsky also remembered how depressing Dubcek's experience had been in Dresden. "It was a different kind of Brezhnev in Dresden than the one whom Dubcek had known from hunting trips to the Tatras," Smrkovsky said. It was in Dresden, in Smrkovsky's opinion, that Brezhnev had for the first time threatened to intervene militarily in Czechoslovakia "if things went too far." According to the same account, Dubcek was also told that the Soviets had been pushing to station their troops in Bohemia since 1964, using the low birthrate in Czechoslovakia during the war-time—and therefore the shortage of army draftees in the midsixties—as an excuse.

When this writer told Dubcek in early May that he would publicize the overwhelming demand, in Party organizations, for a speedy convening of the Party Congress, Dubcek did not refute the facts. With tears in his eyes, he just said, "That will lead to many complications." He did not say that the Russians were at the root of these complications.

In fact, the modest personnel changes made in April, and the "action program" itself were already unacceptable to the Soviets. That was apparently no secret to the leading Czech conservatives, who had their own connection to Moscow. Soviet criticism of the developments in Czechoslovakia, however, were released in their usual cryptic coding, and it was not so easy to guess where exactly the line demarcating their displeasure started. We were, in fact, never quite sure where that line was.

The Party leadership itself did not provide any clues, either—not even during several meetings with leading political editors in July and August. It looked rather as if the politicians, including Cisar and Cernik, were expecting the journalists to offer some opinion. Evzen Erban, a member of the Secretariat and a former Social Democrat observed during one of these meetings: "This is a conflict between two different civilizations." Only Indra and Mlynar, each for different reasons, seemed to understand what the Russians wanted most—the reimposition of complete censorship. Whether that may have prevented the invasion is, however, an entirely hypothetical question: the reimposition of censorship was simply domestically unacceptable.

On the whole, the media handled the growing external pressure cautiously and with great reserve. There was no substantive criticism of Soviet policies and practices, and polemical articles were entirely defensive. That applied even to satirical forms and cartoons. While it was easy and attractive to ridicule the Russians, the criticism resorted to irony, the indirect, the low-key, and the inoffensive. One way we did it, for example, in *Reporter*, was to run a full translation of a particularly mendacious story by Yuriy Zhukov in *Pravda*, without any commentary. Surprisingly, he did not like it.

To say that there were no expressions of the notorious Bohemian light-mindedness in the behavior of the media would, of course, be untrue. But the press as a whole and the broadcast media, including the Russian-language program of Radio Prague, adopted a distinctive measure of self-restraint in the face of Soviet intimidation. In the critical several weeks before the invasion, the main sin of the journalists was in reporting how resolute was the Czech and Slovak public demand not to abandon the policy of reforms. That was especially true during the conference in Cierna on 29 July-1 August.

The interpretations of the Bratislava declaration of 3 August did not differ much in the media community. While the document—phrased in heavy orthodoxy but quite vague in terms of specific commitments—was unequivocally approved in published commentaries, privately the conference was seen as providing breathing space, either short or long. In spite of some warning signals we did not perceive as a serious possibility that it would be followed by a massive military aggression only three weeks later. Not well versed in Soviet history, we were not ready for such complete foul play.

The agony

The era following the return of the kidnapped Czechoslovak leaders from Moscow was termed "normalization," a word with almost perverse connotations for the large majority of the people. What kind of normalcy could the Russians have been expected to establish?

After his return, Dubcek made a helpless, depressing speech on the radio which speeded up the exodus of those who decided to leave their country rather than to wait for the consequences. Some quietly resigned; a few, like Husak, made a turn-about. The majority was still resolved to resist. This period, lasting until the final crackdown in April 1969, was a strange mixture of resistance, accommodation, desertion and betrayal.

Pledging with other groups of intellectuals to stay and to fight, the journalists were caught in the same quagmire as the rest of the society. By virtue of their profession, of course, they were bound, once more, to be in the forefront of a losing battle.

The chronology of this period marks the positions of the gradual retreat. First, the forced departure of Dr. Frantisek Kriegel from the Presidium, and Josef Pavel, the first decent person in the office of the minister of interior since prewar times, from his position. More personnel changes —including those in the media—seemingly strengthening the centrist position, in fact weakened the capacity to resist. On 18 October, another sorry capitulation took place—the approval of a humiliating "treaty" by the National Assembly, formally legalizing the occupation. In November, a C.C. meeting gave substance to the Soviet accusations that those resisting the surrender were "antisocialist forces." The traitor Bilak was reinstated in the Party Secretariat and another one, Strougal, took control of the Czech Party affairs, in preparation of the coming purge. A month later, the state was federalized, and Slovakia reacquired its statehood, under circumstances even worse than in March 1939. At that time, it had at least not been occupied. In January 1969, the act of federalization was misused by Husak to break the front of the resistance by forcing the removal of Josef Smrkovsky from the chairmanship of the Parliament.

The Russians took good notice of Husak's services: he was to be their next bet.

A twenty-year old student set himself on fire in January to protest this gradual disintegration of the defensive front of the reform movement. A few weeks later, nevertheless, the final act arrived. The Soviets installed Husak in Dubcek's place. "Normalization" was replaced by "consolidation." Its first step was to finish off the remnants of the independent press.

Throughout the "normalization," the media, although more and more muzzled, still recorded the events with remarkable courage and openness, maintaining public opinion as an important part of the struggle. Otherwise, the process would have been more sudden.

Censorship was reestablished as early as September 1968—a top priority point of the Moscow Protocol imposed upon the kidnapped leaders. The new censorship authority, called the Office of Press and Information, was reasonable and moderate at the beginning, but it added pressure as time passed. The media operated directly by the government, such as radio and television, were affected more than those belonging to independent organizations. In the last months of this period, only a few weeklies and two Prague dailies *(Prace* and *Mlada fronta)* were still defiantly publishing critical editorial opinions. According to Pierre Broue, the author of the two best works on this period, this was the most glorious time in the whole history of the Czech press, with four independent weeklies bearing the brunt of this last struggle: *Listy, Politika, Reporter*, and *Zitrek.*[9] These four were the first to be terminated soon after Husak's takeover, and their editors were the first to be professionally destroyed.

There were remarkably few traitors among the journalists during the "normalization" period. A handful of them ran to the Russians at the time of the invasion, and until April 1969 they operated a "Czech" radio service from Dresden. The same group was editing a Czech-language newspaper called *Zpravy* (News). When Strougal's bureau for Czech Party affairs was established in October 1968, it launched a pro-Soviet weekly, *Tribuna*, edited by Svestka. This whole group consisted altogether of about twenty-five people, mostly known down-and-out types, rarely seen sober in previous times. There was not one single well-known journalist among them.

A typical issue of *Zpravy* or *Tribuna* was a poorly edited collection of diatribes, slander, and calls for revenge. The printers of *Svoboda* publishing house, where *Tribuna* was produced, initially refused to print it, and we had to come to their meeting to persuade them to do so, arguing once more that freedom was indivisible. The publisher of the weekly ordered

40,000 copies to be printed; the actual circulation was unknown. That there were 40,000 friends of the Soviet Union left in Bohemia and Moravia at that time seems to be quite possible.

On the whole, the record of Czech journalists throughout the "normalization" was honorable. The last public opinion poll conducted in February 1969 showed that journalists were the only group still enjoying the confidence of a vast majority of the public. Some months later, blacklisted, thrown out of the editorial offices, and forced to make their living on construction sites, in factories, as truck drivers and window cleaners, these former journalists continued to enjoy the confidence and sympathy of the ordinary people.

Twenty years later, bundles of yellowed newspapers and magazines of the 1968-1969 era still belong to cherished remembrances in thousands of homes in Czechoslovakia. The memory has not died, and where there is memory, there is hope.

Conclusion

Between the invasion and the end of the mass purge of the Union of Journalists in 1970, approximately 2,560 editors left the profession. 180 emigrated, 1,400 were expelled from the Union (losing their jobs before or after that), and the rest were forced to leave their jobs under a variety of pretexts: "loss of confidence," expulsion from the Party, etc.[10] Among them was the cream of Czech journalism—the best and most respected reporters and commentators. Some of them, but only few, came back to their readers and listeners on the waves of Western radio stations, such as Radio Free Europe, Deutsche Welle, and the BBC. Dozens were jailed, some several times, and in some cases spent years behind bars. The leading television journalist, Vladimir Skutina, served four and a half years in prison, and Karel Kyncl, a well-known foreign correspondent of Prague radio, served over three years. Many-sided and persistent persecution affected hundreds of journalists and even their wives and children, and twenty years later, blacklisting is still in effect.

Before the end of 1971, those forced out of the profession during the purges were replaced by about 1,000 persons recruited in various institutions outside the field of mass communication.[11] Most of them came from the Party apparatus. Simultaneously, salaries in the profession were doubled to make it more attractive, and a system of extra premiums for published or broadcast articles was introduced in 1972. The purges were particularly thorough in the cultural and foreign policy sections of all central media, where almost none of the old editors survived. The latter field was conveniently staffed by army and state security officers. The

39

standards of the media sank to those of the early 1950s, and sales of print media went down, in many cases to less than 40 per cent of the sales of 1967.

In the course of time, the profession could not, of course, be maintained by such extraordinary measures. Within a few years, younger people had to be recruited, including graduates of the journalism schools. While screening was thorough, the environment could not be changed. Nowadays, the media present a picture of absolute compliance and loyalty. They looked the same, of course, in February 1968.

According to the last figures, there were 6,787 journalists in Czechoslovakia in 1986, almost twice as many as in 1967. Over 4,000 of them were reported to have a college education.[12] That is a good sign. They cannot be sufficiently primitive to believe in the system of which they are a part, certainly not any more than their predecessors twenty years ago.

The journalists of the Prague Spring were the children of the Great Depression, of Munich and the Nazi occupation. They lived through their illusions and fallacies, but they found their place on the side of their people in 1968.

The journalists of today are the children of the Russian occupation, of national humiliation and defeat. They can have no illusions comparable to those of another historical era. Deep in their hearts, they are certainly even more prepared to stand up when their time comes.

Economic Reforms of 1968 After Twenty Years

Radoslav Selucky

AFTER TWENTY YEARS, the Czechoslovak economic reforms of 1968 look even better than they did during the Prague Spring. They look better not because they have improved with age but because in the context of the late 1980s they can be reassessed in a new light.

The new context began to emerge three years ago when Mikhail Gorbachev introduced his policy of *perestroika* or "reconstruction" whose objective, supported by *glasnost*, was to put the USSR on the track of economic modernization. China had already started its policy of four modernizations in the late 1970s, and Polish leaders had already tried, after a period of military regime, to initiate reforms conducive to their country's economic modernization. By the early 1980s, the notion that the Soviet-type command economic system ought to be revitalized and that this could best be achieved by introducing market-oriented economic reforms had become familiar not only in the USSR, China and Poland, but also in Vietnam, Angola and Bulgaria.

At the same time, however, no ruling Communist party anywhere in the world has yet clearly recognized, let alone openly admitted, that systemic economic reforms cannot work properly unless they are supported by structural political reforms such as those initiated by the Czech Communist party in 1968. In other words, the leaders of the countries now experimenting with reforms have not recognized that in order for market-based economic reforms to work in Communist countries, the ruling Communist party must give up at least some of its direct control over all spheres of society. As a minimum, the Communist party must give up its leading role in the economy, in science and in technology. In addition, it must also show support for the development of an autonomous civil

41

society and restrict its direct control to the sphere of politics alone. In a socialist market system, the state/Party has a limited role to perform in regard to the economy: its intervention is needed only to protect society from the negative social consequences of the market and to provide some kind of indicative planning and regulation. So far, only the Communist party of China has recognized that market-oriented economic reforms need to be accompanied by changes in the country's political system. Unfortunately, the Chinese have yet to go beyond merely talking about it.

Revision of the fossilized doctrine

Viewed in this context, it becomes apparent that the Czechoslovak reforms of 1968 were, and still remain, unique in the entire Communist world. They were, first of all, comprehensive in scope. The Czech leaders of 1968 initiated not only economic but also political reforms, and developed a democratic/liberal revision of the fossilized Marxist-Leninist doctrine. Although they did not give up the principle of the leading role of the Party, they substantially reinterpreted the Party's role not only in the economy, but in other spheres of society as well. For instance, the Party was willing to refrain from exercising its control of society until it had consulted (semi)autonomous social and political groups and organizations. Where the economy was concerned, the Party allowed economic units to pursue their own economic and social interests and restricted its role to ensuring adherence to the legal rule of the (market) game.

In the public sphere, the Party accepted the notion of freedom of the press and abolished censorship by a special law, although that did not necessarily mean that the Party was willing to implement any of the policies, priorities and changes that emerged from public debate. The Party also stopped exercising its nomeklatura rights in social and professional organizations, cultural and scientific institutions, and so forth. The most reform-minded of the Party leaders were even willing to accept an *opponentura,* the officially recognized right of citizens, and especially of social organizations, associations, pressure groups, and marginal political parties to question, debate and openly criticize the Party's decisions.

Quite clearly, a semi-autonomous civil society was beginning to have an impact upon, and contribute to, decision-making by Party/state organs and agencies.

This unique attitude of the reform wing of the CPCS leadership would have been impossible outside the context of Czechoslovak culture, especially Czech political culture, with its long tradition of an autonomous civil society, of self-government, of economic, social, political and ideological/religious pluralism, and of a long plebeian democratic tradition. Since neither the Czechs nor the Slovaks had their own nation-state for centuries, the state appeared as a foreign, alien force. Their national survival/revival, as well as economic advancement, was possible only through civil society. People traditionally felt themselves to be citizens, and this feeling was not alien even to reform-minded leaders in 1968. The Party was willing to democratize its own statutes (to allow deviations from the strict ban on factions; to relax its interpretation of democratic centralism and to federalize the Party), to give up most of its direct control in favor of indirect social regulation; to live with a degree of officially recognized economic, social, political and *ideological pluralism*, and to directly intervene in civil society only if and when the latter had refused to accept the Party's guidance/leadership on the most fundamental political and ideological issues.

Although most of the 1968 changes were of a cultural, political and ideological rather than of a structural (systemic) nature, some structural changes were introduced in the spring of 1968 while others, namely of a legal, economic and institutional nature, were set to be implemented in the second half of 1968 and in 1969.

The most important structural (systemic) change that took place in 1968 was a special law passed by Parliament abolishing censorship. Although the Party did not give up its influence over the mass media, publishing and the arts, it certainly did give up its direct leading role in this sphere of social activity. The abolition of censorship opened up a sort of ideological pluralism. Not one other ruling Communist party in the world has undertaken, before or since, such an important step towards legally guaranteeing the freedom of ideas. In some other countries, such as the USSR at present, there has been a degree of liberalization or relaxation of censorship; the screws keeping intellectual/ideological life under control have been loosened. However, what is loosened may be tightened again, and although even a limited relaxation is significant, it does not represent a structural shift in the nature of the system. That is why such changes as the 1968 Czechoslovak relaxation of foreign travel had been changes of a lower order.

Where the economy was concerned, one will not find much to criticize in the 1968 Czechoslovak blueprint for economic reform even today. The reform was prepared as an alternative model to the traditional Soviet-type command planning system and, as a model, it remains acceptable even today. As any model, it is, of course, a simplified structural/functional paradigm which ignores culture, ideology and the rational/irrational economic behavior and prejudices of both government and autonomous economic units. That was not where the problem lay; no model can assume irrational or dysfunctional economic and political behavior on the part of its constitutive institutions.

The real problem with the Czechoslovak 1968 reform model lay elsewhere: we had no concrete set of alternative economic policies for the transition from one economic system to another. The absence of such transitional economic policies can be explained by two factors. First, the reform model had been constructed by theoreticians whose practical experience, taken together, barely amounted to having run one business enterprise. And second, the people in charge of the economic reform were (understandably, given the pressure of circumstances) preoccupied with the political and ideological problems of the day.

But even these shortcomings were not as serious as many outside observers may believe when one considers that even the initial pre-1968 reform measures, distorted though they were by the pre-1968 Party leadership, worked better than had the old inflexible command planning system. For instance, between 1967 and 1969 alone at least one negative long-term trend (the steady growth of capital-output ratios) was successfully reversed. Even if some inefficient factories were closed, this could not create any serious threat of unemployment since the Czechoslovak infrastructure, as well as the entire tertiary sphere, were so underdeveloped that the service sector was able to absorb all the redundant industrial workers. As the five-year post-invasion period has shown, a mere shift in investment priorities from heavy industries to consumer products, infrastructure and services was sufficient to accelerate economic growth. Even more important, the reversal in capital-output ratios from 1967 to 1969 demonstrated that even the first steps leading toward intensive economic growth could produce quite remarkable results.

There was, of course, a degree of naïvete among the economists and politicians of the time. Both expected too much from the reform and would have inevitably been disappointed had the reform been allowed to continue. While abstract economic models can be worked out to perfection, concrete economic systems cannot, even at best, do more than approximate the models. In the economy, the good and desirable things are apparently always mutually exclusive, while the bad and undesirable things seem to always coexist without the least difficulty. There are many countries with low wages and high prices, but countries with high wages and low prices simply do not exist. By the same token, there are many countries afflicted with high unemployment even though no disruptive technological innovations or structural changes have been introduced into the economy, but no economy which does produce rapid technological innovation and structural change can escape significant levels of unemployment. Each positive economic phenomenon also brings about some socially undesirable results. That is why it is so difficult to create a good economic system. Since it is impossible to maximize two mutually exclusive goodies, the best one can hope for is a reasonable degree of economic efficiency combined with a reasonable level of employment, security and stability. In retrospect, Czechoslovak reformers and the Czechoslovak public certainly did expect too many goodies from the economic reforms in 1968, and while the reform would no doubt have eventually improved the state of the Czechoslovak economy, it would never have been able to create a genuinely good socialist economic system.

The 1968 economic reform was also hampered by a least one ideological bias—its Marxist labor theory of value. Although the authors of the reform tacitly appreciated the value-creating function of capital and were willing to build scarcity and supply-demand relations into their calculations, they were incapable of casting off the ballast of the labor theory of value. As a consequence, they found their road to a rational price reform blocked.

In spite of this, I do not wish to overlook the many achievements of the Czechoslovak reform model. Most notably, the reformers wanted to promote those structural branch changes which would render it possible to synchronize the allocation of resources with innovative technological trends and to take into consideration the concept of comparative advantage for Czechoslovak foreign trade. And, above all, they clearly envisioned the need for noninterference of Party/state bodies in economic decision-making at the enterprise level.

In the summer of 1968 a representative group of reform theoreticians prepared a draft of their reform proposals to be presented to the XIVth Party Congress in September 1968. The draft represented a collective standpoint of maximum authenticity. If taken as a programmatic statement, it reflects their desire to achieve an equilibrium of economic optimization and humanization in the economic sphere. The draft stated, among other things, that:

> A rigid doctrinaire application of the concept of state ownership of property cannot provide an answer [to the question of how to give the workers an interest in socialist enterprise]: it must, therefore, make way for the concept of structured social ownership according to the standard of the skills of workers and the size and nature of each enterprise. Depending on how social productive forces are formed in each particular case, and depending on the degree

to which they are in practice truly social, a socialist society makes use of a broad range of forms of ownership from large state-owned enterprises to socially but not state-owned enterprises, cooperatives and small private undertakings...Independent socialist enterprises are set up as the basic elements of a socialist economy and as the agents of a market economy; they are autonomous from the state, entering into economic associations of their own choosing, exposed to the pressures of the market and of economic competition...These economic conditions—influenced by the central authorities in a planned manner if necessary—can link maximum output with maximum consideration for the needs of both the individual and of society as a whole. If a socialist enterprise is to hold its own under such conditions, it must be capable of harnessing all the skill of its workers, it must choose the most capable executives with the most up-to-date ideas, and it must succeed in combining management by experts with democratic self-management by employees...Socialism will not reach the point where it can stand on its own feet until it creates an economic system of its own which will generalize socialist enterprise and open the sphere of human interests to new impulses of civilization and culture.[1]

This lengthy quotation clearly shows that the Czechoslovak economic reform of 1968 was supposed to go beyond mere changes in the economic mechanism and that it soon grew into a new concept of socialism itself, combining a market economy with indirect (indicative) planning and with political and economic democracy. Although the passage is couched in traditionally Marxist language and is perhaps not readily comprehensible to the Western reader, it nonetheless succeeds in reflecting the libertarian *spirit* of the 1968 economic reform.

I have no intention of passing judgment on how realistic the project was. No attempt at reforming the traditional Soviet-type system can succeed without an element of trial and error. It is possible to construct various simplified and general models at a purely theoretical level, but in practice it is difficult to create a more subtle system which can meet all the varying needs of a particular society. In the final analysis, as long as reforms are open to pragmatic economic, political and social considerations, a reasonable, if not an altogether ideal, system can emerge. At least some of the Czechoslovak reformers knew that the most they could hope to achieve was some new space for initiative and some sort of a self-regulating mechanism in the economy by providing the system with elements of feedback and homeostasis. But because these objectives were intended for the political sphere as well, they exceeded by far the narrow bounds of the economy.

At the time, there were two schools of thought among the intellectual fathers of the Czechoslovak reform. One group of reformers believed that the events of the Prague Spring represented an opening for a new social synthesis which would incorporate all the valued humanistic ideas of European civilization and suggest a solution for the emancipation of man. The other group was more skeptical: it was content with a more down-to-earth approach which focused on creating a society in which life would be liveable. The latter group merely wanted to combine three things: economic efficiency, social justice and individual liberty. The pre-1968 system lacked the first and the third item in the equation, while the second, social justice, was undermined by the inefficiency of the economic system and by the lack of personal freedom.

Self management
Once the question of the relationship between economic efficiency, social justice and individual liberty had been raised, it unavoidably led to the most controversial issue of the 1968 reform, the issue of self-management.

Marx's concept of a positive supersession of capitalism may be deduced from his definition of capital as "the governing power over labor and its products."[2] Be it the capitalist or the State, it is the owner of capital who dominates labor. In order to escape the external domination of their labor, workers themselves must become the owners of capital. And since the essence of the ownership of capital lies not in the title to property but in the exercise of effective power over labor and its products, the "worker is free only when he is the owner of his instruments of labor — this can be the case in either individual or collective form."[3]

How can this proposition be operationalized? In the *Communist Manifesto* Marx and Engels suggest that:

> the proletariat will use its political supremacy to wrest, by degrees, all capital from the bourgeoisie, to centralize all instruments of production in the hands of the State, i.e., of the proletariat organized as the ruling class...[4]

This is very ambiguous. As long as the means of production are "centralized in the hands of the State," then the proletariat, dispersed in thousands of economic units across a country, has no access to central decision-making. And since no member of the proletariat as a class has any social power in his own right, it is out of the question for any proletarian to exercise direct social power. As an individual, the proletarian (unlike a capitalist) cannot rule or govern others. Even as a class, the proletariat cannot exercise economic power directly except in the system of economic self-management.

However, in any centralized economic system, economic power has to be exercised on behalf of the proletariat (rather than by the proletariat) by a special, elite group. And even if this elite group were made up entirely of proletarians, these ruling proletarians would, by definition, become *former* proletarians as soon as they joined the elite group. In the meantime, the actual subordinate position of their class would remain unchanged. The number of individuals who can actually rule in any centralized system is rather limited. There is no way that it can include the proletariat as a whole, as a class. Thus, as long as the means of production are centralized in the hands of the State, economic class rule (self-management) by the proletariat is by definition impossible. Furthermore, if one extends the argument to include all working people and not just the proletariat which, in modern post-industrial society, increasingly becomes a minority of the working population, then self-management truly becomes the only means whereby the working people can exercise the economic power which stems from the socialized means of production.

This reasoning acquired great importance during the Prague Spring and immediately after the invasion by the Warsaw Pact troops. Since it was unlikely that the political reform would be allowed to run its course, self-management was considered by a growing majority of industrial workers and other employees to be the only vehicle for the continued democratization of Czechoslovak society.

In its early stages, prior to 1968, the Czechoslovak economic reform was technocratically oriented. The revived market mechanism was initially intended not as a means of providing an economic base for self-management, but merely as a means of creating a more efficient economic system. In May 1968 when conservative criticism of the reform was growing both at home and in other Soviet bloc countries, two prominent reformers, Josef Smrkovsky and Ota Sik, publicly called for the establishment of democratic organs in factories. Ota Sik came up with a detailed concept of economic self-management. At first he favored councils composed equally of workers/employees, outside experts and representatives of the Party/state. Later on, however, he changed his position by calling for the councils to be democratically elected by all employees and he helped, in his official capacity as the deputy prime minister in charge of economic reforms, to introduce government guidelines for establishing factory councils.

While the majority of reform economists was in agreement with Sik's concept of self-management, some social scientists wanted not just factory councils but genuine workers' councils. They were not so much interested in economic efficiency as in shifting power from managers and technocrats to workers.

It is worth noting that Czechoslovak workers were not initially very enthusiastic about economic self-management. In spite of their positive experience with powerful worker control (exercised from May 1945 to February 1948 through trade union-controlled enterprise committees in both the nationalized and private sector industries), twenty years of bureaucratic planning had alienated them from politics in general and from economic reforms in particular. It was not until the summer of 1968 that they became interested, once again, in active political, social and economic participation. They took part in discussions concerning the separation of the economy from the State (i.e. the transition from State-owned to socially-owned enterprises administered and controlled, on behalf of society as a whole, by self-managing bodies at the level of economic units), a new relationship between labor councils and trade unions, and the composition and functions of the self-managing bodies.

The workers' interest in self-management further increased after the Soviet invasion of Czechoslovakia on 21 August 1968. This makes perfectly good sense when one considers, as I have already pointed out, that the Soviet military intervention meant the end of any radical reform aimed at the creation of a pluralistic political system; as a consequence, the Czech public in general, and the workers in particular, now saw self-management, insofar as it promised the creation of pluralism in the economic sphere, as the only remaining means of keeping the Prague Spring alive under the new circumstances. While there had been only 19 factory councils in existence in September 1968, another 143 were elected as of 1 October and an additional 117 were scheduled to be set up by the New Year. New councils continued to be formed throughout the spring of 1969 and by the end of June, some 300 councils and 150 preparatory committees were reported to be in existence.[5]

The actual behavior of these industrial collectives ultimately rendered irrelevant earlier debates about the composition of the factory councils. About 70 percent of all the elected council members were from the technical staff and middle-management while blue collar workers occupied slightly under one quarter of all the seats. The balance went to clerical staff. In addition, 29 percent of all the council members had a college or university education. In contrast to the composition of these self-management bodies, trade union factory committees remained under the majority control of blue collar workers.[6] These figures suggest that there was a degree of mutual trust between blue and white collar workers in

1968-69 Czechoslovakia, unprecedented in other Central/East European countries including Yugoslavia, and that the education and skills of the technical/economic intelligentsia were appreciated rather than resented by the working class in a self-management context. Indeed, the figures suggest a sort of informal division of functions whereby the better educated white collar workers were delegated to keep the management in check while the blue collar workers assumed the task of defending employee interests on trade union committees. Not su prisingly, however, this very promising system of self-management was eventually dismantled and the old prereform bureaucratic political and economic system was reinstated by the summer of 1970.

Personally, I was in favor, at that time, of a loose self-management model whereby each single economic unit would have been entitled to choose the pattern best suited to its needs. The economic sphere is, first of all, a goal-oriented system and its first objective is to satisfy, as far as possible, both individual and social needs. The system thus cannot ignore the social and political aspects of economic activity. A socialist economic system in particular ought to appreciate the principle of equal access to participation in decision-making in the workplace for all employees. A purely technocratic system of management would probably be more efficient economically, while an entirely self-managed system would be more conducive to increased cooperation, worker satisfaction and greater social harmony. However, only a reasonable compromise between the two is likely both to produce a fair degree of economic efficiency *and* allow for a fair degree of humanization of economic activities. And since both objectives are legitimate in a socialist economy and at the same time mutually exclusive if applied in a pure form, neither the technocratic/liberal nor the democratic/radical approach alone leads to a balanced synthesis.

Had the reforms not been violently halted, we would of course know by now which of the disputed conceptions is best able to bring about comprehensive libertarian reforms. We would also have had the chance to observe how a democratic-socialist system would have dealt with the world oil crisis and inflation, with the transition to a post-industrial stage of development, with the electronic/computer revolution, and other contemporary challenges. None of these major developments of the 1970s and 1980s was anticipated by Czechoslovak economic reformers, nor could they have foreseen the impact of a service economy on employment in Prague of the 1960s. The reform would have pragmatically continued by trial and error, and some degree of both economic and political modernization would no doubt have been achieved. Unfortunately, we can only speculate about the outcome. Indeed, the Soviet-led invasion was a crime if for no other reason than that it deprived us of the fruit of an unprecedented experiment, the opportunity to see how a freer and more open version of Marxist socialism would have handled the complex problems of modern society in a highly educated industrial country.

The Short Spring of a Major Industry

Jiri Loewy

WE WILL PROBABLY never know who first used the term "Prague Spring" to denote Czechoslovakia's political development in 1968, thus lending new meaning to an expression which up to that time was connected exclusively with the well-known musical festival. Most likely the expression was coined by some Western journalist stationed in Prague.

In any case the term came into use in spite of its inaccuracy as to time and locale. After all, the political "spring" lasted throughout summer and was experienced not only by one million residents of Prague but by the rest of the 14-million people of Czechoslovakia. The events in the capital—in the limelight of mass media and foreign correspondents naturally drew and received the most attention. These events are well-documented and have been evaluated from many diverse points of view.

The developments outside Prague—their specific regional expressions and problems, specifically the influence which the events exerted on individual industries—are still awaiting chroniclers. If we do not want to succumb to the erroneous idea that it was a development exclusively limited to Prague, to government departments and the secretariats of the leading Party, to university lecture halls and literary cafes, we will need plenty of testimonies, hundreds of tiny fragments of evidence to reconstruct the intricate mosaic of the Prague Spring.

The cotton industry

The aspect which I would like to address has to do with an industry in which I was employed as a press officer: the Cotton Industry—then Czechoslovakia's fourth largest branch of industry. Its 200 enterprises held a workforce of 83,000 employees and produced 6 billion Czechoslovak crowns worth of goods annually. This industry consisted of sixteen organizational units, i.e., large companies, and three research institutes. Its headquarters was located in Hradec Kralove, the capital of Eastern Bohemia. In the system of centralized planning, the board of directors of this industrial branch—which, interestingly enough, came to be called at that time, in quite capitalist spirit, a "trust"—functioned as a connecting link between the State Ministry of Consumer Goods Industries and the individual cotton companies. The executive board, therefore, played a coordinating role, receiving directions from above and passing them to those below, following the practice adopted by the nation's entire system of centralized planning. The Cotton Industry belonged to the Czechoslovak textile industries—then the employer of a quarter of a million people, predominantly women—and was known for superb inventions (open-end spinning), as well as for hopelessly outdated machinery and the lowest wages in the entire republic. So much for an introduction.

Early Spring

At first nothing happens at all. Early in January people accept with satisfaction the news that Antonin Novotny, who never enjoyed great popularity, is no longer the Party leader. The name Alexander Dubcek, however, does not mean much to them. After twenty years of the Communist regime people receive news of changes in the leadership with severe skepticism and no enthusiasm.

The January and February 1968 issues of the press bulletin, *B-expres*, published monthly by the Cotton Industry (B = *bavlna* = cotton), do not show any sign of departure from hitherto existing norms. Nevertheless, in March the liberalization and finally the abolition of censorship already begin to show even in this organ of the Cotton Industry. Of course the March issue editorial at first maintains that nothing is really happening:

> Recently we received a phone call from a certain editorial office: "What about you, in the Cotton Industry? Is nothing going on there? No stormy meetings? No resolutions being sent to Prague?" We could do nothing but disappoint the inquirer. In the 200 cotton and silk factories in Czechoslovakia there are no political sensations; people are working—intensively.

But the article immediately proceeds to adopt a different tone:

> However, this is not to say that the employees in this large branch of the textile industries are indifferent to what is happening in society and to the course which public and national affairs will take.

It will be necessary to take a look at the sad development in wages and salaries policy in the Czechoslovak textile industries—the lowest in the entire economy, with the exception of agriculture. And it will be necessary to remember how long it took before the return of investment was achieved again in the industry's investment policy...

Up to that time the subject of wages and salaries had been taboo for the Czechoslovak press. Censors did not allow the slightest criticism of the payment policy. Yet *B-expres* is not content with stating plain facts but, very openly, it begins to trace causes:

For years now we have been killing the geese that lay the golden eggs; for years the consumer goods industries have been neglected and degraded in an unparalleled way. (There are people who will call all this an allegedly 'inevitable stage of development'—a poor justification!). We should not daze ourselves with illusions; the odd, underrating, irresponsible, thoughtless approach to this industry has not been fully overcome to this very day. We will be burdened with its after-effects and consequences for years to come. State planning directives, tight centralism and its iron discipline, short-sighted, inefficient management, subjectivist decision-making and an unscientific approach to problems have inadvertently brought us this far; they have gotten us into a situation which we do not want and could have avoided.

The editorial furthermore addresses those who expect remedy from an "economic reform" which has been announced for a long time:

Any economic reform must necessarily remain half-hearted and ineffective, if progressive political solutions continue to be delayed. It really is not enough any longer to change a thing here and a thing there and to smooth things over, as if putting another fresh coat of paint on leaking eaves...

Spring is here...

"In troubled times it is difficult to prophesy," says the April issue of *B-expres*. "Only a month ago we claimed on these very pages that 'no stormy meetings took place, no resolutions were being sent to Prague.' Since then the development has taken a different course in many cotton and silk companies. It is a healthy, natural and normal course."

On 27 March trade union officials from all cotton companies convene in Pardubice. All day long they discuss the situation. At this forum, for the first time, the call for a "rehabilitation of the consumer goods industries" is voiced in rare unison—a demand which will continue to be high on the agenda of both trade and management. At the close of the day the trade union delegates approve a letter to Premier Oldrich Cernik, which says among other things:

> In the past years the Cotton Industry has helped to finance the development of other industries. It has especially contributed to the advancement of the heavy industries. Despite the fact that our output, produced by 83,000 workers, amounts to more than six billion annually, the Cotton Industry has been drawing on its capital most of the time during the past twenty years.
>
> We do not have enough funds at our disposal to provide for the most essential requirements. The problems of reconstruction and modernization as embodied in the resolution passed by the Czechoslovak Communist Party's XIIIth Congress cannot be tackled. Yet, we cannot help notice that vast projects amounting to billions are being adopted to the ultimate benefit of industries which during the past twenty years have already absorbed a considerable portion of resources produced by the nation's economy.
>
> In the future the employees in the Cotton Industry will not lessen their efforts to fulfill production targets but they expect the restitution of means that were diverted to foster other industries over the past years.

To fully understand this demand it is useful to know that from 1948 to 1968 the Communist state—fully controlling the centralized economy—was using the consumer goods industries as cash generators, and kept milking them thoroughly and mercilessly. All surplus earnings were squeezed out of the consumer goods industries and invested in heavy industry, particularly in the production of arms. As a result, the armament industry was equipped with the latest technology and boasted the nation's highest wages. The twenty years of such management methods had left the traditional consumer goods industries—deprived of most means—utterly exhausted.

The very next day, on 28 March, the board of directors of the Cotton Industry, together with managers of all companies that form the trust, holds a meeting in Hradec Kralove. The joint committee basically agrees with the demands that have been raised by the trade unionists. The participants of the meeting write a letter to Prague—this time, however, to Party leader Alexander Dubcek:

> Neither the existing means nor the minimal relief payments which the Cotton Industry has received to this date are sufficient to cover its needs when faced with the current price structure. Over the years

the Cotton Industry has contributed a significant portion of its resources to the development of other industries, most of all to the
expansion of heavy industries. As a result, a large portion of the
enterprises is run in two shifts—in some cases even in three—and
is using an outdated equipment, not to mention the fact that 67
percent of the Cotton Industry's employees are women. In spinning mills their number reaches 80 percent.

The importance of the Cotton Industry is not only substantiated
by large domestic demand for its products, but also by the fact
that up to a third of its output goes to exports, chiefly to capitalist
countries. It is necessary to stress that the high degree of labor
productivity—achieved despite relatively labor-extensive production
—is accompanied by a low income level in comparison with other
industries.

If the fundamental tasks, as set by the XIIIth Congress (of the
Communist party), are to be accomplished by the industry, it is
absolutely necessary that the Cotton Industry be compensated for
the means that have been taken from it during the past years for
the benefit of other industries. We ask the central organs to respect
this urgent demand.

Finally, the managers inform Dubcek that they have "critically assessed
the internal relations between the individual companies and the management of the trust" and arrived at the conclusion that it will be necessary
to improve considerably their own performance and "to reorganize the
trust—to decentralize its power." From this moment on, the demand of
decentralization will never quite subside.

The seamy side of "democratization"

The human mind is apparently equipped with strong filters. How else
can we explain the fact that we tend to forget negative impressions and
experiences so quickly, that we press them into the recesses of our
consciousness as time goes by—up to the point of not knowing? When
I listen to eyewitness accounts of the Prague Spring, this strange mechanism is often strikingly confirmed to me: The further the distance from
the 1968 events, the brighter the sky of that Spring looks. Now, it appears almost absolutely cloudless in our memory. In reality, the sky of
that Spring was not permanently clear but overcast from time to time.
I am not alluding only to the impending Soviet intervention which we
began to anticipate roughly in May, 1968. I am thinking of internal phenomena. The April issue of the bulletin *B-expres* mirrors these events:

Many of those who have sincerely advocated the reform process are now alarmed by some extreme occurrences. They are concerned about numerous instances of local egoism, and about efforts aiming at separation, fragmentation and disunion. They also point to the resurgence of sentiments reminiscent of the post-war period, when, at some places, exacting, dynamic foremen and executives would be condemned and defamed as asocial blackguards simply for not tolerating slovenliness, idleness and disorder on the job. People also lament (in many instances justly so) that here and there a formerly dreaded Stalinist quickly turned his coat, memorized the fashionable vocabulary, and now again strains his vocal cords and again tries his hand at the only activities he has really mastered: the spreading of demagogy and terrorizing of decent people.

A personal reminiscence: In *Pruboj*, a daily published in Usti nad Labem, a Communist demagogue publicly attacks one of the most decent managers of our industry, Frantisek Lamac from Benesov nad Ploucnici in Northern Bohemia. I knew Lamac well having worked for several years in companies that were run by him. He had given me a chance after my release from a Communist prison, although this favor involved considerable personal risk for him. When he hired me he was rebuked by the district Party official for "not having acted as a Communist."

Therefore, I feel obliged to come to his defense against the unjust defamation. So I write a letter to the editor of *Pruboj*. It is not published. I write to the editor-in-chief. He does not respond. I call on the deputy editor and discuss the matter with him. He is not helpful.

This is not an isolated case. Communist journalists, not long ago humble servants of the regime, slowly become aware of the immense power which falls upon them after the abolition of censorship. And sometimes they misuse their newly acquired power to disgrace innocent people. There is no authority to appeal to, no rehabilitation.

The long years of totalitarianism have left their mark; the journalists are unfamiliar with, and at odds with, pluralism of opinion. It is impossible to reeducate an inveterate Stalinist in the course of a few months. They have turned their coats but remain the same underneath.

The May issue of the *B-expres* complains about the behavior of the journalists, who are still obsessed with the "iron conception" (i.e. the priority of heavy and armament industries over all other industrial branches) and ignore the justified demands of workers employed in the consumer goods industries:

The iron conception has been firmly instilled in people's minds, and is accompanied by certain stereotypes in the mass media as well. Today every rumbling in the tubing of any steel mill will instantly receive wide publicity whereas the situation of the consumer goods industries, so it seems, does not get anyone's attention.

The proof: On 19 April the official press agency CTK issues a report to all Czechoslovak dailies on the subject of the cotton, silk and linen manufacturers' conference in Pardubice attended by more than 200 delegates: industrial leaders, representatives of labor and party organizations. The spokesmen for 115,000 employees pass a resolution which calls for the following measures: a systematic and extensive rehabilitation of Czechoslovakia's textile industries, their reinstallment to the eminent rank they deserve in the nation's economy; effective steps to swiftly adjust the industry's income lag; an allocation of hard currency resources for the industry to purchase modern technology; prompt solution of the absolutely intolerable pension situation which was caused by incorrect reorganization of the wholesale prices and by restrictive measures from the center of power; and finally, a thorough investigation into the amount of labor required in the major textile professions and analysis of the results of economizing in comparison with other industries.

The representatives of the textile industries stress that their demands are important to the entire society. They express this idea with the motto: "Without modern, sound, and prosperous textile industries there will be no modern, sound, and prosperous economy in this country!"

The CTK news agency report on the textile conference is sent to every daily in the country. They all receive it but do not print it—not even in the form of a brief notice—not one of them. *B-expres* states the fact with bitterness. Now, in May 1968, the tone of urgency in publications begins to increase; criticism of the system emerges in an completely undisguised way:

> The conception of the so-called 'iron axle'—hailed as the only valid economic doctrine of the state—has done immeasurable and inexcusable harm to our economy. It degraded a modern, sophisticated European country almost to the level of a developing one. It caused the standard of living to stagnate and is to blame for the sad fact that even the smallest apprentice waiter somewhere in the Balkans will nowadays sniff at the incovertible currency of this republic.
>
> No capital is so large that it cannot be squandered away. For two decades the iron conception has relied on supplies which the heavy industries had not themselves created. Now that this conception is overcome at last (?), we are left with mementos of gi-

gantism. Hundreds of investments have been lost. Millions out of
the pockets of society and the resources of the national economy
have been squandered. And we are left with crippled, undernourished,
exhausted consumer goods industries...

The conclusions do not sound optimistic:

> The failure of this one-sided policy, which dictated to produce thou-
> sands of tons of steel to the disadvantage of anything else, is readily
> apparent, at least in *theory*. But in practice it will probably take
> a long time yet for it to disappear.

Public debate

In the companies and individual factories of the cotton and silk industries an almost unceasing public discussion is now going on. Much attention is devoted to the "Theses and Suggestions for an Action Program,"
formulated by the management of the trust. The theses are sent to the
enterprises for evaluation and suggestions. As the comments and general feedback flow back, a few expert teams start to work on the final
definition of the action program for the cotton and silk industries. The
theses deal with the questions of management pertaining to the following
term. They deal with unsolved problems of 1968; with care for workers
and clerical staff; and with an assessment of the future development of
the cotton and silk industries. Basically, the theses advocate the abolition of administrative interventions in individual companies. Furthermore,
the theses aim at "the creation of conditions which could precipitate a
transition to greater self-management and better representation of interests of employees. That should be achieved by means of a sensible division of tasks—as a joint effort of the board of directors and the executives in the individual plants. It is also important to ensure that the
companies become genuine entrepreneurs in relatively short time."

Premier Oldrich Cernik receives another open letter from the Cotton
Industry. Its sender is the director of the Tepna company in Nachod,
Jaroslav Vecera, a nineteen-year-veteran in this position. In the letter, Vecera asks where the consumer goods industry is really heading in the future.
He points out that the employees in the consumer goods industries have
previously cautioned against unfavorable developments which unduly favored the heavy industries and constantly prevented the modernization
of the consumer goods industries. Vecera assesses the current situation
in the consumer goods industries as more serious than is generally assumed: "The restrictive policy of the government has steered the cotton
manufacturers to the brink of disaster...Our investment situation is almost

ridiculous. Annually we receive only 12.1 million Czechoslovak crowns in long-term allocations for renovation and innovation. This amount represents a sum so small that in order simply to meet our most fundamental requirements it would take seventy-one years."

This time the letter attracts the attention even of the official Party organ *Rude pravo* and, what is more, the Communist daily quotes from it. It is not known whether Premier Cernik answered the letter.

Late in May Cernik receives a delegation of six trade union representatives from the cotton and silk industries. The premier summons prominent figures to flank him during the meeting: Deputy Premier Lubomir Strougal; Minister of Consumer Goods Industry Bozena Machacova-Dostalova; the Deputy Chairman of the State Planning Commission Dvorak.

Re: The situation of the Czechoslovak textile industries, the demands of their workers. *Major items*: the demand for a total, moral and material, rehabilitation of the textile industries, problems of investment policy, the solution of the intolerable situation after the absurd reorganization of whole-sale prices, reduction of working hours.

The trade unionists:

Conscious of the necessity of building up the heavy industries, our workers—at a great sacrifice—accepted the full responsibility for the creation of resources in our national economy. But now, twenty years later, they are no longer willing to look on in silence when resources are distributed. They expect a portion of the means which have been channeled away to flow back to their plants. The amount of labor required in our industries is so high that it is no longer possible to ensure a rise in average incomes—which already rank among the lowest in the entire economy—without an immediate modernization. It is impossible to reduce work hours without subsidies. Eleven companies in the trust are nineteen million crowns short in their budgets.

The government:

We are aware of the necessity of modernizing the consumer goods industries. It is necessary to correct the mistakes committed in the restructuring of wholesale prices. However, the demands for investments and funding, filed with the government by various branches of industry, already amount to thirty-three billion crowns. It is impossible for all projects to materialize at once...Under no circumstances will the government accept the demand for a reduction of working hours to a forty-hour week, despite the fact that in most of the plants in question the majority of workers are women. The situation requires not only solutions for 1968 but necessitates

economic measures until 1970. The errors in pricing are currently being corrected; the Cotton Industry will receive what it needs.
Much more difficult is the fulfillment of demands for investments.
The situation may improve as a consequence of a credit granted
by the USSR, a part of which will be allocated to cover the needs
of consumer goods industries.

The surviving record reveals that in the course of the meeting the
premier and his colleagues had to listen to words unfamiliar to Communist
ministers' ears—manifestation of distrust and the threat of strike:

> The demands raised by our workers are very modest. The work-
> ers do not trust our government because comrades who headed the
> "iron policy" are still part of it. That policy is still in effect, while
> nothing has been done to improve our situation. If the demands
> laid down in the resolution will not be tackled and solved, the work-
> ers will go out on a protest strike.

The firmness exhibited by the labor representatives impresses, most
of all, Minister of Consumer Goods Industries Mrs. Machacova-Dostalova.
In an interview with the magazine *Slovenka* she virtually identifies with
the position of the labor delegates:

> The current situation is unbearable, and is justly being criticized
> by the workers. I fully support the demands for an uncomprom-
> ising rehabilitation of the consumer goods industries. And I advocate
> the raise of the allocations for the consumer goods industries. This
> should be achieved by a redistribution of means in the national
> economy. We owe this to more than half a million workers who
> have always bravely and honorably fulfilled their tasks in the con-
> sumer goods industry and now expect an improvement of their work-
> ing, and their financial, conditions.

Minister Machacova-Dostalova even goes so far as to confess publicly
how small the share in total investments that has been allotted to the
consumer goods industries for 1968 is going to be: 1.507 million out
of a total of 14 billion Czechoslovak crowns. When asked who is to
blame, the minister declares:

> It is the whole political and economic conception which is imposed
> on us by the State Planning Commission, and the Ministry of Finance;
> in other words, by the guardians of the treasury. I have constantly
> pointed to these anomalies, both in the government and in the Na-
> tional Assembly; there was hardly a conference or congress without

their agreeing with us. However, in practice nothing has come out of it.

As the Prague Spring progresses the old lady becomes increasingly radical. She appropriates the vocabulary of the workers, and proclaims demands of the trade unionists as if she were one of them. She completely forgets that she herself, for years, has been a member of governments fostering the "iron conception" and that, as a minister she was coresponsible for the situation in the Czechoslovak consumer goods industries.

However, in one respect Mrs. Machacova-Dostalova does not diverge from her traditional position: in her love of the Soviet Union and her boundless faith in Soviet representatives. I am interviewing her in July 1968 at the Liberec Trade Fair. After raising a couple of professional issues, I ask her the question which is currently being raised by millions of people in Czechoslovakia: "What will be the outcome of the negotiations in Cierná nad Tisou?" (Brezhnev's Politburo was just trying to bring Dubcek's team back to reason in a railway wagon on the Czechoslovak-Soviet border). Minister Machacova-Dostalova replies without hesitation: "The negotiations cannot end but positively. After all these are talks between friends!" Perhaps she really does believe it. In the meantime, the armies of our "friends" are just completing preparations for the invasion of Czechoslovakia.

Minister Machacova-Dostalova's staff is discussing an important report on the state of affairs in the consumer goods industries, prepared for the Governmental Economic Council. Apart from an analysis the report also contains a number of concrete suggestions on how to aid the modernization and reconstruction of the consumer goods industries. Even the official party dailies, including *Rude pravo*, give a full account of it. The hopes increase; at the same time, worries grow about what the next day will bring.

At that time I am visiting the three largest companies in the trust, Tiba in Dvur Kralove, Tepna in Nachod, and Hedva in Moravska Trebova. I interview managers, and talk with trade unionists and with workers. The fear of a Soviet intervention is wide-spread and becomes topic number one. It overshadows the yet unsolved question of the rehabilitation of the consumer goods industry.

There is plenty of arguing but, most of all, people work intensively. They entertain hopes that their lot is changing for the better. They have the feeling that they are working for themselves, for the nation—with which they can identify themselves at last. And many of them hope, as if catching at a straw, that a Soviet invasion will not occur as long as there is peace in the country and an orderly working climate.

In early August the tension is relaxing; the campaign against Czechoslovakia in Soviet media subsides; a great many people in the besieged country heave a sigh of relief and truly believe that the crisis has been overcome. It is a beautiful summer, students and many people are still on vacation. The blow comes when we least expect it.

After the invasion

Ten days after 21 August 1968, an editor of *Rude pravo* talks with Cotton Industry's General Manager Josef Machacek about what the invasion entails; Machacek carefully weighs his words. He asks Machacek how the *previous period* influenced production in the plants; we should note that he uses the word *period* instead of invasion or occupation. Self-censoring begins to function even though official censorship has not yet been reestablished. Machacek replies: "None of our plants has been directly occupied, nor has the equipment suffered any damages. The production, however, was substantially impaired by the departure of Polish female workers...The situation is most serious in the silk industry where raw material shortage threatens the production. We cannot expect to be able to make up for the losses in a foreseeable future. It is simply beyond our power."

B-expres is much more outspoken. The September 1968 issue presents detailed information on production losses following the invasion: 4 million meters (13.12 million feet) of fabric and almost 600 tons (= 661.38 U.S. tons) of yarn. *B-expres* asserts that workers spare no effort to make up for the losses, but adds: "Unfortunately we have also suffered losses which cannot be compensated—the tragic events in Liberec claimed the life of Stanislav Vesely, employee in our plant Tepna 5."

During the following months, practically until April 1969, the picture of the situation in industries presented in *B-expres* as well as in other news media is peculiar and full of contradictions. A constant tension is being felt between the extremely negative external impact of the invasion and a creeping "normalization"; between the desperate striving for self-preservation and efforts to stabilize at least some of the partial successes achieved in the reform process. There is a conflict between hope and resignation; a conflict between attempts at "business as usual" and futile rebellion. In newspapers and magazines, it is still possible to read a lot between the lines as well as in the actual lines themselves. Editorial offices remain as yet unpurged. So far no staff is being replaced in the management.

On 23 January 1969 a bill is introduced for debate concerning a "Law on Socialist Enterprises," which is projected to become one of the pillars of economic reform in Czechoslovakia. Six months earlier the bill would have looked much different. Now, all the passages likely to irritate occupation authorities have been moderated. Nevertheless, even in this form the law is a decisive step forward and instantly triggers a lively discussion in enterprises, the press and the public.

Although the bill has not yet been passed, the Cotton Industry's board of directors takes the initiative: It anticipates the major principles of the new law and transforms the trust—which until that time has been directed centrally—into a group of autonomous enterprises. *B-expres* characterizes the step thus:

> Though the actual agreement on integration will be signed later, the establishment of an executive board endowed with decision-making power, effective immediately, provides the enterprises with the improvements they have long been calling for: autonomy, participation in all decisions pertaining to important matters of the branch, abolition of the subordinate status.

But the initiative of the Cotton Industry is still lacking a legal basis: The Law on Socialist Enterprises has not yet been passed. Another bill, on Socialist Entrepreneurship, becomes the subject of a vehement debate. The advocates of reform have apparently realized that time is working against them and they are desperately seeking to institute swiftly what has been accomplished—to enact in law some of the results of the Prague Spring before a total darkness sets in. There is reason for haste.

Freezer

In April 1969 Alexander Dubcek is forced to resign. Gustav Husak becomes leader of the Czechoslovak Communist Party. The discussion on the Law on Socialist Enterprises is silenced almost immediately; the underlying idea of the bill is termed "anti-Socialist." The economic reform is put on ice for two decades. Purges soon follow. Hundreds of thousands of people are affected by them. Reformist managers, liberal-minded Party officials, journalists and rebellious trade unionists are ousted from their positions and forced to take up mostly manual jobs. Their successors are inexperienced and quite incompetent but all the more docile and obliging.

The acute problems of the Czechoslovak economy, some of which the Prague Spring attempted to solve, are also put on ice for the time being and their solutions "postponed" by an inflexible regime represented by the name Gustav Husak.

Perestroika again

Not until Gorbachev introduces his *perestroika* twenty years later does the ice in the freezer begin to melt. All of a sudden a bill emerges again— this time it bears a slightly changed name: the "Law on State-Owned Enterprises"—and is put up for public discussion. The arguments in support of the bill do not differ basically from those in 1969 except that, this time, it is strongly emphasized that the Party and the government must have the final say in decision making.

Thus we are witnessing the Czechoslovak reform making its second appearance on the scene—this time as a farce. The problems the Czechoslovak economy faces are worse than twenty years ago. They have not been solved but aggravated by rejecting the reform for such a long time.

Is there a genuine chance for a delayed new attempt? I doubt it. To be successful and effective, any kind of reform in Czechoslovakia, in the Soviet Union, and other totalitarian systems, is lacking the most essential prerequisite: political freedom.

Translated by Dana Loewy

The Russians Are (Really) Coming!

Vladimir Skutina

IT WAS AFTER midnight, Wednesday, 21 August 1968. About half past midnight. A hair-splitter would write 0:28 A.M. But I am not sure whether the clock was accurate, and after all, it does not matter. It could have been 0:28 A.M., it could have been 0:35 A.M. What difference does seven minutes make in a historical period whose time unit is "now?"

I was sleeping, filled with indomitable optimism that after the Czechoslovak Spring and the turbulent summer, a golden autumn of socialism with a human face would finally arrive. The telephone rang, and I, sleepily, reached for the receiver, expecting either a dumb joke from one of my colleagues or a vulgar offense from some drunken enemies. Rarely does anyone call about anything reasonable at this hour, but, neurotic as we have been made by these times, we will not unplug the phone and will answer every call, worrying that if we do not, we will miss something vitally important.

This midnight ring on 21 August 1968 was precisely one of those important cases among thousands of useless awakenings. Boys from the *Literarni Listy* called and asked me to turn on the radio. They said we were being occupied. I—since I lived at the Western end of Prague and possessed passports and valid visas for my entire family—could make it to the border via Pilsen before the tanks of occupants reached Prague. It was a paradox and a naïve idea. A paradox, because Czech history has been one huge chain of defense against occupations from the Germans or some other side, but never from the Slavic side. However, this time—without even spelling it out—the word "occupation" was associated only with the bloody claw of the Soviet imperialist autocracy. My colleagues were very naïve about the technical realization of the invasion because, at this very time, one heavy airplane after another flew over my head every twenty seconds, and from the Ruzyn Airport one transport after another was pouring into Prague.

A paradox and a naïvete

"What technology!" a teacher from the Union of the Czechoslovak-Soviet Friendship would exclaim during public lessons of the Russian language. A paradox. A naivete. These were my first impressions of the newest period of Czech history that started shortly after midnight on Wednesday 21 August 1968. A paradox and naïvete—but double-sided paradox and naïvete on the sides of both antagonists.

The sovereign, untouchable territory of an independent state was invaded by an army of rabid bands from five backward countries whose self-appointed leaders expected that an hour after the occupation, power would be in the hands of a puppet government composed of frustrated nobodies, and that at high noon, a mob of fanatic alcoholics would brandish a sickle and a hammer at the Old-Town Square and, while doing so, scream with happiness over freely flowing discount vodka. Sadly, the blood-drunken Soviet usurpers did not realize that had unofficial and sincere fondness between the peoples of two countries existed anywhere, it was here. The fondness of the Czech people for the Russian people and Slavic people in general is centuries old, as our national enlightener, Safarik, would say. On the other hand, the relationship between the people of the other four satellite countries and the superpower in the East had traditionally been even worse than our relationship with the Germans. All the talk about friendship and fraternal alliance had simply been a cheap pretense of this East pseudo-socialist bloc.

Perhaps I do not have to emphasize that I did not think of an escape from my homeland for a split second. I was born in this country, and if everything ends well, I would like to die here, I thought. Let them flee who have nothing to do here.

I turned on the radio and was lucky to hear the beginning of a broadcast! In midsentence the voice was suddenly severed. That was due to the interference of the prostituting hand of collaborators who had been trained to act in advance. They were later called "the only faithful bearers of the Marxist-Leninist ideas."

That is how 21 August 1968 started for me. It was the beginning of the episode of the modern history of Czechoslovakia which we first called occupation, and for which our leaders—when they started playing with words—invented names such as "transiency," "normalization," "fight against rightist-opportunist forces," and "consolidation." At its core, it was nothing but the disintegration and decay of a living organism. The people called this joyless era "a road to the absolute asshole."

I got up, dressed, and opened the window. "Anduly"—heavy transport jet-planes of the Warsaw Pact armies—flew over our roof toward Ruzyn. I was tempted to curse the heavens, but I did not—it would have been a useless gesture. From that moment on, I refrained from all gestures.

For a while I waited wondering whether the Czechoslovak radio would broadcast again. But only squeaking and rustling noises could be heard from the radio. In the meantime, several people called and asked me whether I knew that we were being occupied. As the minutes and hours went by, I knew I had to go to the TV station. In critical moments, man should be with those with whom he has decided to tie up his life.

I called the apartment of our editor-in-chief. He lived near the embankment of the Vltava river, not far from the National Theater. He picked up the receiver and mumbled something, irritated. Then he said: "Wait a minute! I cannot understand you, I've got to close the window. Some late street car is rumbling right underneath it." After a while he returned and unsuspectingly announced: "Listen, it was not a street car. There are tanks. Probably some military exercise, again." I corrected his error. "That is what I wanted to tell you. Those are Russian tanks, and we are being occupied."

At 3 A.M. I got into my car and went to the TV station. I had been going infrequently and without pleasure to that place—the "Stock Exchange"—where the Central Headquarters of Czechoslovak TV was located. This time I subconsciously knew that I could not go anywhere else. Throngs of helpless and desperate inhabitants of Prague wandered in the streets. Czechoslovak radio began to broadcast again and the announcer was saying dire things. Disoriented armored vehicles of the "glorious Soviet Army" were passing through the streets. People were awakening from the first shock and raised their fists and spat on the passing tanks.

In the office of the director of Czechoslovak TV, all of us, for whom TV work had become the chief meaning of our lives, gathered. Slowly, dawn came. Members of the National Assembly began to come to a building across the street that during the reconstruction of the National Assembly building served as a National Assembly site. Twice or three times armored vehicles of the occupants passed through Gorky Square, back and forth, as if they were looking for direction, as if they were searching for something.

69

Later they returned from somewhere around the Main Railroad Station and turned their guns against the building of the National Assembly and partly against the building of the Czechoslovak TV. Then stupefied soldiers with loaded automatic weapons jumped out, ready for a clash. We heard them stamping their feet on the stairs and then in the studio on the first floor. We sat down in a half circle and expected the worst. Finally, with a kick, the door opened, and several fussy soldiers of the Soviet Red Army barged in with submachine guns aimed at our chests. Behind them stood an office with a gun stretched out in his hand.

The general director of Czech TV was sitting behind his desk and with a gesture of his hand invited the officer to sit. The officer had apparently never seen that gesture and did not understand. He aimed the gun at the director and in confusion shouted: "Give me the stamp!" There are countries in the world, where—if you have a stamp—you can do anything. If you don't have a stamp, then you cannot get even cauliflower. Well, a different country, a different custom.

The director knew the customs and habits of the bureaucratized "country of wonders," and therefore the officer's request did not surprise him very much. He opened a drawer and gave the officer the official stamp of Czech TV. The Soviet officer examined the stamp, then pressed it against his palm, spelled out the text, and rubbed his hands against each other in satisfaction. At that moment, something happened that not even the best director could have timed better. On the shining TV screen, the face of a TV announcer appeared and the first (extraordinary) broadcast of the occupation began.

The Soviet officer entrusted with occupying the headquarters of the Czech TV building, looked first at the screen and then at the director. Then he pulled out the stamp from his pocket and, as if he believed that a miraculous power to broadcast or not to broadcast was hidden in the stamp, guilelessly asked: "Is this a right stamp?" When assured that it was indeed, he shook his head in wonder and exclaimed: "What anarchy!"

The occupying soldiers set off to look for the studio from which the broadcast was emanating. For the entire fifteen years of our TV existence we had cursed improvisation. Wise leaders of "the country heading by mile-long steps toward socialism" (as it was often written then) placed, for example, the Central studio (in its time the only one in Czechoslovakia) in a building which was to have been demolished in 1913 by the order of the Hapsburg bureaucracy because the building was in danger of collapse. Exactly forty years later, the latest TV technology was placed in the building (dilapidating "Mestanska beseda") with few construction modifications. (These consisted of propping up the falling ceiling with wooden beams.)

I remember that in 1953 when we were preparing the first New Year's Eve program, the minister of information and enlightenment, Vaclav Kopecky, visited us (then he was not yet famous by his nickname Cassius Clay, but was called the "Big Mouth") and depicted in rosy colors how in five years, in 1958, we would be broadcasting from a new studio on the Kavka Mountains. Ten years later, in 1968, we only cherished hope that—if everything went well—a trial broadcast from Kavka Mountains could start on 9 May 1970.

In August 1968, Prague TV studios were scattered in seventy-two places all over Prague—in various shops, stores and apartments. During the occupation, this dispersion proved to be, for the first and last time, a big advantage. Russian occupants, enraged by the smiling face of the announcer, set off to look for the source of the broadcast. They scoured the entire building of the "Stock Exchange." During the first search they managed to break several valuable machines. They confiscated several wireless radios in front of the owners' eyes.

They did not discover the studio from which the broadcast was coming, but on every floor they did find several clean minirooms serving as lavatories and restrooms. About these rooms they shook their heads in bafflement and wonder. The scouting of the building was held up as each of the soldiers tried the flushing mechanism. When, after the fourteen-day occupation, the soldiers had to leave the building, we found the toilets undamaged and unused! It was the only equipment that was not demolished or stolen. However, on a handmade carpet in the center of the office of the director was a huge heap of human feces.

I remember how many of us, upon this discovery, ridiculed and condemned the Soviet soldiers. How naïve we were! Narrow-minded Central Europeans! Not without a reason, the great teacher Lenin urged that we study, study and more of the same. But we would not. We, in our guilefulness were making fun of the beautiful Soviet people.

And yet, there is a valid saying that the culture of a nation can be judged by its toilets. We, in our philistine Central European ignorance built and are still building miniature rooms where people can relieve themselves in privacy—leaving collectivist spirit outside. We had to wait for glorious Soviet soldiers to bring shame on us. Miniature rooms with the signs "Ladies" and "Gentlemen" were left provocatively unused. In exchange, the soldiers left their smelly "calling cards" on the carpet

71

in the center of the biggest and most representative room—the office of the director. So that is how it is, you Czech revisionists. Grab your noses!

"Counterrevolutionary" TV and radio

The complex layout and equipment of the TV headquarters made examination of the building complicated and drawn out. This made it possible for the first group to continue broadcasting from Mestanska Beseda. In the meantime the second group had moved to the former movie house "Skaut," where another studio had temporarily been built. "Vlastovka" and other programs for youngsters had been broadcast from there.

A sign, "The Czechoslovak TV Prague" was hanging on the house. Our technicians—those clairvoyant men—removed the sign and moved it to the other end of the Karel Square, where they placed it conspicuously on the famous Faust House, a part of the General University Hospital.

When the Russians finally took over Mestanska Beseda and dispersed the broadcasting technicians and commentators, they found—to their great surprise—that the programs on TV screens ran undisturbed. So they set off in search for other studios. They passed the movie house "Skaut" and stopped in front of the Faust House. According to unconfirmed reports they are still guarding the bladder cases who lie inside.

The studio in the former house "Skaut" was—despite all the cunning arrangements—too conspicuous. Then someone from the technical department came up with a solution that proved to be the simplest of all— once it was spelled out.

The picture spread from Prague into the entire republic from the transmitter on the Cukrak Mountain. As long as the transmitter on Cukrak operated, we were able to broadcast. As soon as the Russians discovered Cukrak, all programing efforts would be brought to an end.

This was logical, and it is a wonder that no one had been struck by the idea earlier. Fortunately, the commander of the Soviet occupation armies had not gotten the idea either. Not even that genius of diplomatic strategy, the Soviet ambassador to Czechoslovakia, Chervonenko, had realized this fact. Instead he pounded a table with his fist and screamed that "We must gag the mouth of the counterrevolutionary television and radio."

In case of emergency—and we had had many of those during the fifteen-year history of Czechoslovak TV—a small trailer-transmitter was standing at Cukrak. Now this improvisation came in handy. A small group of people in the car of Vladimir Tosek, and I, in my car, started up toward Zbraslav and Cukrak. The technicians had been already waiting for us there. Everything was ready for the extraordinary occupation broadcast. In the meantime, remaining colleagues from the movie house "Skaut" and people from studios in Brno and Ostrava—from where our colleagues supplemented that extraordinary TV orchestra—took turns on the screen.

We knew that all Prague bridges were occupied. The tanks had completely barricaded the entrances. Moreover, some of our faces could be remembered too easily, and there are no shortage of traitors and collaborators in critical moments of emergency. I was going ahead with my Fiat 850. Vladimir Tosek followed me, always in sight. We passed through Prague without difficulty, shortly before the Russians began to pick off Emauzy and the General University Hospital. Our colleagues reported that in front of the building of Czechoslovak Radio, two tanks were in flames and brave Soviet soldiers, in a helpless rage, set fire to a bloc of apartment buildings across from the Radio Building, and were shooting at the landmark building of the National Museum at the top of the Wenceslaus Square. Later the results of the shooting were called "frescos of El Gretchko."

Behind Modrany, we came across a group of Soviet tanks with machine-gunners aiming at anything alive along the way. We turned down a side-street and, as if by miracle, found the bridge across the Vltava river near Zbraslav unoccupied. It was about half past 10 A.M. when we at Cukrak took over the relay from our friends from the movie house Skaut. At that time the Brno and Ostrava studios had been silenced.

Anyone who had their television sets turned on at that time—several million people followed our broadcast, as we later found out—will never forget that strange emotional broadcast, which ended so symbolically at five minutes to twelve due to the siege of Cukrak and the invasion of the transmitter by submachine gunners. The cameras showed all of that.

When I look back—from a distance—conjuring up the dramatic moments of those thrilling days, I have to confess that those ninety minutes at Cukrak were the only moments when I felt fear. I would be lying if I did not admit that I was really afraid. Heavy airplanes of the occupation armies were still flying over our heads, and someone knowledgeably explained that if just one bomb hit the slender transmitting tower our broadcast and our lives would be over—as at the end of Romain Rolland's *Peter and Lucia,* when a slender cathedral column buried both lovers.

Vladimir Tosek was evaluating the current situation in Prague, and he very accurately termed the entry of the five armies onto our territory their total defeat. They could have planned for everything—perhaps even for armed resistance—but they were not ready for the spontaneous derision and contempt of the Czech and Slovak people. Then Vladimir Tosek turned toward me and asked the slightly modified question that I had asked Jan Werich on TV every Sunday: "What do you say about that, Mr. Skutina?" That modified version of the question later became a synonym of guilefulness.

I said that any haggling and negotiating with that self-complacent, cruel country in the East is useless. And I used the parable that negotiating could turn out to be the same as when a vegetarian invites a cannibal to lunch to convince him that vegetables are healthier than human flesh. The cannibal sits down in front of a bowl filled with vegetables, looks at the vegetarian, tears him into pieces, eats him, and has the vegetables after that. Only later someone tells him that the whole thing was intended otherwise. The original plan of a vegetarian makes the cannibal laugh. The events initiated by 21 August 1968 showed the entire world that any negotiations with the Soviet dictatorship were only the naïve hope of a vegetarian that a cannibal can be persuaded—by good example —to deny his natural instincts.

It was a quarter to twelve. The technicians from the tower reported to us that Russian tanks were approaching us from Zbraslav. We conveyed this to our viewers and we also said that since it did not matter anymore, we would broadcast as long as possible.

Of course, we wondered why they had taken such a long time to occupy us, for according to a telephone call from Prague they had set off for Cukrak at 9 A.M. The trip could take only about half an hour, at most, three quarters of an hour.

Only later did we learn that good and jovial inhabitants of Prague had sent the soldiers first to the film studios at Barrandov when the Russians trustingly asked them, "Where is the picture being taken?"

At the time, the Americans were shooting at Barrandov a film "The Bridge at Remagen," based on the story of a battle for crossing over the Rhine river during the last days of the World War II. A bridge over the Vltava river in Davle—not far from Zbraslav, and directly below the transmitter Cukrak—was chosen as a shooting location. Interior sets had been built in the Barrandov studios. When disoriented and counterrevolution-seeking soldiers of the occupation forces made it there, they *finally* discovered the up-to-the-teeth-armed counterrevolutionaries dressed in American uniforms with their guns hanging under their bellies. It took the Russians a long time to understand that the soldiers were hired extras.

In the studio, the commanding officer was ecstatic when he found American tanks. However, since those were mere dummies, their fronts were made out of plastic. So when the dumbfounded officer poked into the front of a tank with his bayonet the blade went through. The officer, accustomed to peasant carriages pulled by horses, shook his head in wonder: "What technology!"

The confused armored vehicles finally arrived at Cukrak. Since the Soviets were not sure what else to expect from those "damn Schweiks," they jumped out of their tanks, surrounded the building and advanced in jumps, forming a big circle around the transmitter, hiding behind trees.

Just then it was my turn. I said good-bye to our viewers, described the situation and then told the cameraman to turn the studio camera to the window so that the viewers could see the comic moves of the occupation forces. We, of whom the improvised staff of the extraordinary broadcast was composed, came out in front of the transmitter where our cars were standing. Many viewers later asked me how was it possible that they saw me come out together with two coworkers, get in a car standing near garbage cans, back out and leave amid creeping Soviet soldiers.

That was one of the mysteries of the first day of the occupation. Soviet soldiers who were expecting counterrevolutionaries in American uniforms, and under all circumstances heavily armed, probably took us for tourists who were at Cukrak picking mushrooms. So they let us pass without taking their watchful eyes off the transmitter even for a minute.

When they finally entered the transmitter, they found only automatically running technical gadgets and a deaf janitor who was so afraid that he had hung a framed picture of Lenin next to a boiler. I am not certain, but a story has it that the Soviet soldiers guarded that eternal light of the boiler by Lenin's picture till Lenin's one hundredth birthday.

Since Ambassador Chervonenko still hoped at the time that the resistance of the handful of hardened revisionists (how they were described repeatedly in the messages having been sent to Moscow before August) would be broken, he ordered that the transmitter stay undamaged because a transmission trailer of the Soviet television in Kiev was on the way to Prague.

As known, the trailer made it to Prague no sooner than Saturday, and because the "handful of hardened revisionists" numbered 14 million of determined inhabitants of Czechoslovakia, the transmission trailer had to be placed—for security reasons—in the garden of the Soviet embassy.

75

Despite the efforts of several untalented collaborators, the Soviets did not succeed in showing on the screen more than a picture of the Prague castle (which was ready at Cukrak for an emergency), and after a super-human effort they exchanged the picture for a photograph of the cathedral of St. Nicolas. This trick was repeated ad nauseam.

What technology!

And What If the Russians Did Not Come...

Pavel Tigrid

MORE THAN ONE hundred books and an infinite number of articles and essays have been published about the Prague Spring of 1968. Many of them maintain that the reform experiment would have succeeded—the Spring would have turned into a Summer and yielded fruits—had it not been suppressed *manu militari*, by the military intervention of the five Warsaw Pact countries. (For example, the title of the extensive study *Czechoslovakia's Interrupted Revolution* by Gordon Skilling reflects such a belief.) Simultaneously, the essays and books point out that it is impossible to show what would have happened *if*...since a serious historian cannot take into account events that did not take place. Yet, some of the authors of these publications—above all those who stood at the cradle of the Prague Spring—conclude, or suggest, that had it not been for the invasion of 21 August 1968, something that had not occurred in any country ruled by a Communist party would have taken place in Czechoslovakia: by a nonviolent reconstruction, the centralized, autocratic system would have been transformed into an ideologically, politically, economically and culturally more open society, perhaps ultimately a pluralist one. There is, however, no proof for this belief.

Therefore, allow a journalist, not a historian, to play a little bit with the "if"—allow him to use it as one of the "models" and, simultaneously, let him lean on the documents and studies which the 1968 Prague reform Communists worked out on the presumption that the process they initiated would not be interrupted by force.

In our model, the Soviets and their class brothers do not come in August 1968. The Prague Spring is developing according to the plan called the Action Program of the Communist party of Czechoslovakia. The Program is properly approved by an extraordinary Party Congress, which itself is conducted calmly and harmoniously, and whose conclusions are accepted in Moscow without big problems (as they would be almost certainly accepted today under Gorbachev's leadership).

It may be proper to point out that the Prague Spring was officially called "the process of renewal." In the Czechoslovak case, what was being "renewed" was a Party that had found itself on the brink of disintegration. To remedy that situation was the first and main goal of the reform Communists. Their thesis went thus: "If the Party—the leading force in the country—succeeds in revitalizing itself, society, too, will be revitalized, above all in the areas of the economy, politics and culture. That will lead to a higher responsibility of citizens, a better sense of honest work, and to decent relations among people." One of the teams of experts appointed by the Czechoslovak Communist Party to examine the problems scientifically stated that the crisis in the country "has afflicted all spheres of our life." But the team also claimed that those who initiated the process of the revival were exclusively Communists, and that they had to remain in the forefront of the process. It was said that "after the election of comrade Dubcek in January 1968, the *power* preconditions for the start of the process of renewal were created."

The promise of many delights...

Therefore, in our scenario, the sky of the Prague Spring is as blue as the triangle in the Czechoslovak state flag. Society lives according to the Action Program, and the Program promises many delights. Take, for example, the political ones: anticipated future freedoms and rights of the citizens. This charter of the immediate Czechoslovak future asserts that the Communist party—still the main political power in the country—wants to earn its "leading role in our society." It will put into practice "socialist democracy." It does not intend to be "a universal manager of society" anymore, to control and manage everything from the center, to "rule over the society." The program states explicitly that "the policy of the Party must not create a feeling among non-Communist citizens that they are being limited in their rights and freedoms by the leading role of the Communist party. On the contrary, they should see in the activity of the Communist party a guarantee of their rights, freedoms and interests." Such a statement really is not a trifle, even though in a parliamentary democracy it is always a constitution which guarantees rights, freedoms and interests of citizens, never a political party. The latter must always act in accordance with the constitution. The Action Program also promises to remove the so-called "cadre ceiling," meaning the system in which only Communists can hold certain posts, certain jobs, be entitled to a higher education, etc. The program also promises the constitutionally guaranteed rights of free speech, freedom of movement ("especially travel abroad"), and a thorough rehabilitation of both the Communist and non-Communist victims of illegalities of the previous era. It outlines a broad democratic concept of political rights of citizens, extended jurisdiction of the parliament, control over the police, the growth of nominal wages and, with it, the overall standard of living. "The ideological and political role" of the culture, education and science must not be overemphasized. The federalization of the state will take place, and the Slovaks will have their own Slovak Socialist Republic. Moreover, the goals of the Action Program, and its intentions, will be put into effect in "the immediate future." They should be implemented within a year to eighteen months.

...and "Socialist democracy"

However, the same Action Program contains directives which weaken or entirely contradict its good intentions. The rules of our game are such that we have to follow these directives as well. So, for example, the Communist party still holds its leading role in the society, though it wants to deserve it. But how? The Party explicitly rejects competition from other political parties—even the socialist ones. It also repudiates a pluralistic and unmanipulated election, which can only rightfully decide who rules in a state and for what reason. So, in fact, the proclaimed "socialist democracy" is no democracy at all, and it cannot be one. The Action Program does not talk about political parties; it mentions only political *forces* which can function only in the framework of the National Front based on a "joint socialist concept of politics." It therefore talks only about shadowy parties, as it has done so far, and it does not mention the right of such parties to a prospective election-mandated share of ruling power. That power remains in the hands of Communists and the Communist controlled "organizations of interest," which, it is asserted, must not be "excluded from direct influencing of state policy." The National Assembly, to which the Action Program—in its "good" part—guarantees the position of "the highest organ of state power," is only several lines later described as a "socialist parliament," and thus, in two words, both the Assembly's sovereignty and independence are abolished.

But this is not all. Two months after the declaration of the Action Program in June 1968, the Central Committee of the Czechoslovak Communist Party publishes directives that amount to further limitations of the freedoms and rights of citizens. Here it is, black on white: No political party or force is allowed to "develop political activities"—not even legal ones—aimed against the existing socialist society, for that would "threaten the socialist character of social development." Thereby, the good intentions of the Action program to end the limitations imposed on the rights and freedoms of citizens are abolished. The directives also demand from all "an agreement with the socialist class arrangement of social relations." That amounts to an Orwellian definition according to which all are equal but some are more equal than others, and the latter decide about all essential matters. The program materials of the XIVth Congress of the (reformed!) Communist Party of Czechoslovakia read: "The leading role of the Communist party must be secured institutionally...by a number of measures...which would secure...the hegemony and preference of the Communist party in such a way that a minority representation of the Communist party in the National Front and representative state organs could not occur."

The enumeration of such demands could be continued, but perhaps it is sufficient to conclude that all the rights and freedoms that the reform program of the Communists offered to the citizens were negated in the very same program. Some could object: Well, perhaps it is not possible to ask for everything at once, perhaps it will get better with time. After all, the Action Program was drafted as a political platform for only a short period of time. In two years, it will be clear whether the majority of the nation is satisfied with the reform program of the Communists, and, above all, whether the authoritarian regime can bear the systemic changes without disintegration. If yes, then perhaps the questions of a pluralistic system and of independent political parties, as well as of risks for "socialist democracy" that are inherent in such developments could be put on the agenda of the ruling—yes, still ruling—Communists.

Two preconditions were manifestly present in such reasoning. First, Moscow would have to accept the gradual development toward democratization and not strangle it before it had a chance to develop. (However, Moscow's behavior does not much interfere with our game anyway, for while the Kremlin masters experienced a nervous breakdown after eight months of "the process of renewal," the patience of those in Czechoslovakia who were immediately concerned with the process ran out after only five months.) The second precondition was as important as the invasion and, in contrast to the the first precondition, we cannot exclude it from our game, because it was an integral part of the social movement which took place in Czechoslovakia in 1968. The second precondition for the survival of the Prague Spring was that the society

—in this case the Czech and Slovak people, or at least its active parts mobilized by the Prague Spring—would view what the Communist program offered as sufficient. The society would have to be willing to wait for two or even ten years for the results; it would have to accept the snail's pace of halfhearted reforms; it would have to be satisfied with democratization and not ask for democracy; and it would have to find sufficient the truncated civil liberties and promises.

All that did not happen, because people did not see the Party's promises as enough. The second precondition was not fulfilled. One of that time's ironies, of which history is fond from time to time, is that the Party intelligentsia managed to rouse wide circles of people, radicalized the situation in the country, and thus contributed heavily to the failure of its own Party's reform.

"Where and with what goal?"

This engaged intelligentsia could be heard almost without interruption in the news media free of censorship, which in many cases had more power and influence than the official leadership. Take, for example, *Literarni noviny,* the weekly of the Union of Writers and, according to moderate reformists, "the bastion of radical" Communist intellectuals. Already in March 1968, *Literarni listy* put a question to their readers: "Where and with what goal?" The newspaper (circulation 100,000) received and published unheard-of answers and even more unbelievable demands: the liquidation of the monopoly of power of the Communist party. Free elections. A Parliament with a functioning opposition. Freedom of thought and expression. The equality of civil and political rights for the "four fifths" of Czechoslovak citizens who are not Communists. Obviously, the authors of the answers wanted a dark night to become a white one.

And the process did not stop at appeals and demands; people began to act. KAN (Club of Committed Non-Partisans), and an organization of former political prisoners came into existence. A Club of Democratic Youth was founded, as was a section of independent journalists and writers. The foundations of Social Democratic Party were created. In the entire country, public discussions took place in which the Communist party was often mercilessly knocked out. All this was already taking place in February and March. So when the Action Program was finally published on 10 April 1968 it was a stillborn baby. What the program, this Magna Charta of the Communist Party of Czechoslovakia, was saying and promising already lagged far behind the demands of the society, which wanted more and much faster. The strong pressure from below caught hesitating Dubcek and his colleagues by surprise. While they needed the pressure,

81

because without it the dogmatics in the leadership of the Party would have made sure that even the cautious reform program could not have been approved, the pressure from below was even more unrestrained than it originally looked. (Within the Party the term "eruptive character of the Prague Spring" was being used.) But above all, the popular movement was of a different kind and had a different source than the one from which the reform group in the Party leadership drank. The reformists promised to relax the totalitarian system; the society demanded freedom. The reformists offered democratization; people wanted a democracy.

At the end of June, the *Two Thousand Words* manifesto was published. It was written by a writer-Communist Ludvik Vaculik, and signed by hundreds of Party members and non-Communists (as well as several members of the Central Committee of the Communist party). It was addressed not to the holders of power in the country, but to "workers, farmers, officials, scientists, artists and all others." The manifesto represented a challenge to the Action Program and put against it its own program. It criticized the hitherto slow development of the reform and simultaneously expressed worries concerning the reform's fate. It asked the leadership to get rid of all dogmatics. If that could not be achieved without coercion, the best thing to do would be to organize a strike! It was topped by a proposal that even Dubcek must have considered as counterrevolutionary: people should start founding their "own civil committees and commissions," which would be independent of the Communist party.

It should be clear from what has been said so far what would have happened if the Russians had not come: not a gradual, half-hearted reform of the power structures, which no one wanted anymore, but a quick liquidation of these structures; not ascending, shining tomorrows, but— let's call it finally right—the beginning of the end of communism in Czechoslovakia. Could the possessors of power so visibly endangered look on inactively, while at the same time promoting a reform process now deluged by the wave of real popular demands? Certainly not. And that is why they were left with no choice when considering the next step. The retreat from the original intentions—the radical strokes in their own, already truncated program—represented such a next step. The order had to be renewed, and the old order was the desired result.

If it is impossible to prove that the reform Communists, under extreme circumstances, would not have hesitated to save the regime even by force, at least two other things can be said. First, the order (at least then, at the Brezhnev times) would have been reinstated by the Russians. But we are not concerned with that right now. Second, the domestic power elite would have had to suppress the pressure from below, if the ruling Communists intended their power to survive. The Prague Spring, which started as a limited, centrally directed, and carefully planned auto-reform of an authoritarian party and its way of governing, changed very quickly into a national movement for a structurally different system. This unrestrained movement, initiated from above, would have had to be liquidated just as another "movement of renewal" was destroyed twelve years later, (this time movement from below)—Solidarity in Poland.

The *Two Thousand Words* manifesto was seen by the Dubcek leadership as a signal to start a counterrevolution. Some members of the Central Committee saw it as a declaration of war on the Soviet Union; for others, it was an analogy of the situation that existed in Hungary in the Fall of 1956; still others saw it as a call for a civil war. The entire leadership, in a special declaration, rejected the *Two Thousand Words* manifesto. Regional committees of the Communist party received instructions for imposing emergency measures, and dogmatists pointed their fingers at the reformists (and reported their names to Moscow): "This is how it ends when the Communists credulously play with such a basic principle as the leading role of the Party."

"Not the best found solution"

One of the closest collaborators of Dubcek, Zdenek Mlynar, (today in exile in Vienna) wrote in his book *Nightfrost in Prague:* "Today I am not at all convinced that even if everything during the Prague Spring had happened according to my ideas about the real possibilities of the development, it would have been possible to achieve the goals I set for myself at the time. There would probably be less political democracy in Czechoslovakia today than I was convinced that there could be. It was also obvious that reform communism was not the best found solution." Two hundred pages farther, Mlynar describes how, after the invasion, in Moscow "half as a hostage, half as a state guest," he was, deeply depressed, thinking: "We are actually stupid, but our stupidity takes the form of reform communism."

There are of course more learned formulations of the same reflection. Leszek Kolakowski summed it up approximately thus: The goal of communism and Communists is gaining the monopoly of power and holding it. The monopoly of power cannot be only partial. All suggestions of change, or changes, in the system of indivisible power are necessarily only superficial, fleeting and unrealizable—if supposed to last. Stalinism is not a deformation of the system, but its fulcrum. Communism is a petrified system, deprived of self-regulating mechanisms. Such a system embarks on a reform course only when it is threatened with catastrophes, big economic crises and ideological revolts. However, even these reforms are only partial, usually temporary, inconsistent, and they do not touch the basic structures of the regimes.

Other observers point out that the Soviet model of socialism (no other, when all its variants are taken into consideration, really exists) cannot be fully reformed, because a thorough reform would not be a reform anymore but a disintegration of the system. The system has the form of a pyramid, and everything is being controlled, planned and managed from its top: from gigantic construction projects to the size of meat portions in factory dining rooms. Attempts at a structural reform, even those initiated by the power elite, sooner or later threaten the entire structure, and must therefore be canalized and neutralized. It is a vicious circle. Democratization is only a chaste word for pluralism—ideological, political, economic, social and cultural—and therefore, once again, the beginning of the end of the power pyramid. The closed character of the system demands that its functional defects are concealed and manipulated. A really free criticism of the system is therefore inadmissible. An informed citizen is dangerous. He or she wants a remedy, and as the pressure on power grows, it threatens the system and must be therefore broken— one way or another. Therefore, a vicious circle again.

Shortly, in both theory and practice we can see the basic contradiction between the democratic, parliamentary system of the open society and a regime that is based on a guaranteed—sometimes even constitutionally —unlimited and uncontrolled power of one party, even though this power may exist within certain limits and may be in certain situations regulated by the needs and desires of society which is thus ruled. Czech political scientist Ivan Bystrina thinks that the Stalinist and post-Stalinist regimes are unable to have permanent changes and reforms—they have never existed and could not exist in a democratic form. Bystrina says that just as the Hitler regime—if it had escaped destruction by the war —could not change into a democratic system through a reform, so the post-Novotny regime in Czechoslovakia could not have changed from a non-democratic into a democratic one.

Ivan Svitak, one of the active participants and later critics of the "reform process" made in Czechoslovakia, put together a list of illusions of reform Communists: the illusion that totality can be detotalized, democratized, made more humane; the illusion of an "open Marxism," according to which Marxism can absorb the results of contemporary science, philosophy, and culture without losing its essence; the illusion that free or freer market relations are compatible with the centrally directed economy, which, in essence, even the reform Communists wanted to keep;

the illusions about the human face of the totalitarian dictatorship—one excludes the other. So, concludes Svitak, the Czechoslovak experiment of the Spring of 1968 was doomed to be wrecked because of its own paradoxes—the bizarre role of a Communist party that wanted to step on the historical scene in a costume of a democratic institution. The attempt was, in fact, liquidated before it was wrecked.

I think that the Prague Spring was doomed to fail from the beginning, even if the tanks had not come. Because, really, something that is a total cannot be simultaneously a half; if the regime is anti-liberal it cannot be also a little bit liberal, and if so, then only for a short while; if the ideology dictates to a political party that the Party must get all political power in a country and never relinquish it, it is obvious that such a Party cannot share power. To take a liberalization process all the way to its end, with all the consequences that ensue from such a notion, would amount to laying the foundations of a system that would be in sharp conflict with the principles and above all the application of power of Marxism-Leninism as we know it—in all Communist countries.

Dubcek and his colleagues did not intend to do anything like that, and would not have allowed anything like that. (And Gorbachev won't allow it either, otherwise he would be swept away.) After all, the best and most devoted reform Communists were also at least as devoted comrades who believed that Marxist-Leninist ideology is a miraculous ailment for all social ills. And even if their belief had been shaken, they would not have known where to turn because they were neither liberals nor democrats, nor democratic socialists. Dubcek and his colleagues attempted to reform a system paralyzed by a rigorous application of a one-hundred-years-old doctrine, which itself was the main cause of the paralysis. In short, they wanted to cure not the causes but the symptoms of the illness. And so the reformists, wherever they moved—as long as they wanted to call themselves reform Communists—were faced with an anachronistic ideology that forced them to damp down their own initiative, to truncate their own reform. Slowly, but surely, they closed themselves again into their own fortress of power.

Expulsion from Paradise: The Bypassed Generation

Eva Kanturkova

TWENTY YEARS IS a long time in human terms—one fifth of a century, a third of an adult life. The last twenty years in Czechoslovakia have been a period of decline, but it can't be said that this decline has resulted in a worsening situation. In a famous passage of *To The Lighthouse,* Virginia Woolf describes how time takes its toll imperceptibly in the short term, but in the long term with far-reaching effects. Dust settles in an abandoned house; mirrors become blind; things rot, wood dries up; spiders take over; trash and leaves are blown about by the wind; and all is covered by weeds.

People abandoned the house of Virginia Woolf; our land was abandoned by freedom. But under the hard cover of the anesthetized public life, under the many folds of the tough crust of simulated ideological life, time too creeps in. Movement takes place imperceptibly in small, minute shifts which we don't even notice, shifts which are recognized only after they have become part of us. Time and motion are half-conscious; the changes are impossible to verbalize. On the outside, silence. Nonetheless, under the self-confident surface of crass power, change smolders.

I do not want to write about how, during the past two decades, the republic has deteriorated contrary to the plans and hopes we once had. What is evident, what everyone knows, is of no particular importance. Rather, I would like to capture that creeping of time inside us. Inside we have certainly not changed. We haven't lost our creativity, hope, willpower, talent, imagination or skills. It is only that all these valuable properties clashed with the impossibility of their realization. Like the person in the fairy tale, we all had to penetrate beyond the door of the thirteenth room. With the creeping of time grew our understanding, optimistic certainty inside us, thanks to which nothing is ever completely lost. There is always something that's new, something to be understood, and one's life is to be arranged accordingly. Maybe it's in powerlessness that one's understanding transforms into something substantial.

On the outside this shift, manifesting itself as a shift into separation, "dissidence," could be expressed in what is almost a slogan: from a loyal citizen to a prisoner of the regime. At first glance this is a dramatic depiction, but it does not express what sort of loyalty was entailed and what sort of slave the one-time loyal citizen had become.

My generation

It could be said about a substantial, numerically strong part of my generation that the start of their careers chimed in with the spirit of the times. At least that's what I am able to deduce from the fate of my high school and university classmates and friends. When we left the university in the midfifties our hands were still clean, for the revolutionary terror had taken place at a time when we were still too young to take part. We were, therefore, entering ready-made conditions but with (fortunately for us) awakened reason, for at the start of our adulthood great upheavals were taking place in the Soviet Union, in Hungary and in Poland. In 1956 I saw Poznan with my own eyes; my husband was studying in Moscow at the time of the 20th Congress.

We were strongly critical even as we enjoyed all the advantages of our succession: the revolution, whether we realized it or not, had created a place for us. This fact will one day be the cause of traumatic thoughts within many of us. To the credit of a majority of my friends I must say, however, that the two main circumstances of our entering into society —the possibility of a career and a critical eye—remained in balance. Our fathers' generation tried to win us over, and it really was quite impossible not to accept the advantages presented to us. But it went against our grain to abuse the advantages. We used them according to our talent, knowledge and skills.

Our conscience functioned inside us. The focus of our critical sense was not ourselves—after all we were secure—but rather the people who had suffered under the revolutionary terror. Our critical sense protected our moral sense and we entered into social ties with a high degree of idealism, refusing to identify with Communist excesses—as they were called at the time. But, influenced by the times, we remained loyal to the regime. We wouldn't have dreamed of wishing for its downfall. The only thing we asked from the regime was to be ideally just. And so we became the loyal opposition. There was no distinction between those who were and were not Party members. In any case, opposition from outside the Party was impossible at the time; members of the opposition had been either scattered or placed inside camps and prisons. And people were arrested not only for outright animosity to the regime but for nondestructive rebukes as well. In 1966, at the time of the partial awakening, the trial of writer Jan Benes took place. His "crime" consisted of corresponding with an emigre magazine.

I began to write relatively late, when I was almost thirty. My husband and I had been poor for a long time—we never thought of trying for an easy career. This wasn't naïvete, it was the trend of the times. To this day I see the 1960s as years made to measure for me, as a time when I fought to be able to do that which I wanted and for which I was suited. However, I lived through failures and painful falls as well. There had been a political prisoner in the family and my father's means of livelihood was destroyed by the regime. Nonetheless, I never felt that I had been bypassed. There were plenty of opportunities and he who knew something, he who had a goal along with the willpower and talent was sure to find a place for himself. And this began to be true—albeit more difficult—even for those who had been prisoners and people who had once been persecuted. Time had started to favor that which was natural. Our generation was also mutually supportive; almost everywhere there were people who thought and felt the same way, although this support was quite harsh to itself, critical and not willing to compromise its values.

During the next five years I published four books and wrote several movie scripts. I didn't need to worry that I was being successful with something that was artistically without quality, that the support we were giving each other was really unprincipled protection. We were quite different from today's young generation; we did not enter official structures the same way.

The impact of critical thought and views came to an end when they encountered a brick wall—21 August. I can still hear the droning of the Antonov planes over Prague. That night I was awakened by the jarred window panes. The radio, which was still broadcasting, told what had happened. My husband was shooting a television program in northern Bohemia; he found his way back to Prague inside a recording van that made it through the columns of Russians. He arrived in Prague in one piece, perhaps thanks to the fact that he spoke Russian with an acceptable accent. I and my son sat on a bed until the morning, holding each other, trembling inwardly with tension. In the morning we left our apartment.

89

My husband went off to broadcast against the occupation from secret television studios and as we were saying goodbye we couldn't be sure that this was not the last time we would see each other alive. The whole street saw us and understood.

Undecorated by illusions and ideology, naked reality emerged immediately in all its power: the internal opposition was too weak to be able to reform Soviet style socialism. Quite simply, Soviet imperialist interests were much more powerful than anything else, even socialism. After 21 August I certainly found it more difficult to come to terms with my loyalty. I would have felt guilty, had I not possessed a critical sense from the beginning. But because I had been critical there came an open conflict. Having once been the generation of succession we became, almost without exception, the persecuted generation.

We were excluded from succession and from its link with influence and action; we became a generation which was to be bypassed. As the revolutionaries had once courted and cultivated us, the conservatives started to court and cultivate the youngest generation. People who had been persecuted during the fifties had lived through it all before. For those who experienced it for the first time only after 21 August, it felt something like an expulsion from paradise. Not only did they experience disillusionment with the very ideas to which they, in good faith, originally devoted their lives, but they also experienced a great loss in the means of their existence. Yet, despite all this, I do not see this loss as a historical punishment for our previous good fortune, our succession, because the entire country suffered through the destruction of this opposition.

I don't like to make too much of a woman's intuition because it sounds too much like a Cassandra, but I had been skeptical as to the possibilities of 1968 from the very start. Not that I wished for the downfall of the regime while realizing that it wouldn't come true. Quite the opposite: I became a loyal citizen all the more because our criticism was reaching its height and because for the first time in twenty years other people could speak out—people who were not Communists. But I didn't believe in the ability of Czechoslovakia to wean itself away from the influence of the Soviet Union. We are too small a country, strategically placed in too important a spot. Also, and this is less often written about, we are a nationalistically fragmented country. The end of the Prague Spring fit not only Brezhnev's plans but also the plans of ambitious Slovak representatives. For them Alexander Dubcek was a welcomed Trojan horse.

Despite all that happened, 1968 was a happy year for me. I can't remember when I worked with such intensity, though even that was an expression of our skepticism. We tried to fit everything that we could into the upsurge and finish it before all the threats around us came true. At the same time it was an intensity born of relief because we were able to do all that we had wanted to.

The movie coffin

At the start of that year my novel *Smutecni slavnost (Funeral Celebration,* or *The Wake)* was published and Barrandov Studios bid on it. We worked on the script with director Zdenek Sirovy all that spring, always under pressure from two sides. First, we knew that we mustn't miss out on this opportunity when the state-owned studio was willing to provide the means of making a film such as ours. Then there was also the pressure of the material itself: it was to be a black and white film, a tragic story in which black and white played a graphic role. It had to be shot in winter and this was why the script had to be finished and accepted in the fall.

As is known, the clever Czechs with their August Party congress in Vysocany made sure that the Soviet assault did not succeed 100 per-cent. Brezhnev had to release his prisoners, and the prepared group of leaders-collaborators did not dare to take over immediately. And during those strange months when everything had already been decided but had still to be gradually realized—by those who had been in power before August—we started to shoot. Because of the beauty of the countryside the director had chosen Vysocina, where people were poor and life was hard. The studio rented a farmhouse near Pelhrimov and when word got around what it was we were shooting, people came from far and wide to watch. But not to earn the hundred korunas fee.

The film tells of the death of a farmer who has been evicted from his native village because he fought collectivization. In offices still con-trolled by people who have evicted him, his wife obtains permission for the body to be buried in the family crypt. She brings the body to the ruined farm and there in the courtyard places it on a raised platform inside a casket. It is accompanied by a funeral procession through the black and winter countryside. One former farmer, who in real life had been evicted, came from far away and asked to be in the procession without pay; he saw in it personal satisfaction. We even hired a local amateur brass band which sounded a bit squeaky and slightly off key. We had a chance to think about what was illusion and what was reality. The country was occupied and we all knew that it would be for a long time. Nonetheless, we saw nothing illusory about the fact that people manifested their resistance only behind a movie coffin.

Local authorities complained to Prague, but we managed to finish the film; unfortunately not soon enough for it to be released. Along with many others it is locked in a safe. Reportedly, the bosses of Barrandov Studios used to show it to Soviet delegations in order to document the presence of counterrevolutionaries in Czechoslovakia. Lately they can't even do that. But the film, *Funeral Celebration*, is reported still timely; the director Zdenek Sirovy considers it to be his best.

Separation

At first through the main shock of the occupation and then through minute shifts, we were being further and further separated from society. The great numbers of those affected are well known. Because of their dismissal from institutions, offices, science, industry and schools the country is wasting away. Most members of the internal opposition were Party members; some were dismissed, some left on their own. During the purges only one symptomatic question was asked: Do you approve or disapprove of the entry of the armies? All the newly founded structures were gradually destroyed. The country was covered with an impenetrable and self-promoting police-protected bureaucratic stratum all the way to the management level of industry and agriculture. You must understand: I am not trying to describe affliction and deterioration but separation.

Those who felt their separation only on the institutional level see their dismissal, to this day, as an injustice that has ruined their lives. They maintain the illusion that it is possible to develop democratic socialism, even under the rule of a Communist monopoly, from the top—through the "progressive" will of the leadership. Today they expect a revival through the policies of Gorbachev. Historically, and during the past twenty years quite convincingly, the destruction of internal opposition has proved the inability of Communist socialism to liberalize itself solely through the power of enlightenment created and active inside the Party. With socialism which is unaccompanied by pluralism, the country can only continue on its road to slavery and backwardness.

As I see it, what was positive about the "expulsion from paradise" lay mainly in the fact that the one-time critical loyalists finally found themselves in the same position as the rest of the nation. Actually, they were now in an even lower position: university professors, directors of companies, secretaries, journalists and scientists became, in the best of cases, lowly clerks, in worse cases, workers, and in the very worst cases, unskilled help such as window cleaners, watchmen and fire stokers. Perhaps I am ready to accept that as punishment for our one-time superiority. But I would like to see that those discarded in 1948 were able

to mix with those discarded in 1968 as an opportunity for a deeper conversion than that based on the loyal criticism of the previous decades.

I am not an author who can write bestsellers. I am more interested
in what I am writing than how favorable are the conditions under which
I am writing, or what sort of response the book will receive. Even so,
had the conditions which had developed during the 1960s continued, I
would probably have achieved a certain amount of success and popularity. As things were, I was still able to publish the novel *Po potope,*
(After the Flood), but there was no longer any place for it to be re-
viewed. In the end it was taken out of the libraries. The theme of *After
the Flood* is concerned with the hero's spiritual breakdown and his find-
ing new courage to live. The censor connected the image of the flood
with the takeover of 1948, the time during which the book takes place.
As the Czech saying goes: every gypsy tells fortunes according to his
horoscope.

To document the base vengeance that governed the decision making
of the rulers: Secretary Jan Fojtík made into pulp the entire press run
of my novella *Pozustalost pana Abela (The Inheritance of Mr. Abel)* because my husband signed a protest petition on behalf of the first of the
new wave of political prisoners—his friend and colleague, the journalist
Vladimir Skutina.

Suddenly there wasn't a magazine or a publishing house that would
print a single line by me. I mention this not as a complaint but to emphasize the situation. Our problem was not how to come to terms with unfavorable conditions. It wasn't that simple even for those who had not been
affected by the political conditions. Everyone had to find a way out in
his own life. Those who were not directly affected have learned during
the last twenty years how to turn inward into their private lives. The
regime accepted this—it prefers people who are socially indifferent to
those who are restless. Many also went into exile.

For me emigration was not a choice. He who remained began to wrestle
with a paradoxical mechanism absolutely unimaginable for someone living under normal conditions. The totalitarian arrangement of society controls everyone to the smallest detail: which dentist to visit; what sort
of shoes to buy; whether there will be beef or pork on Sunday; tasty
bread or bread without taste; whether one has a place to live; whether
one's children can study; whether one can travel abroad; whether, whether,
whether. For each of these "achievements," as they are called, one pays
with servitude. The basis of this type of government is an absolutely
monstrous type of reasoning. When my friend was being dismissed from
her writing job she defended herself by saying that according to the con-

stitution she has a right to work. They laughed and told her that indeed she has but that nowhere in the constitution does it say she should not be making her living as a cleaning woman.

I read a review of a young author's book, penned by one of today's university professors of literature, a man who during the 1960s had no chance of making it higher than an official of the apparat. He said that the author had not properly used his talent to benefit society. An author's talent, wrote this cultivator of literature, belongs to the society. According to the precepts of this new age of slavery the "society"—as this parasitical class likes to call itself—is free *not* to make use of talent and to send an able literary critic to wash steps.

The situation is made more difficult by the fact that a certain psychological deformation takes place in people who are disposed of by the regime in such ways. Those who can't find a place for themselves through their independent spirit of entrepreneurship apart from the state begin to place their demands on the state and no longer upon themselves. In effect they are coming to an agreement with it.

I too first tried to find a place for myself inside this enclosed social structure. Three things were important to me—that the regime wouldn't succeed in proletarianizing my husband, that we wouldn't endanger the children who were still in school, and that I would manage to successfully defend my ability to write. The old publishing house personnel and dramaturgists were largely gone, but not so completely as to make it impossible for forbidden authors to publish under a different name. Not under a pseudonym, because through the central control of all payments that would be easily discovered, but under names of other people. Some of my friends use this method to publish to this day. I know of a case where the bogus author was even accepted into the writers' union on the basis of a good book. The real author's name, of course, had been kept strictly confidential.

Some day it will be hard for literary historians to find their way through such a jungle. And jungle rules predominate not only in the way such works are published but also in the division of royalties. This is done in various ways, according to how the bogus author values his name, how he regards the risk of such undertakings. It has been known for the bogus author to retain the entire payment for himself when the real author was unable to prevent such a theft. Several bogus authors have published my works under their names. They were friends and accepted no payment. Except for one—he took ten percent and was quite lovely in addition. Having acquired such a pleasant feeling about becoming a playwright, during rehearsals and especially on the evening of the premiere (I even bought some flowers for him), he started to advise me how to improve my dialogues. And this despite the fact that he found it difficult to write even a simple letter.

My first bogus author was a good friend, a talented director, now dead, who used to introduce himself on the phone as "your agent 007." I regret that even now I am not able to name him and express my gratitude. He looked around for acceptable material with which to counterbalance the various ideological garbage he was forced to direct. He chose my text and also signed it. We were a happily matched pair, seeing things similarly and with a related poetical sense. The production, which was the result of our cooperative effort, was quite successful; it was even made into a film. The entire company, except those who were not to know, had been told. The secret and dangerous nature of the production provoked the actors, costume designers and even the scenery movers into an exceptional effort. We were living through something which a few years later, in connection with the birth of Charter 77, was described by philosopher Jan Patocka as the solidarity of those suffering from shock. Faced with the same risk people sometimes became lifelong friends.

Emigrating books

But in the end the mechanism of those in power proved to be too strong. With subsequent materials it was no longer possible for my friend to be both author and director, and other directors ruined the productions. Since I no longer wanted to write things for the purposes of contraband livelihood, I had to opt for a higher level of separation. My books emigrated in place of me.

To Czech authors, there is a difference in importance between a book published abroad in a foreign language translation and a book published there in Czech. A foreign language edition means success; it reaches many people. A Czech version published abroad, even though it is salvation for the written work, reaches few people abroad and readers at home sporadically or not at all. For a forbidden author to publish abroad is full of risks. Long ago, when Jan Benes was on trial, I felt a revulsion over the guilty verdict. But I also felt admiration for him: at that time it never occurred to me to publish in Czech with an exile publisher. In 1981 I was in jail precisely for that reason—my book was published abroad. When I let it out of my hand I knew what could happen to me as a result. Yet I did not want to tempt fate—that's not my nature. In the book itself I was trying to get a friend fresh from prison to tell me about her experiences.

When the time came I did what I felt I had to do. Within the stench of an unaired cell, while climbing steps and walking through corridors that, during the 1950s, had seen the passage of so-called enemies of state sentenced to hang or to serve long prison terms, I felt many things. Dressed in a worn flyer's shirt and running pants loosened by time, I also felt relief. My institutional separation had reached its summit. A prisoner is not dragged behind bars with his loyalty intact.

The shock of one's drop in social standing does not always lead to far-reaching changes in viewpoint. Inside many of my friends the ideals of 1968 remained fixed as permanent values to which a society must return. It remains their hope existentially and as a means of their livelihood. Because of these ideas they believe in their future only in terms of their own importance and a return to their former position. The truth, however, remains, that he who has allowed social demise to transform the defeated ideal into a fixed idea is in danger of succumbing to soured discontent, bitterness and also opportunism.

The salvation of conversion probably rests in the fact that under the pressure of a situation one examines as deeply as possible one's spiritual equipment and its potential. And when one discovers its limits, he looks for other options, other spiritual solutions. I, however, have no faith in conversion to the opposite side and I respect those who were able to free their spiritual horizon of ballast, yet did not fall prey to pressures of current fashion and opinion. I am someone who needs to form and renew a harmonious state within herself. I understand reserve in others but in myself I view it with revulsion. Harmony probably lies in making one's actions and thoughts into a unity. Even in my books I notice how my view and depiction of the world is balanced by my understanding of the new situation.

The film version of *Funeral Celebration* differs from the book in that another central hero is accented in it. I wouldn't be able to say how much this is caused by the differing requirements of film and literature and how much by my own inward shift. In the novel the hero is a worker, a carpenter and master of his craft. He is a small town man, considerate, wise and honest. After the war he becomes a functionary of the Communist party. The novel tells how power which had been won and put into practice is no longer a mere vision of movement but is its reality. It destroys not only ambitious people with base motives, but also those who are noble. The film script, on the other hand, was based on the opposite thought, that there are values before which even power (which is not choosy) must bow down. In the film, power has to retreat before the dignity of death despite the fact the man who was being buried did not possess much dignity during his life.

The problem of power has always fascinated Czech writers. Revolutionary violence, its aftermath and guilt feelings cried out to be analyzed —becoming part of the spiritual climate. My third novel, *Cerna Hvezda (The Black Star)*, was written under the immediate influence of the 1968 tragedy. The theme had been chosen earlier. I began writing it in 1970 and the writing was accompanied all day long by the radio as a monstrous stimulus. The country was under the rule of the victors of 1968, and their outrageous lying and agitation only strengthened my determination. We were being hosed down by ideological sewage. Its stench settled like poisonous gas over the entire land. Those whom the book meant to warn against had become victors. There were days when I wrote as if in a wild dream. The protagonist of the novel is similar to my father in some of the circumstances of his life. The time span of the book is from the 1930s to the start of the '60s. It is a book about how one fights for power and how, after the victory, one deals with it on the highest level.

In the then-current anti-Communist atmosphere some of my critics felt it was wrong that the hero of the novel should be a Communist, but I regarded such criticism as facetious. I was proud that I had captured this general social danger called communism from the inside, through its internal functioning. And I do not consider it a mere facile argument to say that communism is one of the basic phenomena of our time, that it's impossible to avoid and that it is useful to describe it from the inside. In any case, many readers whose experience did not reach beyond the 1970s wept over the fate of my father who died in the 1960s as if that fate were their own. Also, one could use another facile argument: other movements besides communism ruled through their monopoly on opinions as well, for example religious movements. In the case of Czechoslovakia's own dramatic history, until the dissolution of the Austrian monarchy the Catholic church had monopolized ideas.

But all this outside evidence is not important. I saw the problem of a limited view in something quite different. The hero of the novel is a man not particularly strong; in his youth he joined the Communists for sentimental reasons and also because of his own weakness: he did not want to remain an outsider. It was the way many an intellectual joined the Communist movement. He is talented, moves up and becomes a famous journalist, but never stops being split by the chasm between his own decency and the indecency of power. His decency prevents him from using his power several times and, in the end, the unscrupulous rulers of the Movement wipe the floor with him. And the limited viewpoint? The hero of the novel is without an alternative viewpoint, remaining inside himself. He defends himself, hesitates and when he harms someone it is only himself. But he is still a prisoner of the power monopoly; failing to find a way out he dies by his own hand.

Of course, while writing the novel I would not have been able to formulate an explanation of it so clearly; the convenient view from the inside also constituted my limitations. In this case the circumstances were useful and fruitful, but in the future they could deteriorate into a hollow, claustrophobic shell. I don't know what it was and how it resulted in my realization that a criticism of power can become a fascination with power, that when you begin to criticize it too much, you find yourself within the sphere of its influence. In the full freedom of his exile, Czech writer Josef Skvorecky wrote his novel *Mirakl (The Miracle)*. He had been unable to achieve such a clean incision in any of his previous works written at home. In *The Miracle* he described the conditions through the eyes of another type of existence. He wrote about our times through the eyes of "the others," those whose connection with power was such that they were being choked by it. That was an alternative, a liberating stance which, when applied to myself, I accepted as justly critical.

As part of my own, complex research I wrote the novel *Pan veze (Master of the Tower)*. Its form is that of an intrusion of planes—what is current mixes with distant history, reality with imagination, fact with parable. Because the hero of the book, a writer, sold himself, he is unable to finish the most important work of his life, a novel about Christ. Upon dying he is resurrected for eternity by love; he lives through all that he had been writing about during Easter Week in Jerusalem. It is a novel about a novel and also about guilt and desire for expiation. The writing does not strictly adhere to the gospels; Jesus is not God to the writer, but a man with actions so principled that he could be pronounced God. Mainly due to this, the book got the reception which usually befalls books asking questions with such a vehemence: at times enthusiasm, at other times violent antagonism.

That ideas permeate the world has been proven for me through an outstanding philosophical study *Kristus pro ateisty (Christ For Atheists)* by Professor Milan Machovec, and also through the excellent essay *O povaze nasi kultury (On The Character of Our Culture)* by Professor Vaclav Cerny. Machovec examines the possible factual basis of the gospels and the roots of that which shapes us, while Cerny looks into that special mix of ancient paganism and eastern Christianity, two sources of European spirituality, which again and again knot themselves so painfully through European history. Of course a writer draws from his own feeling of the times, not from previously thought-out theories. A writer searches for an explanation of his time; in choosing the theme aside from the atmosphere of the times I was also influenced by the roots of childhood and early adolescence. In those two books I became aware of the complex background of even my own thought.

It seems to me that the spiritual aspirations of a particular time tend always to deal with central themes, stressed independently by various people. Correct or not, I believe in the vitality of my novel; for me, it has already provided a sharp ray of light. The realization that the truth of the world is comprised of all that which is complex and paradoxical, calls for one to differentiate and to be as precise as possible in one's explanation. In order for a person to understand the world, he must keep creating a spark within himself, remain open. Only with such openness is it possible without mutilation, without one-sidedness, to study everything without destroying it: the genuineness and falseness of this world, the past and future of humans, the existence or not of God—whatever it is that shapes and deeply affects us. Only in openness is there such a great spiritual strength and freedom.

"Trust nobody!"

In the transformations of our two decades we saw the other face of liberty, and we were to engage it in practice as well. I will attempt to express it via a small detour. My last book was about prison, the novel *Pritelkyne z domu smutku (My Companions from the Bleak House)*. Some of my friends say that my prison experience helped me to write my best work. The prison experience is a good experience, so good that to have been in prison constitutes (in Czechoslovakia) almost an honor instead of shame, but I still do not consider it indispensable to a writer's creativity. Something much more important than the mere acquisition of material developed through my own prison experience. Whenever a human being becomes powerless, the poles between those who rule and those who are ruled are drawn astonishingly far apart. The imprisoned pariah becomes a real pariah only when the warden reveals how much of a master he actually is. This is probably true everywhere, but in relation to regimes with a monopoly of power this drawing apart of the poles so faithfully expresses the condition of the entire society that to describe a prison, the fate of imprisoned people, means to describe our society. One recognizes himself in the fate of the prisoners even when one has never been in prison, even when one is afraid of it. Unfreedom, exposed in its nakedness, is an indictment of unfreedom disguised.

For me the distance between the poles had been personified by two people—my interrogator and one of my prisoner friends, a young gypsy woman. The interrogator would arrive well dressed, shaved, perfumed, carrying a cup of fresh hot coffee which he refused to provide for me when my lawyer asked him. He was about thirty-five with a recent law degree which he acquired not at a university but at a school for state security. He was starting his career with my case, proud of his cultivated life, the amount of reading he had done. "A book is the only thing I could ever steal," he said as he lovingly went through a laundry basket full of books and manuscripts which had been confiscated in my apartment. He considered them a transgression and conducted his interrogations on the basis of the material. To this date they have not been returned to me, despite the fact that our group has never been brought to trial.

On the other hand the gypsy woman, who carried the delightful nickname of Rum Praline, could neither read nor write. I wrote her letters for her and she would then shyly print her name at the end—she didn't know how to do more. She arrived in the cell with a monstrous black eye and a severed nerve in her lip. According to what she said, she had been arrested either for kidnaping a child, for not paying the upkeep for her child in a state institution, or for stabbing her lover in the stomach. But everything she told us could also have been the product of her imagination—telling stories was an activity very much favored by prisoners. Once Andy—Rum Praline—returned from an unexpected medical examination. During a walk in a remote corner of the prison courtyard where we couldn't be heard she said to me: "Eva, trust nobody, nobody!" And then she added, in an even lower voice, "Not even me."

This is exactly how, under collective danger, under mutual inhuman pressures, something develops which for a person's freedom is as important as his separation from the institutions and that of his opinion. His own community is thereby created. Andy, because she refused to be an informer, had joined me against the interrogator; a community of the powerless had been created. And with Andy's help I am now coming to the pinnacle of our separation, our solitude, our freedoms: the development of independent communities and activities. Our experience with totalitarian power resulted in a practical and at the same time basic decision to simply circumvent power wherever this becomes essential. To create one's own, parallel structures is a far-reaching thing. Inside a totalitarian system, cells are being born to provide other solutions in the future.

That is how editions of typewritten manuscripts are born, how periodicals are circulated in typewritten form in twelve copies, how Charter 77 was born. That's how people's spirits are being revived, not only in churches and at religious services, but also at jazz and rock concerts and in movie houses.

When the English film *Ghandi* was released in Czechoslovakia, people remained seated as if glued to their seats even after the movie had ended. And in those seconds a community of people with the same feelings and thoughts was born. An ozone of unity flowed through their consciences. And it remains a mystery why the factual, sober and circumspect Czechs felt Gandhi's way to be their way, especially when far and wide in this land no leader resembling Gandhi can be detected.

Under the impenetrable cover of fake reality the fruits of change are ripening. And they seem to me to be more important and consequential than attempts to tear off the cover which is already rotting anyway.

Translated by Jan Drabek

From the Prague Spring to a Long Winter

Jan Kavan

I WAS BORN into a highly political family in very political times. I was six years old when my Czech Communist father was sentenced to twenty-five years imprisonment in Communist jails, for allegedly being "a traitor." He was relatively lucky because he was still alive, though not for long, when several years later the Communist party switched the labels and began to reverse some of its policies. Much later, in a macabre move, his executed friends were readmitted to the Party in memoriam.[1] My English socialist mother brought me up to understand that if socialism is not married to democracy but instead to totalitarian "democratic centralism," it can give birth only to a nightmarish dictatorship.

Primarily, however, my mother stressed—and my experience as "a son of a traitor" underlined—that genuine socialism is incompatible with injustice. Realizing as a teenager that many people knew the truth about the Stalinist fifties but were cowed into silence by fear, I began to see that through their ostrich behavior many of my father's generation shared responsibility for the judicial murders.

Indifference unjustified by fear of persecution was beyond contempt. It was, therefore, inevitable that when the Party confronted me as a university student and official of the youth union with the choice between silence, which would ensure my smooth career, and outspoken defense of a student leader persecuted for his belief in pluralism, my response was unhesitating.

The birth of the student movement

The student's name was Jiri Muller. He invited the wrath of the authorities in December 1965 when, at a national student conference, he presented a political program that would have transformed the only sanctioned youth union (CSM), controlled by the Party, into a genuinely representative youth body and "if necessary, a certain corrective to Party policy."[2] The then president and first secretary of the Communist party, Antonin Novotny, saw the proposal as an attempt to institutionalize opposition outside the Party. Muller was expelled from the union and the university and drafted into the army. Ironically, the repressive measures taken against Muller furthered precisely those aims they were intended to stifle. More students wanted to learn about the ideas deemed important enough by the Party to make Muller into a martyr. Muller's supporters, including myself, were elected to the leadership of the Prague University Council of the Youth Union (VOV CSM), the highest position within the union that we could reach even against the Party's will. The Council became the *bête noire* of the authorities.

To understand the authorities' anger it is necessary to remember that public opinion in Communist societies was largely reduced to the opinion of the official organs. These were formed and controlled by the power elite. We were supposed to defend the power elite's conception of grassroots opinion as if it was real. By refusing to do so, we threatened to expose the "as if" game on which the whole system was based.[3] This was the beginning of institutionalized opposition.

The Communist party leaders were well aware that they had virtually no allies among our generation, the first to be educated in postwar Czechoslovakia. Those who took Party propaganda seriously and identified socialism with the trials and Orwellian controls of individuals from cradle to grave rejected both the Party and socialism. Others like myself, who began to contrast the humanistic content of socialism with the reality of policies designed solely to preserve the Party's power at all costs, rejected the Party for being the major obstacle to socialism. The Party could thus rely only on a handful of spineless careerists willing to serve anyone in power. It was, therefore, understandable that the youth union was the only mass organization to be put under direct Party control.

With the progress, albeit desultory, of de-Stalinization in the sixties, it became obvious that the mass social organizations were not functioning as efficiently as the power-center would have wished. The Party fully appreciated the danger of decentralization, namely loss of control, and therefore tightened its grip on the largest of these organizations: the trade union (ROH) and the youth union (CSM).

This pressure to conform was exerted on us even by some reformist Communists, including those who later in 1968 embraced the concept of "socialism with a human face." The reformists gave us very little support. For them the way we expressed our ideas and, hence, our relationship to the power structure was more worrying than the ideas themselves: they expressed similar ideas in internal, confidential Party papers prepared by "expert committees." However, by attempting to put the ideas into practice we had shot ahead of our time. Some of those ideas found their way into the 1968 Prague Spring's Party Action Program, but by that time the program was already lagging behind the times. Many people, especially students, no longer merely questioned the methods the Party used to control society; we rejected its leading role altogether.

Many of us became involved in politics primarily for ethical and moral reasons. One of the main differences between us and the reformist Communists at that period can therefore be illustrated by the explanation offered in 1968 by Major Raska, a reformist, who a year earlier had been a member of the CSM Presidium and head of the commission that was supposed to inquire into Muller's expulsion: "I was faced with an inner conflict: should I save one person, risk a split, weaken my position and that of the progressive forces, or was it not my duty to promote the progressive trend and to that end sacrifice sympathy for one person?"[4]

The main student leaders became known as the Prague Radicals. Our attitudes and activities were once summarized by Lubos Holecek: "...no power is omnipotent. It creates a certain empty space, the boundaries of which are not precisely known to it. Only by constant activity on the boundaries of the permitted can one gain the information and experience necessary for independent political activity."[5] I recalled this remark ten years later when Charter 77 was born. Lubos, tragically, did not live that long. Still in his twenties, he was killed in a mysterious hit-and-run accident by an employee of the prosecutor's office.

In Czechoslovakia, as in all East European countries where the power and monopoly role of the Communist party are anchored in the constitution, the scope for expressing political views outside it was very restricted. Students were among the most outspoken critics, and at that time they were the only group to oppose the regime at the grassroots level. The problem we faced was the same as that faced by most East European opposition groups: is the optimal form of opposition from within the Party, from outside the Party but through its institutions, or from outside the entire power structure? Eventually, following our brief encounter with such structures, we abandoned the idea that change could be achieved through positions of power. Jiri Muller explained our attitude at the time: "We are not interested in power. Our strategy is to restrict any power. We make politics in order not to have to make it. There are people who want to restrict power by rising in the social hierarchy and who say to themselves: 'When I reach the top, the rule of good will be established at last.' When they actually reach the top we find that due to various circumstances their initial conceptions of the good have been lost. Our alternative is to gradually limit the sphere of the functioning of power..."[6]

In 1967 we still explored the possibility of achieving change from within the youth union. Exploiting the workers' inherent distrust of the intelligentsia, Novotny launched a campaign to drive a wedge between the students and young workers. The regime has always regarded horizontal contacts across social groups as inadmissible, and fearing the results of student-worker cooperation the Party ordered that such contacts be exemplarily punished.

It did not work. At the Prague CSM conference in May 1967 we managed to get the support of the majority of worker delegates and were elected to the highest policy-making body—the CSM congress, held a month later. Here the Party took every precaution, including ordering Communist delegates to vote automatically against anything we cared to propose. The reform programs were shelved. Even so, minor successes were achieved, including the legislation of discussion clubs that became centers for political exchanges between students and the rest of the intelligentsia—especially writers, who challenged the regime at their congress later the same month. The role that such clubs can play can be seen even more clearly in the Soviet Union today.

This experience and the budding cooperation with the writers proved to be very useful in the tense atmosphere that followed a clash between police and students at a demonstration that October against inadequate study and living conditions at the Strahov dormitories in Prague. Both the Strahov demonstration and the political pressure we were able to exert in its aftermath proved to be a catalyst that helped to overthrow Novotny and his neo-Stalinist hardliners.

It also highlighted the pathetic inability of the youth union's national leadership to defend its members' interests, especially when these clashed with the government's wishes. Its attempt to suppress our account of what happened proved to be the final straw. We abandoned CSM and without waiting for anybody's permission began to create our own student parliaments. I was elected chairman of an interfaculty commission which helped to coordinate student protests and to formulate our demands for a basic change in the political conditions which made the repression possible.

Not long afterwards I was awakened by the proverbial early morning doorbell. My interrogators played the usual nice guy/nasty guy game. The 'nice' one (who after the invasion became a deputy minister of the interior) made chilling references to my father's fate and questioned me about my links with "British imperialist circles." The similarities with the fifties, however, ended there; by the end of 1967 the threats had a hollow ring. Student anger was widespread. Our talks with the authorities were stalled by the government. We were prepared to go into the streets and risk a bloody confrontation with the police. We were dissuaded by the Party reformists, some of whom, like Dr. Frantisek Kriegel, began for the first time to exchange information. Kriegel also intervened on my own behalf.

Students in 1968-1969

The decisive battle took place on Party—or more precisely, Central Committee—ground, when on 5 January 1968 Alexander Dubcek replaced Novotny as first secretary of the Communist party. The loose coalition that toppled Novotny soon showed signs of disunity. Conflicts arose among the Party reformists who had come to power. Outside the Party many intellectuals pointed with cautious skepticism to the Stalinist past of some of the top reformists.

The students were probably most critical, but we did not proceed immediately to outright opposition. In March we helped organize the first genuinely mass political rally in decades. We acknowledged that it showed great progress that we were able to speak out openly and we expressed our belief that "it would be wise and prudent to avoid obstructing the progress achieved with such a struggle." Nevertheless we made it clear that "our momentary support" for Dubcek and his fellow reformists did not mean that we would stop pressing for the "adoption of a program of our own generation." This would not include a leading role for the Party, and we warned that "if, for any reason whatsoever, the Party's political monopoly proves incapable of rallying the people, we shall be obliged to seek a different system which will not be a mere surrogate solution..."[7]

Soon afterwards Dubcek *de facto* abolished censorship. He did so mainly to harness the force of long-suppressed criticism against Novotny, still president, and the remnants of his conservative following who were still entrenched in the Party apparatus. In this Dubcek was fairly successful, but freedom of the press, once granted, could not be taken back without resorting to the very methods of power he had renounced. A mechanism capable of forcing change on the system thus developed outside the Party's control, backed by a free press and the free expression of opinion of many groups that mushroomed outside the power structure.

Some reform Communists, such as Dr. Zdenek Mlynar, warned against this danger, but in vain. What in January had begun as Party coup began to acquire a mass character.

A nationwide discussion on possible developments began to emerge. The least active participants were the workers, whose attitude could be summed up as "wait and see." Twenty years of deliberate depoliticization, combined with inherent distrust of any change imposed from above, could not be effaced immediately. We shared some of their uneasiness about the very technocratic and managerial content of the proposed economic reforms that in their earlier drafts played down the role of the workers' councils.

By midsummer the sharpest controversies had become muted as people rallied behind Dubcek and his Party in the face of an external threat to the whole reform movement. We argued in articles published in July that the government should consider means of defending the country, but our warnings were ignored.

All the films and photographs taken during the August invasion make clear that most people in the streets were of my generation—a generation of people entering their twenties. This does not seem to me to be a coincidence. The invasion was a terrible shock, but for us the capitulation five days later—signed in Moscow by Dubcek and all his colleagues, with the courageous exception of Dr. Frantisek Kriegel—was much worse. Dubcek returned to nominal power but appeased the Russians with one concession after another throughout the autumn. I agree with Jaroslav Sabata that "the blackest day of 1968 was not 21 August, [the day of the invasion] but the last day of August" [the day the Czechoslovak Communist Party Central Committee accepted the Moscow diktat and endorsed capitulation].[8] Sabata and Kriegel were among the few courageous top Communists who raised their voices against an agreement "written with the barrels of cannon and machine guns."[9]

In November the Central Committee, still led by Dubcek, designated the "right-wing opportunists in the Party and anti-socialist forces in the press and various clubs," as the biggest threat.[10] Twenty-four hours later, 60,000 students inaugurated a sit-in protest strike and issued a Ten Point program. Ironically, this program defended the Party's April Action Program against its authors and promoters. Factory meetings immediately adopted the Ten Points as the workers' own program.

The most important result of the strike was the establishment of this close cooperation which culminated in December 1968 and January 1969 in the signing of political agreements between the new, independent student union and all the Czech industrial trade unions. Jiri Muller was the architect of the first such agreement, with the Union of Metallurgic Workers. The two parties to the agreement—the students and trade unions—pledged support for the Prague Spring policies, demanded workers' councils, the holding of general elections and the withdrawal of foreign troops. I helped to reach a similar agreement with some unions from light industry.

I can still recall the workers' unwavering determination to defend the Prague Spring leaders, especially the popular Josef Smrkovsky, whose purge was demanded by the Russians. 900,000 metal workers, 330,000 building workers, 200,000 farmers, 180,000 railway workers, printers and many others announced their readiness to strike on Smrkovsky's behalf. Unfortunately the Party leaders were more afraid of the consequences of resistance than of capitulation.

On 3 January 1969, a few hours after the arrival of a Soviet delegation, the Party Presidium condemned the campaign and the strike threat. Some of us went to see Smrkovsky and asked him to stand firm, assuring him that our trade union partners were able and determined to call the general strike, but to no avail. On 5 January Smrkovsky himself appeared on television and begged the workers not to come out on his account. Two days later he was demoted. In a televised speech Dubcek hinted that "irresponsible actions" could provoke fresh Soviet military measures.

Several politicians later contended that the huge support for Smrkovsky had helped to create a situation which gave Dubcek "a solid basis for going over to the offensive." However the government seemed more afraid of its own people than of the Russians. The dilemma facing those unwilling to stop their compromises and concessions was unwittingly exposed by Smrkovsky later in January when he addressed a student meeting in Brno. "You have recently formed a relationship with the working class," he said. "This is a big thing: it carries weight...But what can happen? If you take action as you are resolved to...tanks may appear in our streets again...a provocation can easily be staged and a massacre may ensue. Then there will be an end to all our hopes."[11]

One wonders what hopes the Dubcek leadership could have still entertained. Preserving their own naive hopes by giving in again and again, they effectively smashed the hopes of ordinary people.

In fact, a wave of hopelessness swept the country. On 16 January Jan Palach, a twenty-one-year old student, set himself alight in a moving and tragic effort to shock the public out of its growing apathy. Hundreds of thousands responded, and the August unity was briefly reborn. This precipitated a further crisis, described by Dubcek as "the most serious since August."[12] The government correctly perceived Palach's sacrifice

109

as a protest against their own policy of compromise and sought to pacify the population by expressing sorrow that "a courageous young man" should have died as a result of "a misunderstanding between government and people, particularly students."[13]

There was no "misunderstanding." There was an unbridgeable gap in our perception of the country's needs and the impact and role of the occupying forces. I was a member of the student delegation that tried to persuade the Czech government to meet Palach's demands to guarantee reform policies. Minister Havelka tried to persuade us that our accusations of government capitulation were only false "impressions and subjective feelings" because "all the main principles" of the reform "are preserved and no one is being persecuted."[14] Czech Prime Minister Stanislav Razl warned us that "if you pressure the government [to take a firm and unambiguous stand] the government has no hope of a success" in its quiet diplomacy.[15] Halfway through the tense meeting, Razl learned that Palach had succumbed to his burns and died, after fighting for his life for three days. I shall always remember Razl's angry outburst: "Now you have really spoiled our hand!"

Palach's death was announced on the radio by Lubos Holecek. Palach had earlier summoned him to his hospital bed and in great pain whispered to him last message: "Tell them [the anonymous group prepared to become new torches] that they should all join you...alive...in the struggle."[16] The tragic news sent many students spontaneously into the streets. This speeded up our talks and we were eventually allowed to address the nation, though our prepared speech had to be "amended" in several places and presented only after Cestmir Cisar, a prominent reformist, had put forward the government's position. The student union's president, Michal Dymacek—today a Charter 77 activist—read the speech on television and I did so on the radio.

When four of us earlier had tried to formulate the proclamation we realized that "in the light of [Palach's] ultimate sacrifices, all words, however radical or sublime, sounded hollow and painfully inadequate."[17] My feeling of pride that we were resisting as much as we could gave way to a feeling of shame and a feeling that we, too, shared a responsibility for his death. Palach held up a merciless mirror to all of us and asked each of us individually whether we had done our utmost to fight signs of apathy and indifference.

Listening to myself promise on behalf of students "a torch of positive deeds so mighty that in its light Palach's friends will see that there is no need for their sacrifice,"[18] it became clear to me that in order not to feel permanently guilty, not to disappoint Palach's trust, I would have to place my deeds on the other side of the scale for the rest of my life. To date it has remained one of the strongest motivations for my work. I still feel that we all have his death on our hands and that we can only prevent it from ever being perceived as useless by continuously struggling against indifference to injustice or oppression wherever it occurs.

Half a million people lined the streets for Palach's funeral. The minister of education—professor Vilibald Bezdicek, who soon lost his job and who today is a Charter 77 signatory—promised never to betray "Palach's legacy."[19] Smrkovsky expressed sympathy, but other Party and government leaders remained silent. Of the politicians, only purged reformists such as Dr. Frantisek Kriegel and professor Jiri Hajek—the latter a former foreign minister and later one of the founding spokespersons of Charter 77—attended. The one politician who had no qualms about linking Palach's act with "dark, antisocialist forces," and the student-worker cooperation with "counterrevolution," was Gustav Husak.[20]

The beginning of the era of normalization

Husak's moment came in April 1969. Dubcek had served his purpose. The reformists had cut all the branches on which they were sitting and become dispensable. By the first anniversary of the invasion it became clear that opposition within the legal structures was no longer possible. There were, however, people prepared and able to resort to clandestine methods. The first such group circulated in August a leaflet appealing to Prague citizens to commemorate the invasion with a day of mourning, and by boycotting public transport, restaurants, cinemas and so on. The response was overwhelming: 98 percent of employees walked out of work, according to an official report. At noon all work ceased for five minutes and factory sirens wailed. Later, 120,000 people packed Prague's main square. Czech police and Czech soldiers were ordered to fire at Czech demonstrators. The country became "normalized."

The student union was banned soon after we refused to join the National Front, the Party-dominated umbrella organization. Jiri Muller then argued to the students' union congress that "...it is not important who will rule us and in what way; it is important that there should not be rulers and ruled...As I do not wish to replace the free student movement by a transmission belt from state to student, I vote against affiliating to the National Front. To rephrase the West German students' declaration, I would say: 'Only the most stupid oxen choose their own butcher.'"[21]

At the same congress, as vice-president for international affairs, I appealed against the continuation of the union's full membership in the

Moscow-dominated International Union of Students. The majority of the delegates supported our radical stand, and soon afterwards the union, with several other organizations and publications, was banned.

The censorship and the banning of civil organizations was rejected and condemned by eleven leading intellectuals, including Vaclav Havel, Rudolf Battek, Ludvik Vaculik and Jan Tesar, who also used the invasion anniversary to make a stand. In retrospect it is interesting to note that their *Ten Point Manifesto* demanded the ratification of the very international civil rights covenants which eight years later provided the basis for Charter 77. Historian Jan Tesar and Rudolf Battek spent a year in prison because of the *Manifesto*. Later, they served five and eight years respectively for their continuing activities in the opposition.

The first opposition group to go underground was the Revolutionary Socialist Party (of Czechoslovakia) led by Petr Uhl. Its program bluntly stated that "we no longer believe the myth of legality because the bureaucracy uses the law in its own interests...Our position differs little from that of the working people in the neighboring people's democracies, and it is with them, first and foremost, that we must join forces..."[22] The RSP was infiltrated by the Secret Service (StB), and nineteen members were eventually sentenced to terms of one to four years imprisonment. The longest sentence was given to Petr Uhl, who later served another five years for his activities in VONS and Charter 77.

More or less at the same time the first people who had begun to cooperate across East European borders were brought to the dock, including my colleague from the Presidium of the student union, Laco Moravec. A group of Prague students was accused of illegal cooperation with Polish students, the production of leaflets and of supplying the Poles with a small duplicator.

By 1970 the Big Purge had really gotten under way. More than five million people were screened. Twenty percent of enterprise managers were sacked, almost half the journalists had to look for menial jobs, and thousands of teachers were found unsuitable to educate Husak's "new generation." Half a million Communists were expelled from the Party.

I did not know what to do. The new minister of education terminated my permission to study in England, and I was accused of "harming the interests of the state abroad" and of similar "crimes." I was confronted with a dilemma: to become an emigre and feel that I was betraying my friends or to return and face the consequences. I was unable to make up my mind and so I returned, illegally, to consult my friends. Most of them advised me to stay abroad and help the opposition from there, or as they put it, "to meet our needs, as we will, in a different time, define them."

Scattered opposition

Most opposition groups during the first half of the seventies concentrated on issuing and circulating leaflets, samizdat periodicals, and open letters, as well as producing samizdat books of good literary value. Purged university professors and expelled students joined together and formed unofficial seminars dealing primarily with philosophy, sociology, political science and religious studies. There was therefore a need for duplicators, for financial help and for Western scholarly books with up-to-date specialized information.

In the autumn of 1970 I helped set up a small group in London called the Solidarity Fund, which by the end of that year began to send many of these items to Czechoslovakia. It did so regularly until 1981, when our van was stopped on the Czechoslovak-Austrian border. By that time, however, a few other groups had emerged, each of them forwarding to Czechoslovakia requested literature and other items.[23]

The flow of information was, of course, not just one-sided. We received copies of almost all the samizdat material that circulated in Czechoslovakia. I received numerous samizdat journals including the regular broadsheet *Facts, Views, Comments*. This was produced by the Socialist Movement of Czechoslovakia, a group whose views evoked the ideas of many reformist Prague Spring leaders. I also read journals such as the Moravian *Behind the Censor's Curtain* and documents such as the little Action Program (MAP), whose socialist authors rejected communism as "utopian and unrealistic" and advocated the concept of "democratic self-government" as a common denominator for all the movements and groups interested in radical democracy.[24] Later I found out that the main author was Dr. Jaroslav Sabata. There were also writings by nonsocialist democrats but, their role, as that of the Christians, significantly increased only in the late 1970s and early '80s.

I was most thrilled, however, when in November 1971 I received a duplicated leaflet entitled simply "Citizens!" and signed by six different opposition groups. Released just as the authorities prepared to hold the first elections they dared organize since the invasion, it reminded citizens that they could express their opposition to existing conditions by refusing to vote or by deleting the regime's candidates from the secret ballot's single list. Although the advice merely reflected peoples' constitutional rights, its use was unheard of and was bound to be perceived by the authorities as a serious challenge.

113

In the event, according to the public prosecutor, at least 70,000 leaflets were distributed. According to unconfirmed reports a significant number of people, especially in Prague, did not vote. The opposition's success, however, overstretched their resources and, in the summer of 1972, forty-six people were sentenced to a collective total of one month short of 100 years of imprisonment. Another fourteen young people were given suspended sentences. Dr. Jaroslav Sabata received six-and-a-half years, Dr. Jan Tesar six years and Jiri Muller five-and-a-half years. The essence of the trial was summed up by Muller, who told the judge that the trial's concern was not guilt or innocence but the need to propel "a policy which could be described as 'Keep quiet and don't step out of line.'"[25]

There is no doubt that these trials were a severe blow to the opposition. The level of activity dropped drastically, contacts between various groups stopped and for a time the audible voice of the opposition was reduced to some of the reform Communists.

The stiff prison penalties imposed merely for typing a clandestine publication were a deterrent. The increasingly smaller number of "virgin" typewriters, i.e., those that did not have their typeface and the name of their owner registered in police files, posed another problem. The main obstacle to the growth of an underground press was, however, a widespread feeling of resignation. The demoralization caused by two capitulations within a generation is certainly crippling; the realization that for the third time (1938, 1948, 1968) in thirty years the extent of their sovereignty is determined by a tacit agreement between the superpowers is discouraging. Attempts to resist were regarded as mere quixotism. The majority resigned themselves to a long dig-in and cultivation of the Czech art of survival.

The government has encouraged this mentality with a smooth application of a kind of stick-and-carrot strategy: a reasonable standard of living and consumerism has been "offered" in exchange for political compliance. The regime understands well that consumer-oriented people everywhere are reluctant to sacrifice material gains for moral integrity. Nationwide corruption was tolerated to supplement the deficiencies of the stopgap economy. Exhortations to support ideological dogmas and promises of future paradise were replaced with a more reliable rule of fear— fear of losing one's savings, one's job, fear of the Secret Service, of imprisonment, and, very effectively, fear of jeopardizing the education of one's children. The courageous minority who still refused to conform was subjected to unceasing repression all the more because the authorities were clearly aware that it said aloud what the majority thought. But by exposing the majority's silence as the unspoken disagreement of a silenced people this minority ensured vital continuity of the opposition and kept fertile the ground for the future.

From 1974 intellectuals concerned about the survival of Czech culture stepped up their activities. Samizdat publishing houses produced more books, many of them written by the best known postwar Czechoslovak authors. At the same time rock concerts and exhibitions organized by young nonconformist groups associated with what became known as the cultural underground began to flourish. By the end of 1975 samizdat books, literary manuscripts, economic analyses and open political letters were being produced in quantities second only to Poland.

The increased quantity of material which the Solidarity Fund brought to London soon underlined the need for its work to be legally protected and institutionalized. With the help of several Czech and British friends I therefore set up in 1975 a press and literary agency called Palach Press. We were also greatly helped by the experience we gained earlier that year when we distributed—simultaneously in thirty-three countries on five continents—Dubcek's first open letter since he became an employee of a Forestry Office, in which he defended the Prague Spring and complained about his surveillance.

Charter 77

I shall always remember the winter of 1976/77 as exciting and full of promise. It started, in fact, in the summer when we tried to publicize the forthcoming trials of two rock groups—the Plastic People of the Universe and DG 307—and encountered among Western journalists much greater interest than we did over any of the previous trials. Even more encouraging news was reaching us from Czechoslovakia where solidarity with the musicians led, as Vaclav Havel, the internationally renowned Czech playwright pointed out, "to the forging of an understanding among former activists including reformists from 1968, Christians and intellectuals and caused them jointly to undertake protest activities."[26]

Then in November the government published the full text of the International Covenants on Civil and Political Rights, and on Social, Economic and Cultural Rights, which it ratified in March thus making them formally an integral part of the Czechoslovak legal code. The small official brochure entitled Law No. 120 became a bestseller overnight. People learned that they had a legal right to freedom of the press, and speech, freedom to strike and set up independent trade unions and so on. The defense campaign on behalf of the musicians spawned an informal organization linking different groups that wanted to close the gap between the letter of the law and everyday practice. In early December the last of the 1972 trial prisoners, including Jaroslav Sabata and Jiri Muller, were released. All the ingredients for the reemergence of a legal opposition were in place.

In January 1977 Charter 77 was born. At first glance the human rights manifesto, with the first 242 signatures, did not look very explosive. The Charter described itself as "a loose, informal and open association of people of various shades of opinion, faith and professions united by the will to strive individually and collectively for the respect of civil and human rights..."[27] The Chartists stressed that they were not a political organization, had no political program and did not want to be regarded as a political opposition. They made it clear they had no intention even of setting out a "platform of political or social reform or change...to conduct a constructive dialogue with the political and state authorities."[28]

Right from the outset, there were Chartists who had their doubts about the feasibility of conducting a constructive dialogue with one of the most repressive regimes in Europe. Internal debate about this and the degree to which the Charter could legitimately become involved with more political issues has gone on for years. The resulting division between the radicals and moderates hearkened back, to a limited extent, to divisions in the society caused by the August '68 capitulation, and to the long-standing argument on the expediency of resistance, both nonviolent and armed. The greatest support for "constructive dialogue" came from the Euro-Communist group whose supporters, although a minority, played a significant role among founding signatories. The first decade of the Charter has, however, seen an upsurge of interest among workers, young nonconformists and Christians (the latter a reflection of the rapidly growing independent Catholic movement), thus diminishing the role of the Prague Spring reformists.

Not surprisingly the only dialogue the authorities permit takes place across the table with Secret Service interrogators. By demanding that the government observe its own human rights laws the Charter has exposed the regime's ingrained hypocrisy and lies. It has exposed not only the myth of normalization but also the myth of the system's legitimacy. The unceasing repression of a group that is today about 1,400-strong can only be explained by the fact that the regime perceives Charter 77 as something that strikes at its very core, the group's supporters being only the visible tip of the proverbial iceberg.

Charter 77 is a remarkable phenomenon. The oldest human rights movement in the Soviet bloc is still both united and politically almost as heterogeneous as the society it speaks for—minus, of course, its current rulers. Among its signatories are revolutionary Marxists, independent socialists, Communist reformists, liberals, democrats and Christians. Many of them continue to work in their own political groups outside the framework of the Charter.

The standpoint of the Charter is basically a moral one and its role primarily that of a catalyst: it offers encouragement and hope, it reveals the limits of what can be done today, and it attempts to create a space that others can use. The last is today most evident in the cultural world. The price which individual Chartists have paid and continue to pay is, however, very high.

Tom Stoppard noted that "the events of 1977 are in a direct line with a process which since 1968/69 has turned Czechoslovakia into a weird, upside-down country where you can find boilers stoked by economists, streets swept by men reading Henry James in English...where millions of crowns per month are spent on maintaining little cordons of policemen... to disarm a handful of dangerous men whose only weapon is free conversation."[29] If I had to describe Charter in a nutshell I couldn't do better than to quote Havel's colorful and pithy description of the movement as "an icebreaker with a kamikaze crew."[30]

In addition to human rights, Charter's concerns cover a wide range, including ecology, questions of peace and security, religious and ethnic rights and those of conscientious objectors, social and economic problems, music and literature. Palach Press has translated into English all Charter 77 documents and all statements by one of Charter's main offshoots, the Committee for the Defense of Unjustly Prosecuted (VONS). To date this represents at least one and a half million words. Perceptive analyses and commentaries have been published in numerous specialized journals and books.[31]

Changes in Communist systems

In my opinion, the most important development during the last few decades is the dialogue and cooperation between the independent movements across the Iron Curtain and especially within the Soviet bloc itself. It is crucially important, in my view, because it can help achieve a genuine change of the political status quo in Central and Eastern Europe or at least influence the nature of such a change.

Obviously there is no blueprint for effecting change in the Communist systems of Eastern and Central Europe. Those who believe that the system is reformable advocate different sets of reforms that can be implemented either from above or below. Given the command structure of the totalitarian state, reform from above is the easiest to initiate and thus, to date, the most frequent. Czechoslovakia experienced the former to a certain extent between 1963-67 and particularly during the first half of the 1968 Prague Spring. The Soviet Union is currently being given a dose of it by Mikhail Gorbachev.

Reformers-from-above initiate reforms not because of their intrinsic support of liberalism or democracy but because they recognize the need to modernize and strengthen the system, or simply to forestall its rapid decay. By implementing their reforms they both respond to pressures from below and in turn stimulate further pressures from below.

A second strategy depends on rallying the Party rank and file, the trade unions, youth unions and so on, in an attempt to democratize existing institutions from below. Some attempts at this have been made, for example, during the second half of the Prague Spring. It is important to note that this has not taken place in the Soviet Union. Both methods introduce functional changes designed to make the political and economic systems more efficient, but the second one can open the door to structural changes that may lead to the emergence of a more pluralistic and democratic system.

Those who believe that the system is not reformable from within its own institutions aim to achieve major structural changes by encouraging the growth of independent groups and social movements which reflect people's aspirations and promote fundamental values that go well beyond the given institutional order. This third approach is not incompatible with reform—especially not with reform from below—and under certain circumstances they can complement each other, as some Prague Spring experiences have shown. It has been embraced by Solidarity, and to a large extent by Charter 77 and independent groups in Hungary, East Germany and Yugoslavia. These groups have already managed to set up certain parallel structures, although their scale in Poland can hardly be compared to that in Czechoslovakia, and have become the germ of an emerging civil society.

The peace movement

Most independent activists agree that almost all the problems they face stem from the undemocratic legacy of the last war, from the division of Europe with which the nations of Central and Eastern Europe have never been reconciled. Their goal is a nonviolent change of the political status quo and a democratic transformation of Europe into "a pluralistic community of sovereign countries with equal rights."[32]

A tacit agreement between the superpowers that any change in the status quo is against their interest has preserved the division of Europe for more than forty years. The Iron Curtain is, however, getting rustier every day. It is encouragingly pock-marked with little holes drilled from both sides by independent activists and ordinary citizens who wish to hasten its collapse, reduce the current tensions and strive for a more just, democratic and peaceful Europe.

This vision is the cornerstone of the dialogue between Charter 77 activists and *that section* of the Western peace movement which understands that peace depends on political as much as on military disarmament. Peace, it is argued, has to be secured by eradicating the causes of political and social tensions as well as removing weapons of mass destruction and foreign occupying armies.

This dialogue, begun in 1981, remains controversial on both sides of the divide. In Eastern Europe many people are suspicious of the Western peace movement because it is praised by their own official propaganda. These suspicions are reinforced by arguments they read and hear in the Western media that the entire peace movement is a naive fifth column of the Soviet Union. This perception is given further credibility by those Western peace activists, numerous particularly in the United States, who still believe that "the enemy of my enemy is my friend," and that the human rights situation in the Soviet bloc should not be publicly deplored simply because it is deplored by the U.S. administration. But a significant section of the West European peace movement and most of the leading representatives of all the East European democratic opposition groups have now reached some agreement.

At the end of 1986 they formulated a joint Memorandum, "Giving Real Life to the Helsinki Accords." The Memorandum was inspired by the March 1985 *Prague Appeal*[33] in which leading Charter 77 signatories emphasized the importance of the Helsinki process for overcoming the division of Europe. They argued that there will be no peace without the eventual removal of this artificial barrier. It took almost a year of sometimes quite heated discussions, in which I participated as a member of the Memorandum editorial group, to reach a consensus on the final text which was signed by about 500 people. Together with Jan Minkiewicz, a Western representative of the Polish Freedom and Peace group, we tried to ensure that the text incorporated many of the East European arguments expressed particularly by Charter 77 and Freedom and Peace and also by the East German Initiative for Peace and Human Rights group, the Slovenian People for Peace Culture group and some members of the Hungarian democratic opposition who send in their contributions. I think that we have been fairly successful.

The signatories made clear that "peace...can only be secure if it is really democratic peace, based on civil liberties and social justice...the implementation of basic civil rights...is an ongoing condition: for societies to be able...to exercise democratic control over their own governments...for safeguarding disarmament and a stable, lasting democratic peace on our continent."[34]

Cooperation across borders

Janos Kis, a philosopher and a leading activist of the Hungarian democratic opposition, has recently acknowledged that more and more people in the East think in terms of the need for the cultural and political reunification of Europe, "partly as a result of the lessons learned from the forcing of Solidarity into the underground and partly through contact with Western peace movements."[35] Such an aim is, obviously, still a very distant prospect indeed but it is less utopian today than ten or fifteen years ago. It will, however, remain an unfulfilled dream, as long as distances between, say, Budapest and Prague remain frozen or grow even longer while they get shorter between, for example, Budapest and Vienna.

The Iron Curtains between Soviet bloc countries are less visible than those between East and West, as they bristle with fewer watchtowers, guns and minefields, but for some people they are even more impenetrable. Vaclav Havel called them "inconspicuous Iron Curtains" when he talked recently to a friend of mine writing for the journal *East European Reporter*, which we have been publishing in London since 1985.[36]

These Iron Curtains are not designed to stem the flow of refugees from communism to the greater economic prosperity of capitalism but, rather, to obstruct the flow of ideas between those determined to democratize the communist regimes. This does not make them any less solid, just more discriminating. Most East Europeans can travel across these borders relatively easily. But as Havel made clear, real obstacles emerge "at the moment that the interest of one nation in another begins to go beyond what can be found in the other country's department stores...The state is clearly attempting to remove any political content, even a cultural one, from people's international contacts, trying to keep them at a level of consumer tourism."[37]

Petr Uhl argues that the authorities place so many obstacles in the way of East-East contacts between independent movements because they regard them "as much more dangerous than East-West contacts."[38] This is partly because they wish to prevent potentially explosive joint public protests, but primarily "because they are afraid of the international movement which this cooperation could bring about."[39]

The successive defeats of individual national revolts or reform movements have finally made many activists aware of the need to learn from each other's mistakes and to search for a common solution. It is no coincidence that since the banning of Solidarity, and especially during the last two or three years, leading activists argue that "any liberation movement in the Soviet Bloc will only succeed if it goes beyond the borders of any single country."[40] Despite regional differences they now realize they are subjected to a similar predicament and they face it in a similar manner. These activists are increasingly aware that they might be able to withstand their oppression and to overcome it the more united they will be. They are also aware that they need to adopt a common approach to the superpowers and Western independent groups and to share their experiences with the Communist reformists.

Of the independent movements, Charter 77 has the longest history of international contacts, both East and West. It has always insisted that human rights and freedom are a multinational concern: "The happiness and freedom of mankind is indivisible and those who are capable of feeling concerned about the fate of the individual on earth cannot restrict such a responsibility by state frontiers and cannot be indifferent to what happens beyond them."

Chartists enjoy closest cooperation with the Polish democratic opposition groups. The history of contacts between independent-minded Czechs and Poles precedes the existence of the Charter. I mentioned the degree of cooperation between the Czech and Polish students that became public in autumn 1969, during the so-called "Alpinist' trials. In March 1968, a number of students were arrested in Warsaw following demonstrations in which students chanted slogans such as: "The whole of Poland awaits its Dubcek!" We immediately protested at the Polish Embassy in Prague and demanded their immediate release. A few months later, when Adam Michnik and others heard about the involvement of Polish troops in the suppression of Czech reforms, they expressed their feelings of shame, anger and indignation.

Systematic contacts, however, date from the summer of 1978, when leading Chartists met with representatives of the Polish KOR in a mountainous border area and agreed on various forms of cooperation. Their third such meeting, in October 1978, was prevented by a joint Czechoslovak-Polish police action. As a result Jaroslav Sabata, one of the most internationally minded Chartists, went back to prison—this time for twenty-seven months—and subsequent contacts had to take on different forms.

During the heyday of Solidarity in 1981 the Czechoslovak government unleashed its harshest repression. It feared that the "Polish disease" might spill over to Czechoslovakia and give Charter 77 a role similar to KOR, which is sometimes described as Solidarity's midwife. The regime relaxed —although never to the pre-1980 level—only after the imposition of martial law in Poland.

Since 1982 there have been a number of joint Solidarity, KOR and Charter 77 statements that expressed support for their common aims and the defense of each other's political prisoners. These have been backed occasionally by hunger strikes or, in Poland, demonstrations. Samizdat books and periodicals are increasingly exchanged and the most important writings translated. New periodicals have emerged, devoted entirely to information about each other's country. Czech opposition to theoretical writing has begun to appear fairly systematically in Poland and has had a marked impact on a number of Solidarity leaders. Zbigniew Bujak, for example, explained that he and his friends were very impressed by Havel's *The Power of the Powerless* and tried to incorporate his analysis into their practice: "Havel gave us theoretical backing, a theoretical base for our actions. He enabled us to believe in their effectiveness. Until I read his text I was full of doubts."[41] In July 1987 the activists publicly acknowledged for the first time that since 1981 many of their contacts had been organized by a "cooperation group" known as Polish-Czechoslovak Solidarity. They named the group's two spokespersons— Anna Sabatova from Czechoslovakia and Jozef Pinior from Poland—and launched a new group, the Circle of Friends of Polish-Czechoslovak Solidarity. This includes almost all leading personalities of Solidarity and Charter 77 and its aim is to act as a public shield for the largely anonymous working group.

The latter's work includes demonstrations, such as that in Polish Wroclaw on behalf of the imprisoned Hungarian conscientious objector Zsolt Keszthely, a joint action on the border at Krkonose against the pollution of their common mountains, and the publication of stamps and calendars bearing a joint Solidarity and Charter 77 logo. The impact of the Krkonose mountains demo was limited, due to police intervention. The group feels, however, that its demonstrations and a campaign on behalf of the Czech civil rights activist, Petr Pospichal, imprisoned last year for his work on Czechoslovak-Polish cooperation, contributed to his release after only four months' detention. Books are being translated, videocassettes and periodicals exchanged and since the end of 1987 the group also publishes its own information bulletin.

Even filming is being commissioned. In 1987 the group encouraged the filming in Czechoslovakia of eight interviews with leading members of the Circle who discuss Polish-Czechoslovak relations and the long-held concept of Central Europe as a historical and political entity. Some representatives of the group sent me a request for technical help with the filming. As I was unable to find a receptive ear among more affluent organizations, Palach Press provided the requested help, and filming finished recently.

Most importantly, the group is involved in the "coordination of a diversity of international activities" between independent groups in the Eastern bloc.[42] In August 1987 Czech and Polish opposition leaders met secretly on the border and agreed on a detailed list of common ideals that have since received support in other East European countries. These ideals were defined as: "a deeper respect for social rights including the right to found independent trade unions; the ideal of political pluralism and self-government; spiritual, cultural and religious freedom and tolerance; respect for a national individuality and the rights of national minorities; the freedom to search for and create a better-functioning economic system which would provide a space for people's creativity and also grant all workers real responsibility for the results of their labor and their share of economic decision-making; and the ideal of a peaceful, democratic environmentally conscious Europe, as a friendly association of independent states and nations."[43]

Some of these statements echo the above-mentioned East-West Helsinki Memorandum and the Declaration issued in October 1986, on the 30th anniversary of the Hungarian revolution. This was signed by 122 leading dissidents from Czechoslovakia, East Germany, Hungary and Poland, and subsequently endorsed by three Rumanians. The Declaration was unprecedented because it was the first time that representatives from democratic opposition groups from several East European countries had articulated the basic common principles of "joint determination to struggle for political democracy in our countries, their independence, pluralism based on the principles of self-management, peaceful reunification of divided Europe and its democratic integration, as well as for the rights of all minorities."[44] They emphasized "support for one another in our current struggles for a better, more decent and freer life in our countries and the whole world."

Many Western journalists at that time expressed their admiration for the organizational feat necessary to reach a consensus on a political statement between so many people across such "closely observed" borders but few knew of or acknowledged the role of the coordinating body—the London-based East European Cultural Foundation.

The need for growing cooperation

The EECF was set up in 1985 following several years of ad hoc contacts between Palach Press and the Polish London-based organizations Aneks and the Information Centre for Polish Affairs. It was prompted directly by requests from Poland and Czechoslovakia for more effective assistance in their efforts to prevent their isolation, not only from the West but also from each other. Similar requests stressing the need for help with communication between independent groups across East European borders came from Hungary. We met with the Hungarian-born lecturer and writer, George Schopflin, and eventually set up the EECF as a charitable foundation.

The need to internationalize efforts to democratize the Communist system has preoccupied me ever since our failure to do so during the Prague Spring. I was therefore pleased when Ferenc Koszeg, editor of the Hungarian samizdat journal *Beszelo*, asked me to help to circulate the draft of the 1986 joint Declaration to as many Soviet-bloc groups as possible, to gather responses and to collect signatures for the final text. It took almost six months but the effort was worthwhile.

Koszeg described the Declaration as "a milestone in cooperation."[45] According to Koszeg all the independent movements share Solidarity's aim of "creating a situation in which those in power would have to deal with representatives of society and try to agree on a social contract with society."[46] Another editor of *Beszelo*, the writer Miklos Haraszti, argued for the need to "carry out on a wider East European level what Charter 77 and the Polish opposition have been doing at their national level. On the one hand we should constantly draw attention to the fundamental values of democracy, political pluralism and self-determination, and on the other hand, we should promote all the reforms that are possible within the system. The first activity looks beyond the constraints of Yalta, the second explores the possibilities of changes within the Yalta framework. Such a dual approach will enable us to form a common perspective on a number of issues."[47]

The idea of formulating a minimum common political program of the East European democratic opposition was raised but it was soon agreed that the safest method of reaching a consensus was to start with agreements on a series of specific issues and stay with those general political principles expressed in the Declaration. A more detailed political consensus will then emerge later more naturally. The first such issues have already been pinpointed by the Czechs and Poles: demands for freedom of travel within the Soviet bloc, the need for a civilian alternative to compulsory military service and a need for a solution to ecological problems, which are among the worst in Europe.

Since its inception the EECF has improved its informal information and coordination network. We try to make available to different groups and samizdat editors their information bulletins and periodicals. We forward documents or analyses, for example on travel restrictions or the environment, to relevant groups in different parts of the bloc. We publish some of them in the *East European Reporter* with commentaries written for us from those countries and we send issues of the EER to Eastern Europe, where English is almost something of a *lingua franca*. The numbers involved are, of course, relatively small as we cannot use the government-controlled postal system but only couriers or helpful tourists. But important articles are translated and reprinted in local samizdat journals.

The EECF, using the experience and contacts built up over the years by Palach Press and others, can respond to East European requests fairly quickly and flexibly. For example, soon after leading East German peace and human rights activists were arrested and charged with treason at the end of January 1988, I was asked by their colleagues from Budapest and Prague to help to coordinate a joint protest. Within days we were able to release an open letter to the GDR's State Council demanding the prisoners' immediate release and the end of the practice of compelling people under the threat of imprisonment to emigrate to West Germany. The petition was signed by almost 300 individuals and several important groups—including Charter 77—from Czechoslovakia, Poland, Hungary, Yugoslavia and, for the first time, the Soviet Union. In some of these countries the petition was sent to the GDR's embassies. At the same time we were helping to coordinate East European responses to Charter 77's call to make 1 February 1988 a day of solidarity with the oppressed people of Romania. This included simultaneous demonstrations, vigils, symbolic hunger strikes and switching the electricity off, as well as petitions in several East European capitals.

The largest coordinated action to date took place in March 1988 when, after almost four months of cross-border discussions, we were able to present an Appeal on behalf of imprisoned and persecuted conscientious objectors in the Soviet bloc. We asked the delegations at the Conference on Security and Cooperation in Europe in Vienna to put the demand for a right to an alternative civil service on the agenda of their follow-up Helsinki conference. The Appeal was signed by almost 450 individuals from six Communist-ruled countries, including nearly a hundred Soviet citizens, among them Andrei Sakharov. Some of the individuals were authorized to sign on behalf of larger groups, including Charter 77.[48] The EECF's work was described as "a triumph of coordination."[49]

Our current coordinating role enables these joint actions to take place without East European activists needing to travel to another part of the bloc and risk loosing his or her passport, as has happened in the past. This should not be allowed to cloud the fact that many East Europeans are denied their basic right to travel, in stark violation of the Helsinki principles; and some have their movements restricted even within their own country.

This issue has been highlighted again by the Czechoslovak authorities who have recently confiscated passports from a large number of Chartists. They had been able to hang on to these documents because these Chartists were relatively unknown and living far away from opposition centers such as Prague or Brno. This latest measure has clearly been provoked by Charter 77's success in sending its representatives as "tourists" to international seminars organized last year by peace groups and some other independent groups in Warsaw, Budapest and Moscow. Charter's potential pool of envoys has thus been significantly reduced. We shall, of course, continue to make available to such seminars the contributions of those Czechs who cannot attend.

I am convinced that this cooperation will help the growth of *de facto* pluralism from below, which could pave the way for the gradual democratization of the Soviet bloc. This would facilitate the ending of the Cold War and in turn further accelerate democratization.

Given the obvious importance of such a development for the West it is surprising and disheartening that these coordination efforts and requests for help have so far elicited only lukewarm interest among Western journalists and politicians. Some of them have explained this to me by saying that exchanges between small and powerless groups have only a marginal value. Vaclav Havel calls this "a typical misunderstanding" among people from Western societies, "where the importance of a social force is measured by the number of its adherents, or the number of votes it can attract, whenever they attempt to assess the conditions in a totalitarian country."[50] The potential support of independent groups, he argues, is to be found in social consciousness and is not measurable by some simple method. "When KOR began its work in Poland, its activities seemed to be little more than desperate attempts by a handful of intellectuals... and yet without it, there would have been no Solidarity."[51] Havel, who perceives the role of Charter 77 as that of a critical mirror held up to the times, explained that "the importance of the mirror far exceeds the importance of the number of people holding it."[52] Those who understand this should be able to comprehend that meetings between Charter 77 and Solidarity "may, one day, be of considerable political significance."[53]

The widespread lack of such an understanding unfortunately plagues the work of organizations such as the EECF when appealing for financial assistance, so much so that we might not be able to support the coordination efforts in the future.[54] The Soviet-bloc establishments, on the other hand, by trying to limit the East-East independent contacts, make abundantly clear their awareness of the threat such cooperation represents for existing power interests.

How to bring about change

Even the reforms designed to make the system more stable and less repressive, pushed through by enlightened rulers such as Gorbachev, have an obvious ceiling: preservation of the reformists' own power. Reforms will not work, however, without some amount of popular support and to achieve this they have to be more responsive to peoples' needs—in other words, they have to introduce more democracy. Reforms from above can thus open a Pandora's box by stimulating forces within the society that can lead not only to some liberalization of the system but to the emergence of genuine democratic elements. A strong and mature independent movement can help bring about such a qualitative change. I believe that for such a change to be achieved and safeguarded, some link-up between the independent movements and rank and file reformists is essential. Such a coalition will reflect the conditions of each country; reformists will play more important roles in the Soviet Union or the GDR, for example, while in Poland a greater emphasis will be placed on the independent groups. Without the reformists-from-above, be they Dubcek or Gorbachev or anyone else, the prospects for change will undoubtedly be much dimmer but without the independent movements the process will, at best, become stuck within the confines of present day perestroika (or economic reconstruction, aimed to reduce waste and increase profits) and glasnost (or openness, including relaxation of censorship). These will not lead to greater liberalization but only to cosmetic changes in the decision-making process and still leave the leading Communist party as the final arbiter of everything.

Certain principles of glasnost can be, and are being, taken up by democratic groups outside the Communist party and used to expose and challenge the establishment's power base. This is obviously clear to Milos Jakes, who last December, with the support of both the Soviet reformists and Czechoslovak hardliners, replaced Gustav Husak as the Party leader. In a country where democratic traditions are stronger than anywhere else in the Soviet bloc, Jakes welcomes perestroika only with silence. The silence is spiced with repressive measures against civil rights activists and those who act on the old slogan: "The Soviet Union is our model."

Joint pressures from outside and within the Party could ensure that the reform from above will open the door to what Adam Michnik of Solidarity calls "the philosophy of compromise."[55] This consists of an exploration of aspects of social change acceptable both to the political elite which needs to gain fresh legitimacy and to the independent groups which desire greater autonomy for society and political pluralism. The stronger they are the greater the influence independent groups can have on the nature of this compromise, but in a crisis situation (a frequent state of affairs in Eastern Europe) their impact is much greater than their numbers would warrant. Mutual coordination of such groups across East European borders and the evolvement of a joint political program and strategy will make it much more difficult for the Soviet Union to resort to its usual divide-and-conquer rule. It will narrow the elite's room for maneuver and thereby improve the odds of a political compromise acceptable for the whole region, especially with pragmatic politicians of the Gorbachev kind.

We have not yet reached such a stage and many other factors such as a deepening economic crisis will influence developments. It is clear, however, that the authorities do not wish to take any chances. To protect themselves they are trying to keep all the Iron Curtains, East and West, in place, and to nip in the bud all attempts to coordinate democratic civil rights movements on an international scale. The accumulated joint experience of activists will ensure, however, that neither hardliner repression nor reformist warnings (endorsed even by some Western right-wing politicians) not to rock the still rickety Gorbachev boat will win the day. People obviously appreciate that it is better to live under Gorbachev than Stalin but, as Havel reminds us, "even under totalitarian circumstances what people might win for themselves depends first and foremost on their own efforts."[56] To wait for those in power to make a gesture of goodwill, in the hope that it would also be in the interests of the ordinary people, is not seen as a viable alternative.

The road to success for the independent groups, alone or in coalitions, will continue to be much more difficult than that of the reformists-from-above. I am convinced, however, that the changes they could achieve would provide greater justice and a greater guarantee of democratic peace than any number of superpower summits or declarations that leave social and political tensions untouched.

The increasingly close cooperation between all the independent movements will also help to create an atmosphere favorable to a comprehensive

East-West political settlement. Major steps towards the democratic trans-formation of Eastern Europe, including the withdrawal of all foreign troops and nuclear weapons from Europe, can take place only as a part of such a settlement. This makes it even more important for those Westerners who would like to see democracy prevail and an eventual end to the bloc system to lend their full support to the independent movements rather than to put their faith in reformists-from-above such as Gorbachev, let alone in harsh Cold War hostility.

Sixty Eight Publishers, Corp.

Josef Skvorecky

GOD KNOWS I never intended to become a publisher, and if I eventually became one my wife is to blame. You see, she was nostalgic when— after the Soviet ambush of 1968—we came to Canada. Nostalgic is probably a weak word: she was dying of homesickness because she couldn't talk to anyone. Her first and second foreign languages were French and Russian, but only Quebecois speak French in Canada, and we lived in Ontario. So I was often treated to the absurdity of listening to my anti-Communist wife talking Russian with a sweet American lady who taught the language of our oppressors at the University of Toronto. She, however, held Brezhnev in the same contempt as we did.

Then the late Mr. Lexa from the Czechoslovak Society of Arts and Sciences in America phoned me with an offer. The Society would publish my novel *The Tank Corps*, the one confiscated several times before publication in Czechoslovakia and never printed there. "Why would you give it to them?" asked my wife. "We can bring it out ourselves. In this country you don't need permission. You just pay a few bucks at City Hall for a license, and you are a publisher."

We paid the few bucks and became capitalists. Not rich capitalists but exploiters (of ourselves) anyway. It was that self-exploitation that saved my wife's sanity. In the excitement of the adventure called Sixty-Eight Publishers, Corp., she forgot about nostalgia, about Prague, about her unfinished studies under Professor Milan Kundera at the Prague Film Academy, about her singing and acting career, and became a maker of Czech books, a preserver of values, that, otherwise, might have disappeared without a trace.

So, you see, I do not pretend that either my wife or I was motivated by noble ideas. I only maintain that we, in the past seventeen years, have served noble ideas and that, perhaps, we did not serve them quite so badly. Our capitalist careers ended soon; in 1979 we changed the nature of our private business into that of a nonprofit, nonshare company and received a charitable status from the government of Canada. We turned back into employees, but unlike in Czechoslovakia, we were now unpaid employees. Not that we would not be entitled to pay ourselves salaries; but in these past seventeen years, that great publishing house, the Sixty-Eight Publishers Corporation, has been chronically short of cash.

On the other hand, it has made possible the existence of many a good book, and of quite a few excellent ones; and although these books, printed on cheap paper, are rapidly yellowing and in a few decades will probably disintegrate, at least we did prolong their lives. As manuscripts they would probably have been misplaced, lost or, at best, forgotten in a few private libraries or hiding places in Czechoslovakia belonging to people who were arrested and sent to jail.

It is true that some would have survived anyway, albeit only in the distorted form of translations. That is certainly true about the brilliant works of Milan Kundera all of which we published: *Smesne lasky (Laughable Loves), Zivot je jinde (Life is Elsewhere), Valcik na rozloucenou (Farewell Party), Kniha smichu a zapomneni (The Book of Laughter and Forgetting)* and *Nesnesitelna lehkost byti (The Unbearable Lightness of Being)*. It is equally true about Vaclav Havel's inimitable plays *Spiklenci (The Conspirators), Zebracka opera (The Beggars' Opera), Horsky hotel (The Mountain Resort), Audience (Audience)* and *Versinaz (Vernissage)* which we brought out as *Hry 1970-76 (Plays 1970-76)*. It can be said about Ludvik Vaculik's novel *Morcata (The Guinea Pigs)* and *Cesky Snar (The Czech Dream Book)*, or about Ivan Klima's *Milostne leto (A Summer of Love), Ma vesela jitra (My Merry Mornings)* and *Moje prvni lasky (My First Loves)*. And God only knows whether Bohumil Hrabal's three-volume autobiography, *Svatby v dome (Weddings in the House), Vita nuova and Proluky (Building Sites)*, with its irreverent description of the "Brotherly Help" of 1968 and of the police activites following that event, would have been published in Prague; that is, God knows it wouldn't.

Next come our literary discoveries: they, too, sooner or later would have come out in foreign tongues, for they are far too good never to make it onto the literary stage. But the authors wrote their books in Czech— at least their first ones, which we discovered and published and thus opened the door for them to Western publishers—and the true provenance of fiction is the mother tongue. In it the work lives its real life; its existence in other languages is just a mimesis, a mirror image, and even the best Venetian mirrors distort, if ever so slightly. Although Jan Novak's moving *Striptease Chicago (Chicago Striptease)* is set in the Windy City, its protagonists speak broken English at best, but their Czech-American slang is a joy to read; its beauty, however, disappears in translation. True, Novak wrote his second book, the novel *Milionovy jeep (Willy's Dream Kit)* in English, but we hired a dissident Prague translator and returned the text where it belongs: to Czech, for it is a devastatingly beautiful love-song about Czech exiles—the first really great Czech novel about the fate of millions of our compatriots. In 1986, it was nominated for the Pulitzer Prize.

The unique stories by Jaroslav Vejvoda also now appear in (German) translation, but we gave the unknown author his first chance with *Plujici andele, letici ryby (Swimming angels, Flying Fish)*. We followed up with *Osel aneb Splynuti (The Donkey or Merging)*, a novel, with another short story collection *Ptaci (The Birds)* and with a second novel *Zelene vino (Green Wine)*. Vejvoda is now reaping Swiss literary prizes and writing scripts for Swiss movies.

Yet another brilliant novelist for whom we paved the way to foreign languages editions: Jiri Grusa whose poetic and penetrating fictional history of post-WWII Czechoslovakia *Dotaznik (The Questionnaire)* we published in two editions, and followed it up with a sardonic love story *Damsky Gambit (Ladies' Gambit)* and with a devastating caricature of post-invasion Czech life, *Dr. Kokes, Mistr Panny (Dr. Kokes, the Master of the Virgin)*. Have I forgotten anyone?

Yes, Arnost Lustig, one of the witnesses of the horrible place called Auschwitz who seems to have survived only to capture the nightmare in a long series of books of fiction, as good as anything written on the subject in major languages. In exile he devoted most of his time to radical rewritings of the works he had written in Czechoslovakia, but he did write a new one, *Z deniku sedmnacilete Perly Sch. (The Unloved: From the Diary of Perla Sch.)*, where, as Byron Sherwin wrote, "the author, unlike other Holocaust novelists, attempts to inform and inspire his readers rather than terrorize them." The book is a touch of loveliness on the nightmarish sky of the camps, and one of the most unusual and humane novels about the gas-reeking chapter of modern history.

Have I forgotten anyone else? You see, we have published a lot of books. One hundred and ninety at the time I am writing this, in January 1988.

Other literary discoveries of ours have not made it to the foreign-language stage yet. They include Egon Bondy, the very first Czech dissident and *samizdat* author who, in the early fifties, wrote and lent to friends poems that made fun of Stalin while Stalin was still very much alive and deadly dangerous. Bondy later switched to prose, and we published two absolute peaches of nonconformist novels: *Invalidni sourozenci (Invalid Siblings)* and *Sklepni prace (Cellar Works)*. They, too, I'm sure, will eventually be translated—but we preserved the originals. And I am equally sure that the most original author of psychopathological-surrealist fictions, Jan Kresadlo, whose first novel *Mrchopevci (The Corpse Singers)* received the prestigious Egon Hostovsky Memorial Award, will find his way to English-speaking readers. His second novel, *Fuga Trium*, with its ingenious word-play (*Fugue for Three* or *The Escape for Three*) is a major work of weird imagination, black humor and political wisdom, which makes for a combination very rare in Western literature.

We are particularly proud of one rediscovery. One day we received a lovely letter from a British nurse by the name of Miss Meachum. She informed us that she had a patient—she was working in a mental institution—who wrote poems in a language unknown to her. She consulted a German doctor in London who thought that the language might be Czech, and recommended that she write to a Czech publishing house he heard about in Toronto, Ontario, Canada. He did not know the firm's name, and it is a credit to Canada Post that they found us. When I received the letter I immediately became alert: this could be Ivan Blatny, the brilliant poet who had left the country after the Communist coup in 1948 and was later reported to have gone mad and, perhaps, to have died.

Indeed, it was Blatny. Miss Meachum sent us a huge box full of old doctors' prescriptions, on the reverse sides of which the poet jotted down verses in four languages. Being no expert in poetry, I mailed the treasure to Antonin Brousek in Berlin, a distinguished Czech poet and literary critic, who patiently went through the hardly legible scribblings and from them put together a wonderful collection of pure poetry, *Stara bydliste (Ancient Dwellings)*.

This collection not only brought Blatny's name back to the pages of Czech literary magazines in exile; it also improved considerably the poet's status in the mental institution, which has been his home since the early fifties. All such institutions, naturally, have their poets, and usually more than one. They also have their Napoleons, their Sara Berhnhardts and their Snow Whites, sometimes even with the Seven Dwarfs. But when the handsome volume of poetry, with a full-color reproduction of a painting by the poet's friend Kamil Lhotak on the jacket, arrived at the institution, the doctors realized that one of their loony poets was a poet indeed. Consequently, the manuscript of his second volume we published, edited again by Antonin Brousek, *Pomocna skola v Bixley (The School for Mentally Retarded at Bixley)*, was much more legible than the original manuscripts provided by Miss Meachum.

Blatny's fortunes further improved when Jaroslav Seifert, the Nobel Prize winner and old friend of Blatny made aware of the looney poet's continuous existence, bequeathed a portion of his Nobel Prize money to Blatny— without the knowledge of the greedy Czech government, I am sure; but since Seifert is now dead, the story can leak. The money made it possible for Blatny to move to private quarters.

And speaking of Seifert: we were worried about the image of our great poet that could be created by the few English translations of his works which appeared after he had received the Prize. The translators, almost invariably, selected pieces from Seifert's final creative period when he abandoned strict meter and rhyme and began to write free verse. But Seifert is loved for his rhymed poetry, for he is a great master of the modernized strict form. That is why we commissioned the translation of one of his best books entitled *Venec sonetu (A Wreath of Sonnets)* because we intended to present to the English speaking *aficionados* of poetry the true Seifert at his best. The poet authorized the translation and it was published as a bilingual (Czech-English) edition in a handsome little volume with striking drawings by Jan Kristofori.

We were responsible for the publication of works of two other truly excellent Czech poets: the first of these has never published any poetry in his native country; the other, a cofounder of the celebrated Prague Linguistic Circle, never published her verse either at home or in exile after 1942. The former poet is Stanislav Mares, who now lives in Australia and whose *Baje z Noveho sveta (A Fable from the New World)* has been acknowledged as the best long poem to have been written in exile. George Voskovec, the partner of Jan Werich, half of the unforgettable couple of anti-Fascist comedians of prewar Prague, and after WWII, a distinguished actor on Broadway *(Uncle Vanya)* and in Hollywood *(Twelve Angry Men)*, loved the poem, taped it for us and, to his dying day, would recite long passages from it by heart. The other poet is the late Milada Souckova, and her *Sesity Josephiny Rykrove (The Notebooks of Josephine Rykr)*, with an introduction by Roman Jacobson, is an undeniable gem of modern Czech literature.

135

World-category writers, discoveries, rediscoveries. But there are others, not as well known in the Western world, some of them quite unknown, but quite a few also world-category, were it not for the "small" language which is understood by only some ten million people (less, because babies don't yet speak it) in the entire world. Karel Pecka, the "Czech Solzhenitsyn," a graduate of the uranium mines concentration camps of the Stalin era, was the first one to have the (considerable indeed) courage to publish with us, although he lives in Prague and *they* would not let him out. (The McDowell Colony in New Hampshire invited him for a three-month stay, but *they* would not permit him to go.) We published his intriguing novel *Stepeni (The Splitting)*, a paralleling of the Czech fate of the seventeenth century when the Moravian Brethren were forced into exile, to become eventually the missionaries of the North American Indians (see the novels by James Fenimore Cooper), and of the post-1968 Czech fate when the best brains of the country had to flee Czechoslovakia invaded by the hordes of chieftain Brezhnev. We also brought out his Kafka-esque *Pasaz (The Mall)* and finally *Motaky nezvestnemu (Letters Smuggled out of the Camps)*, a beautiful and poetic indictment of the class pseudo-justice of Stalinism.

The samizdat of the 1970s and 80s, of which we published many volumes, is fairly well known in the West—or at least the West knows that it exists, thanks to an increase of general awareness of the intellectual situation in Communist countries (perhaps much of the credit for this should go to Amnesty International), and because some of the samizdat stars are internationally known, even famous: Vaclav Havel, to name just one. But there existed a *samizdat* literature in the early fifties, when to be caught with an unprinted "subversive" book in your pocket did not mean just an interrogation over a cup of tea, but quick and reckless incarceration.

That is exactly what happened to Jiri Kolar, the unofficial head of such an underground group who served time because of a satirical poem. He is now a world-known collagist, and we published his *Prometeova jatra (The Liver of Prometheus)*, a volume of poetry and philosophical ruminations; the kind of poetry that had a similar effect on Czech verse that Edgar Lee Masters once had on American poets. Bohumil Hrabal, mentioned earlier, was one of Kolar's group, and so was Josef Hirsal whose originally experimental *Pisen Mladi (The Song of Youth)* received the Egon Award and is one of the books we are most proud of. The shy and beautiful poet-essayist Jan Hanc was also a frequent visitor in Kolar's apartment, and nothing of his penetrating writings of the fifties was ever published at home: he died of cancer in 1963 and had to wait until 1984 when we came out with his *Sesity (The Copy Books)*, perhaps the most penetrating analysis (in the form of mini-essays and diary entries) of everyday Stalinism in Czechoslovakia, and the only book of Hancs ever to come out in print. Vratislav Effenberger, the late doyen of Czech surrealism, was also a force in that dangerous underground of the early fifties, and also one of the original and outstanding prose writers and essayists whose work never appeared at home, except in an anthology *Surrealisticke vychodisko (The Surrealist Starting Point),* which miraculously made it at the last minute in 1969, before the universal clamp-down of everything that was good and beautiful in Czech writing. We published his seminal "film scripts" *Surovost zivota a cynismus fantazie (The Cruelty of Life and the Cynicism of Imagination),* the first, and last, book of his that he ever saw in print—he died soon afterwards.

We did many other books of fiction and poetry, but I am trying to write not an enumeration, a dictionary entry, but hopefully a readable article. So I must mention another side of our efforts which reflects, probably, something of my nature, for I am not an entirely serious person. I love humor, detective stories, jazz and pop, gossipy memoirs—the light touch which can often tell surprisingly much about the tragedy and serious- ness of life, so that one wonders: It may be light—but is it negligible?

We did our share of serious and historically important memoirs, for instance Vaclav Cerny's, unfortunately unfinished, five-volume *Pameti (Memoirs),* one of the most detailed and best written autobiographical works of the anti-Nazi resistance and of the first decade of communism in Czechoslovakia. It also tells the absurd stories of our time, because Cerny, an outstanding Charles University Professor of Comparative Liter- ature, and the internationally famous discoverer of unknown plays by Cal- deron and works by Lomonosov, spent only fifteen years of his long life (he died in 1987 at the age of eighty-two) behind the university lectern: he was deprived of it first by the Nazis in 1939, then by the Stalinists in 1951, and finally by "real-socialistic" Communists in 1970.

We also published the four-volume autobiography *Ceskoslovensko, muj osud (Czechoslovakia, My Fate)* by Prokop Drtina, the justice minister of the short-lived democratic government Czechoslovakia enjoyed between 1945 and the Communist coup in 1948, and President Benes's closest ally during his World War II stay in England. We published the highly successful memoirs of Frantisek Moravec, the chief of Czechoslovak intelligence before and during World War II, the organizer, among many other exploits, of the assassination of Reinhard Heudrich, called *Spion, jemuz neverili (The Spy Who Wasn't Trusted).* Last but not least we brought out the memoirs of Heda Kovalyova *Na vlastni kuzi (The Victors and the Vanquished)*—written in collaboration with Erazim Kohak. The book is another prototypical story of our time: a love story, in fact, of two young Jews who meet and fall in love in Auschwitz, survive and return home only to be separated forever by the noose that takes the life of Heda's husband Rudolf Margolius, a victim of the notorious Slansky trial in the Stalinist fifties.

All these are certainly serious and important books. But we also did the reminiscences of Martina Navratilova *Ja jsem ja (That's Me),* because we as Czechs, are very proud of her success, and besides, it is a lively little big book. We published the witty, sexy, jazzy memoirs of the leading Czech jazzmen of the swing era, Jiri Traxler's *Ja nic, ja muzikant (Don't blame me, I am Just a Musician)* and Kamil Behounek's *Ma laska je jazz (Jazz Is my Love).* And we also brought out two tomes of gossip (but not only gossip) by two Czech prewar film stars Adina Mandlova *Dneska uz se tomu smeju (I Just Laugh it Off Today)* and Lida Barova *Uteky (The Escapes).* The latter was, of course, the notorious *femme fatale* of Josef Goebels, and they both lived through the same events as professor Cerny or Minister Drtina, but saw them from an angle from which the two great fighters could not. Thus, in in our opinion, they unveiled a little part of history similar to that which Malaparte, the reformed Fascist journalist, revealed in his post-war memoirs. Besides, a publishing house needs bestsellers in order to be able to publish poetry, history, philosophy: rarely hot items, even among the cultured Czechs.

They sell relatively well, though; but since they are usually bulky volumes, they rarely reach even the direct break-even point (i.e. the point where the book pays for its production costs but does not contribute its share towards defraying the overhead). We are proud to have published Professor Erazim Kohak's *Narod v nas (The Nation Within Us),* a major work of political philosophy in the spirit of T.G. Masaryk; Jiri Kotvun's *Masarykuv triumf (The Triumph of Masaryk),* an innovative work on the first Czechoslovak president, based largely on unknown documents discovered by the author, who is a librarian of the Library of Congress, in various U.S. archives. We were glad, also, to have been able to bring out Erich Kulka's work *Zide ve Svobodove armade (The Jews in Svoboda's Army)* with its surprising revelation that, at certain times, up to 70 percent of the soldiers of the Czech division fighting with the Red Army in World War II were Jewish; and also Jiri Morava's *C.a.k. disident Karel Havlicek (K. und K. Dissident Karel Havlicek),* a historical study also based on documents discovered by the author in Austrian archives, about the great liberal journalist of the nineteenth century and the most prominent victim of the first "normalization" of Bohemia which followed the revolution of 1848. Two works by Karel Kaplan—the second in collaboration with Vilem Hejl—*Nekrvava revoluce (The Bloodless Revolution)* and *Zprava o organizovanem nasili (Report on Violence)*—are, I think, an important contribution to our knowledge of Stalinist justice, for the author, who headed the so-called Barnabite Party Commission for the reexamination of the misuse of justice in the fifties, based them on documents from the secret Party archives which he managed to smuggle out to the West.

But since the metier of both me and my wife is literature, the nonfiction books we like most are those about literature. Professor Antonin Mestan's *Ceska literatura 1975-1985 (Czech Literature 1975-1985)* is the first history of Czech *belles lettres* since the prewar work by Arne Novak, i.e., the first objective history of Czech writing in half a century. Of course, publishing houses and academic institutions in Establishment Prague did publish various histories, but they were written according to Orwell's recipe. They do not inform, but distort, which in the last analysis, amounts to lying. This can be best demonstrated by several dictionaries of Czech writers brought out in Prague in the eighties. They are work of numerous researchers employed by the Academy of Arts and Sciences, and it shows. The bibliographies of authors included are meticulously detailed and exhaustive. The trouble is that many authors are missing and the criterion is not (very obviously) of literary merit—authors such as Milan Kundera, Vaclav Havel and Ludvik Vaculik are omitted. And even in the case of authors who *are* in the dictionary, the hand of the censor often slapped the hand of the literary scholar when he tried to include a book which the powers that be decided to Orwell-out from the bibliography of that erring, but on the whole, acceptable pen-pusher. This peculiar state of affairs was the main reason why we published, for instance, Zdenek Rotrekl's *Skryta tvar ceske literatury (The Hidden Face of Czech Literature)*, a bio-bibliographical study of modern and contemporary Czech Catholic writers who are either missing entirely from the establishment histories, or are distorted by the mandatory political bias of the unlucky scholars.

The most important corrective to these big misrepresentations is, however, our *Slovnik ceskych spisovatelu (Dictionary of Czech Writers)*, which is, in fact, a dictionary of *banned* Czech writers and, in that respect, probably a reference work unique in contemporary literary scholarship. It was edited by four dissident scholars and writers in Prague; Jiri Brabec (fired from the Academy of Sciences after the Soviet ambush and now a night-watchman in the Loretto in Prague), Jiri Grusa (now in exile),

Peter Kabes and Jan Lopatka; and by Igor Hajek, a professor of Czech literature in Glasgow who wrote the entries of the exiled writers.

Shall I stop here? I have mentioned only a fraction of the one hundred and ninety books on our list, which does not mean that the unmentioned majority is not worth mentioning. I tried to use the objective criteria of literary merit and fame, and of topical interest; but rereading my zigzaggy treatment I realize that, in fact, quite a lot of subjective bias sneaked into my report. But isn't that always so when someone who is deeply involved in the issue is asked to write about it? I won't pretend I am not deeply involved, and therefore partial; and so is my wife, the founder of the Sixty-Eight Publishers adventure. It is, therefore, perhaps appropriate to conclude these ruminations by voicing a certain complaint: my wife is a novelist herself, and not a negligible one. Her *Honzlova (Summer in Prague)* is, perhaps, the most beloved Czech novel of the post-invasion period. It was translated into several languages (including English; Harper & Row), and the great Czech journalist Ferdinand Peroutka, President Masaryk's close friend, wrote that *Honzlova* was "the most important Czech novel of present times." George Steiner, writing in the *New Yorker,* said of the book that "modulations of feeling belong almost to the Dostoevskian world" and Graham Greene "enjoyed it immensely." My wife, however, wrote this little jem before she conceived her big idea of helping Czech literature to survive by founding a publishing house—in California, in the summer of 1969. Ever since she started turning out banned books by other authors, she hasn't written anything. As is universally known, the day has only twenty four hours, and, of these, my wife spends twelve, sometimes fourteen, and if need be even more, drudging at her office.

In the seventeen years that have elapsed since the birth of Sixty-Eight Publishers there was only one exception: the long postal strike of 1975, when activities in the publishing house stopped, for there was no mail and the money ran out. She utilized that critical period for writing another beauty: the short novel *Nebe, peklo, raj (Ashes, Ashes All Fall Down).* She received the coveted Egon Hostovsky Award for it, and her eager readers (and the new English-speaking readers who bought the English translation) loved the book almost as much as *Honzlova.*

Then, if I may boast a little, I made a joke which, unexpectedly, turned into a birthday present for my wife. Unbeknownst to her, I commissioned a translation of her pre-1968 novella *Tma (The Darkness),* a weirdly funny story about two Czech dancers who, on a tour in the Soviet Union, are invited to the dacha of a famous Socialist Realist writer who turns out to be an exemplary dirty old man. The story, as all stories by my wife, is based on her real experience (at one time she was a dancer and toured the Soviet Union), and the model for the old lecher was Sergei Michalkov, best known as the author of the lyrics for the Soviet anthem. I then sent the translation to Utah where the University of Utah sponsored an International Novella Competition, and the story won—just three days before my wife's birthday.

But she had written *Tma* in 1966, and since 1975, when she made use of the posties' strike, she has not produced anything. That is, she keeps working on a novel about Czech immigrants in Canada with the working title *Hnuj zeme (The Dung of the Earth)*, but there are all those other books to be published, authors' egos to be mollified, printers' bills to be paid. I am afraid my crazy wife is trying to square a circle.

I, after all, am also a Czech writer. I have written quite a lot of books, and would have written many more if it were not for helping my wife to cope with the demands of her adventure. But the books we published, most of them, are lovely. *Je ne regrette rien.*

Those Who Left:
A Current Profile

Otto Ulc

IN MY BOOK *Politics in Czechoslovakia*, completed shortly after the Soviet invasion of the country and the advent of *normalization*, I concluded with the expectation that the normalizers would fail to revive a vigorous, rigorous totalitarian order. Instead, a weakened, rather exhausted "post-totalitarian system" would emerge. Soviet power would prevent the regime from falling apart, while lack of mass support along with the thorough alienation of the nation, especially of the young, would deprive the rulers of the kind of strength their predecessors enjoyed shortly after the seizure of power in 1948.

This expectation seems to have been fulfilled. Party rule was restored but commitment to the cause was not. Nothing much was left of the "new socialist man" of the original visionary specifications: instead, there emerged a self-centered, selfish citizen for whom corruption is a way of life.

This failure in appropriate socialization, however, has come to be seen by the rulers as the lesser evil, considering the alternatives. Preference was given to the neutralized and overtly politicized, but essentially apolitical population, rather than to ardent devotees whose approach would highlight the glaring contrasts between ideological promises and bestowed reality. This new situation has taken the form of a social contract: the rulers rule and the citizenry, in return for not meddling into public affairs, is rewarded with the opportunity to attend to its private affairs. Preoccupation with the pleasures of a consumer society—an automobile, a country house built typically with stolen material, a poodle, or a vacation spent in a foreign, preferably capitalist, land—has become the order of the day. "Revenge of the bourgeoisie!" characterizes this state of affairs. The deposed

bourgeois class has revenged itself by imposing its values on the society
of an allegedly new type.

Under this social contract there are neither many model socialist citizens
nor challengers to the system. Apathy and withdrawal from involvement
in public matters have replaced the social activism of the 1960s.

Within one year after the Soviet invasion some 150,000 Czechoslovaks—
one of each hundred—had permanently left the country. The sealing of
the border in October 1969 did not stop the hemorrhage. Today, despite,
or rather *because* of the long period of normalization, people continue
to leave by various means: every four hours, day and night, one newcomer
reaches Austria (lesser numbers flee via Yugoslavia; as tourists or visit-
ors on official business they apply for asylum in Western Europe, even
in Australia), thus committing a felony. Emigration without the state's
consent is classified as a criminal act. This is the largest exodus since
the Thirty Years War in the seventeenth century: not even Hitler caused
so many people to leave.

Rudolf Zukal, the former vice president (*prorektor*) of the Prague School
of Economics and currently employed by the state as a manual laborer,
deduced from various available demographic data, that some 250,000 citizens have left the country in the post-invasion period.[1] The outflow continues and it is the thinking, better educated and more industrious individuals who decide to leave. In the words of Zukal, "a considerable portion of young intelligentsia is leaving also because of the overall atmosphere in the country which inevitably gets on the nerves of a thinking
person."

With genuine love beyond reach, the post-totalitarian suitor settles for
mere pretense of amorous infatuation. In this climate arose the parallel
culture, indeed a parallel life in an alternate society, already an undeniable
reality in Poland where, in Adam Michnik's splendidly apt phrase, the
people "live as if they were free."

This novel societal attitude, most forcefully entrenched in Poland but
not entirely absent in Czechoslovakia, I prefer to call "nondissent": the
people do not challenge the system, they merely try to ignore it. As a
result, such a system, ignored rather than attacked, is put in an awkward
position on how to cope with this kind of elusive challenge.

To find out more about the societal attitudes in Eastern Europe, in the
past two years I have been conducting a survey among refugees from
Czechoslovakia. This research project, delving predominantly into the
phenomenon of nondissent, brought me to Europe to conduct a survey,

along with some in-depth interviews, among the recent refugees. Only those who had left *reálny socialismus* in the 1980s were polled. As it turns out, a substantial majority—almost three fourths—of the respondents have lived their entire adult life in the post-invasion era. For them, the exhilarating, dramatic and ultimately tragic year of 1968 is a matter of distant memory.

The survey questionnaire, its anonymity emphasized to the suspicious exiles, consisted of eighty-five items, divided into three parts:

1. personal data (sex, nationality, marital status education, occupation, socio-economic background, political affiliation, residence), questions #1-#13;
2. circumstances and motivation for leaving the country, questions #14-#52;
3. evaluative, normative judgment concerning the Czechoslovak political system and society, questions #53-#85.

The guaranteed anonymity of the questionnaire notwithstanding, the majority of the target audience proved less than cooperative, suspecting ulterior motives and even involvement with the Czechoslovak secret police in the project—not a surprising reaction given their life-long experience with the state's intrusion into their private lives. I encountered this reaction in Austria, a country uncomfortably close to the Iron Curtain, as well as in the splendidly distant Australia (a country with the highest return rate of questionnaires—50 percent).

The questionnaires were distributed with the help of various refugee organizations in six countries: three in Europe (Austria, West Germany, Switzerland) and three overseas (United States, Canada, Australia). After eliminating those who left Czechoslovakia prior to 1980 and those who refused to reveal anything relating to their person, such as gender, the total of 120 survey samples was assembled, rather evenly divided between those residing in Europe and overseas.

It is impossible to determine how representative the assembled sample really is. The Ministry of Interior in Prague keeps files on all the fugitives but is at a loss to detect the true motives, attitudes and expectations of the fleeing flock. The Austrian authorities are in possession of only approximate figures: some newcomers do not bother to register at all, others proceed to West Germany and other countries, and yet others return to Czechoslovakia, either voluntarily, or, as is suspected with some justification, by force—abducted, kidnapped.

The Vienna office of the American Fund for Czechoslovak Refugees provided me with an opportunity to compare my data with their files.

To my considerable relief it was established that my respondents were fairly representative of the entire refugee mass as regards their gender, composition, marital status, age (most numerous were those born in the 1950s, with marginal numbers being teenagers or of retirement age), education (higher rather than lower), occupational background (technical skills prevailing), and place of residence (urban over the rural).

A representative sample of the refugees and that of the nation-at-large are of course two different matters. For example the 2:1 male-female ratio in exile is surely not the norm in the nation left behind. One third of the refugees are university educated, again, not a national average.

An effort was made to distinguish between the attitudes of the refugees themselves and their assessment of the attitudes of Czechoslovak society as such.

For a number of the respondents this sudden exposure to a democratic probing device could not break the acquired inhibition of hiding one's true views. This reluctance became all too apparent in response to question #52 which asked for their main motive, predominantly economic or political, leading to emigration.

Aware of the rather perversely persistent emphasis of the *real socialists* on the class pedigree of the citizenry, I expected a certain degree of allergy to develop in some of the respondents. Yet, with the exception of two individuals no one minded revealing his or her family background.

The findings would provide little comfort to the defenders of the official Party line: it is not the members and the descendants of the defeated capitalist class who flee. Instead the sons and daughters of the victorious proletariat predominate in the exodus (40 percent from the families of manual laborers, and 38.3 percent white collar officials and professionals).

Furthermore, almost no one flees from the countryside. The villages, the target and victim of deprivation during the very unpleasant rural collectivization drive during the 1950s, have turned into relatively tranquil, fairly prosperous oases, safe from too much injurious interference by the organs of the state. By turning Lenin upside down, not the industrial worker but the farmer is being viewed as a pillar of the system's stability.

A vast majority (93.3 percent) of the respondents asserted they were never members of the Party. Three admitted their past Communist affiliation, and three others (a scientist, a salesman and a repairman), were members of the Party up to the time of their defection. While this ratio substantially deviates from the profile of the nation-at-large, it may well be representative of the exile community.

146

The political affiliation of their relatives left behind in the country proved to be much closer to the national average. Almost one-third (31.6 percent) of the respondents came from families with Party members. A nurse (Respondent #22) chose exile from a family of five normalized Communists in good standing. Another nurse, living in Switzerland (R #49) revealed in an in-depth interview: "I am a daughter of an army officer. I was an ardent member of the official youth organization. When my boyfriend, now my husband, told me about the concentration camps in the Soviet Union, I cried, wept and vowed never to see him again."

It is often asserted that the current emigration is mainly a Prague affair. The statement is inaccurate, but only to a degree. Almost one third (31.6 percent) of our respondents came from there, although only 7.74 percent of the country's population live in the capital.

One third of respondents (33.3 percent) lived in cities with more than 100,000 inhabitants, where 10.13 percent of the country's population live.

Thus two thirds of the respondents stem from urban areas where less than one fifth of all Czechoslovaks reside. Emigration is indeed a predominantly urban affair. Only 5 percent of our sample put as their last address in Czechoslovakia small towns with less than 10,000 inhabitants, i.e., communities in which 43.4 percent Czechoslovaks reside.

The majority of the post-1948 emigration wave crossed the border illegally. In the wake of the 1968 invasion, the vast majority of the newcomers to the West did not undergo the risk of combating the Iron Curtain in the darkness of the Sumava forest; rather they arrived with passports and often by car, fully loaded.

In the 1980s, the typical exile arrives either via Yugoslavia or directly to the West (Austria, West Germany, Italy) as a tourist. Only three respondents had made their way through the Iron Curtain heavily guarded by watchtowers, a plowed death strip, high fence, trip wires to release flare rockets, guards, dogs and the almost equally ferocious civilian auxiliary volunteers.

More a rule than an exception, some family members of the applicants for a travel permit are forced to stay behind as hostages, thus guaranteeing the safe return of the traveller. (I even interviewed newlyweds of whom only one spouse was permitted to undertake a honeymoon trip to Paris!)

Some individuals are blackened with such a negative political evaluation that it precludes any chance to travel anywhere, with or without his/her family. Fortunately, widely practiced corruption often accomplishes what the state tries to prevent.

"How long did it take you to make up your mind to leave the country for good, and what was the last straw contributing to this decision?"

147

This open-ended question generated a variety of reactions. Whereas some respondents defected at the first opportunity and 21 others deliberated not more than one year about whether to make this crucial step, 35 hesitated for up to five years and 21 needed even more time. Several respondents rejected the query as inapplicable. For them exile as a solution was not a matter of time-consuming doubt and/or the last straw but of the first *opportunity*. Some—students in particular—offered a brisk explanation:

"I always wanted to leave" *(odejít jsem chtel vzdy-*R #29).

"The difficulty in obtaining a travel permit made me realize in what kind of a cage I have been living" (R #71).

Some individuals identified more than one last straw. "Discrimination in culture and deterioration of the environment," stated a student, a member of the Jazz Section (R #88) who reached the West by swimming from Yugoslavia to Italy.

For a dentist who emigrated to Australia (R #93), the placement of Soviet ballistic missiles on the Czechoslovak territory along with the prospect of a hopeless future were two equally weighty reasons.

According to official Party propaganda, only the following leave the country: egotists deserting their families and the society which provided them with education, skills, even talent (case of Navratilova and Lendl); the naïve seduced by the glitter of capitalism; the adventurers, criminals, traitors selling out to the enemy; or "bloodthirsty monsters"; the last description being one that Stanislav Svoboda, deputy minister of Foreign Affairs, used in reference to exile Jiri Pelikan, Member of the European Parliament.[2]

The survey included a probe into the specific motives that led to emigration—factors encouraging and discouraging such a decision. Altogether twelve motives were identified and the respondents were asked to rate them all, on an intensity scale from 0 to the maximum 10.

The results: a relatively low weight of strictly personal, existential motivation, and a heavy emphasis on frustration, fatigue, and lack of prospects for betterment in the political realm. The average mean on this scale 0-10 grew as follows:

1. strictly personal reasons: 1.7
2. problems with housing: 1.8
3. lack of opportunity to study: 2.4

A surprisingly low intensity, indeed, in light of Czechoslovak reality—i.e., disharmonious family relations[3] ("every second marriage is facing a crisis"), a calamitously tight housing market in which a ten-year waiting period for one's own apartment is no exception, and the continued "class approach" in college admission policies, only to some degree remedied through corruption of the officials in charge of the maintenance of class purity.

After the three least pressing motivation factors the picture started to change:

    4. difficulties in employment: 4.2
    5. fear of police investigation, eventually of court prosecution: 5.0.

In some in-depth interviews the informants pointed to the creeping spectre of socialist unemployment, especially to the surplus of university graduates whose career opportunities are often blocked by unqualified, yet politically mature office holders. The Czechoslovak media started to touch this very ticklish subject by trying to devalue it as the "so-called surplus"[4] (e.g., Josef Havlin, secretary of the Party's Central Committee). The respondents attributed higher urgency to these factors:

    6. deterioration in human relations in general: 6.5
    7. environmental deterioration: 6.9
    8. economic decline: 6.9
    9. feeling of helplessness, pessimism of a life in a colony as if the last train had departed: 6.9
  10. boredom, exposure to primitive propaganda: 6.9.

Already in the preglasnost era the media started to touch upon the disturbing phenomena of substantial deterioration in human relations, brutalization of society, ranging from vandalism[5] (in Prague 10,000 public telephones intentionally damaged), to thievery of the barbaric kind[6] (a trial with seventy employees of state funeral services robbing corpses).

The environment has, in fact, deteriorated badly. The country, and the province of North Bohemia in particular, rank at the top in ecological disaster accomplished on the European continent. This result has recently attracted the attention of the Western media.

In October 1985, the East European Area Audience and Opinion Research of Radio Free Europe published its survey entitled "Czechoslovak expectations were by far the most gloomy": Only 4 percent of the sample thought it possible that the system could be changed by popular pressure (9 percent of Hungarians and 15 percent Poles expressed this opinion with regard to their own countries).

As to the expectations of what the future is likely to bring, the proportion of optimists versus pessimists attests to the prevailing gloom in the country:

Czechoslovakia	Hungary	Poland
16/78	37/59	30/67

The Czechoslovaks view their predicament in even darker colors than did the Poles after the declaration of martial law in December 1981. Our respondents rated highest the following two factors:

11. politics as such, the need to bow and obey powerful primitives: 8.2.
12. the thought that our children would have to grow up and live in such a system: 8.3.

This highest score was also registered with the childless, single individuals. Some respondents underlined the "10" once, twice, and added exclamation points or extra zeroes for emphasis.

"Jan Hus was a hero, he sacrificed his life for the sake of truth— but he could afford it, he was childless." So the saying goes in a country in which minors are made hostages, guaranteeing the docility of the parents. One's offspring are subject to incessant indoctrination: "What do you wish most to make your life happier?" was the question in a poll conducted in elementary schools. "I wish equality be granted to the Blacks," a pupil replies.[7] Thereafter, the parents along with the articulator of the politically exemplary response flee to America, or to South Africa.

The incessant politicization notwithstanding, the harvest is far from bountiful. The Party weekly *Tvorba* published on 3 August 1987 an extraordinarily frank lament entitled *Otcové a deti* ("Fathers and Children"). In it the author demonstrated against the unfair criticism of socialism and the uncritical admiration of all things Western by the young generation. A teacher, almost with tears in her eyes, related her pain and frustration when, during her lecture on the superiority of socialism, she was interrupted by a student who asked why so many people emigrate— already two of their classmates have fled. "The question of which aspects of our contemporary social reality make socialism unattractive for our young I raised only once. The answers were much too depressing."

Militarization—a factor I underestimated and did not include on the list—often contributed to the decision to leave. Civil defense and military preparedness are taught from an early age, first graders are drilled with gas masks on, and they absorb a curriculum substantially laced with martial ingredients: poems extolling the heroism of armed forces and the border guards, revolutionary battles covered in a geography class, explosives in chemistry, rockets in physics.[8]

All citizenry is subject to defense training[9] and to pretense of enthusiasm for martial matters. Probably the peak in this effort was reached in the campaign to have hundreds of thousands of citizens demonstrate their gratitude for the placement of Soviet nuclear missiles on Czechoslovak territory and protest the intention of the Americans to do the same on the West German territory.[10]

Among the factors discouraging emigration, strictly personal sentiments prevailed: concern with leaving one's parents and close relatives (mean average 5.5.), one's friends (4.3). In contrast, patriotism, feeling some identity with the native land fared at the pathetically low mean of 1.8. The younger respondents in particular turned their back on the fatherland without even token apology.

"Which of the factors, negative phenomena included, tended to discourage you from emigration?"

Again, the 0-10 scale was applied. The results revealed considerable optimism, also thoughtlessness and a vast underestimation of the difficulties the Western world tries to cope with.

Older immigrants, already settled in their new domicile, frequently identify language—i.e., the lack of knowledge of the foreign language—as the greatest handicap they had to cope with in the new country. In the survey, however, this particular factor was rated at the unrealistically low mean average of 3.8. The respondents also exhibited considerable confidence as to their skills, usefulness of their profession and training, and their overall capacity to adapt well in the new environment. (The difficulty of adjustment was rated at the low 2.4.)

Among the most surprising findings in the entire survey were the responses with regard to the preconceived socio-economic difficulties in Western democracies. The official propaganda apparatus, with its megatonnage of vilifications heaped upon the capitalist system, proves to be clearly counterproductive. The black caricature painted by the regime is distilled by the recipients into a vision, which also fails to correspond to reality.

The respondents disbelieved and practically dismissed the existence of economic difficulties in the West (mean average of mere 0.7!). The absolute majority of the respondents (96, i.e., 80 percent of the total) rated this factor with a zero—thoroughly nonexistent. Criminality, societal turbulence and related malaise received the meager rating of 1.1.

For the attainment of successful integration into a new environment, this formula may be offered: satisfaction = reality / expectation. The greater and more unrealistic the expectation, the more acute the disappointment ahead. Frequently, the victims of self-delusion tend to blame the reality rather than themselves.

In its effort to portray the West as a contemporary version of Dante's Inferno, in its overkill and consequent burial of its own plausibility, the state frequently utilizes the testimonies of the infrequent redefectors. These are fairly predictable, periodic exercises that follow a seasonal pattern: a peak in June, before summer vacations and increased opportunities to flee, and another in December, to woo back the nostalgic deserters during Christmas time. The respondents rated the impact of these testimonies at the anemic mean average of 0.6.

A substantial majority (78.3 percent) of the respondents stated that their standard of living in Czechoslovakia was either average or above average. Material well-being did not seem a factor determining one's political outlook. In several instances, individuals who were financially better off expressed a greater degree of hostility toward the abandoned political system than did the less well off.

Overall, the respondents considered their views somewhat but not substantially more hostile (level of rejection of the political system) than the attitudes of their relatives, friends, neighbors, coworkers—in short, people with whose views they have been somewhat acquainted.

The question most ardently debated in exile circles and the exile press concerns the main, fundamental motivation behind the decision to leave the native turf of occupied, normalized Czechoslovakia: is it the yearning for freedom or for economic betterment? Are the two desires complementary or mutually exclusive? Does a solely nonpolitical, materialistic motive behind a person's defection carry an opprobrium, a moral disapproval, as voices from various corners insist or at least imply?

Question #52: *"This is an elementary, fundamental query—your main reason, main motive that made you want to emigrate: 1. exclusively economic; 2. predominantly economic; 3. partly economic; 4. predominantly political; 5. exclusively political.*

Answers: 1.—0; 2.—4; 3.—22; 4.—58; 5.—28. No answer—8.

If the respondents were less than forthcoming, to put it mildly, it was in this instance. If their assertions were to be believed, not less than 86 respondents (71.6 percent of the total) did leave the country for predominantly or exclusively political reasons! Such answers were also given by individuals who further on in the questionnaire demonstrated their total lack of interest in political matters, their ignorance of the existence of Charter 77 and the like. Obviously embarrassed to admit one's economic motivation, the long-lasting habit of pretense is not likely to fade away overnight.

In the third and last part of the survey an attempt was made to gauge the political mood and attitudes not only of the refugees but also of the nation left behind.

Question #53: *"Which form of government would you choose if you had the opportunity to participate in making such a choice through an electoral process?"*

The largest group—33 respondents (27.5 percent, mainly immigrants to the United States) opted for the pluralistic democracy of the American type; 25.8 percent favored a social welfare state of the Swedish or Austrian variety; 10.8 percent preferred a system based on mainly Christian principles. Almost one third (30 percent) either could not make up their mind or checked the column "Other" (R #65, a Slovak truck driver living in the U.S., expressed preference for Italian style democracy). Only nine individuals chose what is undoubtedly the most decent type of political system in the history of Czechoslovakia—the First Republic, 1918-1938.

"How typical was your political outlook, how much did it differ from the views of your friends, colleagues, coworkers, classmates, neighbors?"

This question #65 generated the following response: 1. a majority agreed with my opinions—60 percent respondents; 2. about half of them agreed —27.5 percent. Only 8.3 percent asserted that theirs were minority views in their environment.[11]

A query into the assessment of the true political orientation of the Communist party members rendered this cumulative result: true believers, idealists totaled 4.5 percent; opportunists, career seekers totaled 57.5 percent; the remaining 38 percent basically the primitive mass, were in agreement with whatever the political power of the day was.

Various explanatory notes were appended to this column, such as: "I knew also a few idealists—fanatics—but they belonged to the old guard. They either died or are now pushed aside, without influence. Some of them finally saw the light and rejected the whole thing. I know one of this type who, after a single visit to the West, turned into a ferocious anti-Communist" (R #54, a mechanic living in the U.S.).

Question #65: "Most hated person(s) in your circles in Czechoslovakia."

The clear winner was Vasil Bilak, the Party's secretary in charge of ideology (75 votes). There were plenty of domestic villains but few domestic heroes (Q #69). Among the most popular, T.G. Masaryk received 10 votes, Dubcek 8 (mainly from the Slovaks), Havel 4 votes. Foreigners fared much better: Ronald Reagan—43 votes, Pope John Paul—25, Lech Walesa—17, Margaret Thatcher—11.

Questions #58-#73 encompass the broad topic of "dissent"—awareness of, participation in, and familiarity with unofficial publications, and related themes that frequently attract priority attention of outside observers and publicists.

The further analysis of the data assembled would require elaboration well beyond the expected scope of this contribution. Plenty of work has yet to be done.

Neither proponents nor opponents of the regime have reason to applaud the picture of the state of affairs that has emerged from the survey's findings. Vaclav Havel, the prominent playwright, known to the world but banned in his homeland, addressed the issue most succinctly in his letter to Gustav Husak.[12] His latest essay "A Story and Totality"[13] provides an analysis of original insight into the crushing power of the political system that virtually erases any sense of time and events. The post-invasion Party managers produced a document, appropriately entitled "The Lesson of the Crisis Years." The lesson learned was for the managers to abandon all ambitions except one: self-preservation. "Revolutionary ethos and terror gave way to dull immobilism, alibiism, bureaucratic anonymity and spiritless stereotype."

The system does not need murderers or the murdered any more, and it surely does not need passionate architects of utopias. *Real socialism* —this era's self-diagnosis—makes clear that it has no place for dreamers. The events became nonevents, history was replaced by pseudo-history. The media reporting pseudo-stories (who arrived and departed, who spoke wherever and received whatever kind of medal) have become a reflection of this timeless, grey reality of interchangeable years. Not only the past but also the future is being devalued, deprived of its openness. The faceless bureaucratic order loathes all colors, uniqueness, and strives for total sameness of the citizenry, with standardized lifestyles, and, indeed, lives housed in identical dwellings with identical furniture. Peoples' faces are "strangely empty, worn out, as if without life, hope, desire." Warmth, kindness, openness have evaporated, its place taken by rudeness, the very determining characteristics of contemporary civic behavior.

Havel refers to "an uncertain stress: people are nervous, irritated, succumbing to either anxiety or apathy. They give the impression of continuously expecting a blow from some direction. Equanimity and healthy self-assurance are being replaced by aggressiveness. This is the stress of people who live in a permanent feeling of some danger. This is the stress of the unfree, the humiliated, the disappointed who do not believe in anything any more."

The Dissident Writers: What Are They Saying?

Jiri Pehe

WHEN SOVIET TANKS rolled into Czechoslovakia in 1968 they ended a period of relative liberalization that included all spheres of social life. One of the priorities of the new regime, installed by the Soviets in the Spring of 1969, was a frontal attack on literature, film and theater. Why? In a sense the attack was a logical step because the roots of the Prague Spring were closely tied to the relaxation of restraints imposed on culture by the Communist regime during the 1950s. After all, it was the movement of writers, dramatic artists, film directors and other cultural figures that began the erosion of Stalinism. This process culminated at the Congress of the Union of Czechoslovak Writers in 1967. Demands and criticism raised at the Congress served as a final signal for other social groups to demand political liberalization. Soon, the writers were followed by students and journalists.

The role of the writer in Czechoslovakia has often been more important than it is in free societies. As long ago as the Hapsburg Empire, literature was perceived by the Czech people not only as literature but as a political tool. With the political life of the nation severely suppressed, literature stepped in to express political demands and grievances. Literature substituted for nonexistent politics. This practice was brought to perfection after the Communist putsch of 1948. Along came the mid-1960s and the Prague Spring partially released literature from its political obligations. The language of literature became less shrouded and ambivalent, its demands more straightforward. For a short period of time, politics became politics again. The literature of the midsixties benefited from the process of gradually operating in a free artistic field again. Huge amounts of creative energy were released—a process not dissimilar to the outburst

157

of creativity between World War I and World War II, when Czechoslovakia was an independent democratic republic. From 1964 to 1968, dozens of new literary magazines came into existence. New talented writers appeared as well, some of them publishing works that they had kept in their drawers for many years.

The neo-Stalinist leaders brought to power by Soviet tanks knew that if they let this entire structure exist—however controlled through censorship—the literature and people around it would eventually assume their role of a parallel political structure. To be able to assume absolute control, the leaders had to destroy the entire structure of Czechoslovak literature, that intricate organism that had grown for many years. This destruction was necessary in order to kill a substantial part of the liberal political culture bred by the midsixties. Virtually all literary magazines were banned, editors fired, and unreliable writers—especially those active in 1968—banished, not allowed to publish even a word. Their works were taken off library shelves, and their names obliterated from textbooks. Accompanying this carnage of literature, progressive theaters were closed, film directors were dismissed and even some pop-music singers were banished. When the job was finished, Heinrich Boll called Czechoslovakia "a cultural cemetery," and Louis Aragon described Czechoslovakia as "a Biafra of the Spirit." Years later, in his French exile, Milan Kundera wrote: "I am weighing my words carefully: In its duration, extent and consistency, the massacre of Czech culture following 1968 has had no analogue in the country's history since the Thirty Years War."[1]

Yet, though the regime succeeded in eradicating unwanted writers from the official cultural scene and replaced them with a group of sterile literary cadres who were willing to produce works along the official lines, a strange thing has happened: The last twenty years have been marked by unprecedented flourishing of Czech literature. Works of writers such as Milan Kundera, Josef Skvorecky, Vaclav Havel, Ivan Klima, Jiri Grusa and Zdena Salivarova published in the last twenty years rank with the best in Czech literary history. Alas, though they have been published world-wide, none of these authors has had a book or play published in an official Czechoslovak publishing house since 1970. Tremendous amounts of official effort are devoted to obliterating them from the memory of the nation. Mere possession of one of their works, sometimes even those published officially before 1968, can constitute a crime.

A parallel culture

Although there are several good writers who, for a variety of reasons, have been allowed to continue publishing in official publishing houses, such as Ladislav Fuchs, Vladimir Paral, Jiri Sotola, Milos Horansky and Josef Hanzlik, the boom in Czech literature is due to three other groups of writers. The *first* group is composed of major literary talents who fled the country, or were forced into exile, and established themselves in the West, such as Milan Kundera, Josef Skvorecky, Pavel Kohout, Jiri Grusa, Jan Vladislav, Vladimir Skutina, Zdena Salivarova and Arnost Lustig. The *second* group consists of several writers who, although never fully conforming to the official line, have been allowed to publish some of their works in official Czech publishing houses occasionally. However, they have also been published in *samizdat*. Jan Werich, Jaroslav Seifert and Vladimir Holan have died. The only remaining living author in this group is Bohumil Hrabal. The *third* group is composed of writers banned after the 1968 invasion, and of newcomers as well. Writers such as Vaclav Havel, Ludvik Vaculik, Ivan Klima, Dominik Tatarka, Milan Simecka, Eva Kanturkova, Egon Bondy, Karel Siktanc, Karel Pecka, Lenka Prochazkova, Dominik Tatarka and Eda Kriseova form this group. We may call them *dissident* writers (although some of them dislike the term) for the sake of better distinguishing between them and other writers.

Dissident writers have flourished because they have succeeded in building a truly independent second culture and have found ready consumers for that culture not only within their own ghetto but among Czechs in general. There are now two truly parallel cultures in the country: the official one—sterile and followed by few—and the unofficial one that has produced major works.

Independent literature has been kept alive through the emergence of two major phenomena that had been known but had never reached their full potential before 1968: exile publishing houses and domestic samizdat. There are now several major publishing houses in the West that have been able to publish all major works written by banned writers in Czechoslovakia. Josef Skvorecky, an emigre writer, together with his writer-wife Zdena Salivarova, founded *Sixty-Eight Publishers* in Toronto. The publishing houses *Arkyr* and *Index* are based in Germany, and *Rozmluvy* in London. In addition to these institutions there are emigre magazines, such as *Svedectvi, Listy, 150,000 Words, Pater Noster* and *Obrys* all of which also publish literary works. A healthy two-way exchange of literary works between Czechs at home and publishing houses in the West has been going on for many years. Manuscripts are smuggled to the West and published here; the products of the publishing houses find their way to Czechoslovakia where they often multiply. However, the audience that benefits most from this exchange are emigres. For the Czechs in Czechoslovakia, *samizdat* is more important.

Writer Eva Kanturkova describes how unofficial publishing in Czechoslovakia came into existence: "The power to publish a book has proved far less important than the ability to write freely. At the beginning of the 1970s, banned Czech writers formed their own public, circulating ten or fifteen copies among themselves. Today so many have joined in this activity that the author no longer knows how many times his manuscript has been copied. This nonpublic has its magazines and critical journals."[2]

Why has "the parallel culture" become so successful? The writers came to understand that the regime may control the tools to mass-produce literary works, but it cannot prevent the writers from writing what they want to, if they are willing to take the consequences. "Just what is a 'parallel culture?'" asks Vaclav Havel. "Nothing more and nothing less than a culture which for this or that reason will not, cannot or may not reach out to the public through the media which fall under the control of the power of the state, which in a totalitarian state includes all publishing houses, presses, exhibition halls, theaters and concert halls, scholarly institutes and so on and on. This culture therefore makes use of what is left over—typewriters, private studios, apartments, barns, etc...The 'parallel culture' was born precisely because the official uniform was too constrictive for the spiritual potential of our community, because it would not fit inside it and so it spilled over beyond the limits within which a uniform is obligatory."[3]

The very first well-organized independent publishing activity was formed by the writer Ludvik Vaculik in the mid-seventies and called "Edice Petlice." Since then many similar unofficial enterprises have come into existence, such as "Edice Expedice" and periodicals such as *Kriticky sbornik, Host, Vokno, Prostor* and *Jazz.* They are basically unofficial publishing houses and magazines, with their own editors and regular readership, that produce only several typewritten copies of various works. As small as the initial product of these publishing endeavors is—only several copies— it multiplies quickly because people who read *samizdat* publications are often required to type several copies of each publication and give them to their friends. The number of copies of a good book in circulation may quickly jump from several copies to several thousand. Over the years *samizdat* publishing has become such an integral part of the Czech culture, that almost everyone who is interested in literature keeps at home or regularly follows *samizdat* publications. The latest works of banned writers are often discussed and talked about as if they just appeared on the official literary market. "We have one enormous advantage over the officially recognized authors in that we write as we consider necessary and we feel no censorship over us," says Lenka Prochazkova, a relative newcomer to Czech literature. "For this great freedom which we have taken for ourselves we have, however, to pay every day."[4] Eva Kanturkova writes: "The unnatural conditions in our country give some people the idea that they are dependent on the tyrannical regime, that without its blessing and benevolence they cannot produce any art. That is an erroneous and misleading notion."[5]

Political dissidence

The emergence of the "parallel culture" has been able to keep alive what the regime hoped to crush: a parallel independent political culture. Almost all of the dissident writers represent in one way or another political alternatives to the current Communist regime. The writers' ghetto is a part and intellectual core of the larger dissident movement. The writers often generate ideas of the dissident movement. When the Czechoslovak human rights movement Charter 77 came into existence eleven years ago, some of its first spokesmen were writers. Today, virtually all of the banned writers are signatories of Charter 77, and some of them are active participants in various Charter 77 activities, such as the monitoring of unjust politically motivated persecution. Vaclav Havel, for example, besides being a world renowned playwright, has become one of the leading East European human rights activists. Political thought now constitutes a major part of his writing. Writers have also been associated with other movements, for example the Jazz Section, an association of jazz buffs whose newsletter and other publishing activities became the target of the regime. Some of them have served as spokesmen for Charter 77. They have also sent to the parliament and president of Czechoslovakia a number of petitions asking for artistic and political freedom.

This is an example of how dissident writers understand their role in a totalitarian society. For most of them it is simply impossible to live outside the political reality. The reflections of their everyday lives are in themselves political testimonies because they cannot avoid the descriptions of police persecution and the general distortions of reality in totalitarian societies. "Who knows, perhaps the most worthy task of culture is to struggle for a free message under the conditions of unfreedom,"[6] writes sociologist Milan Simecka.

Although the writers differ in their estimates of the long-term influence of totalitarian oppression on a culture, mostly they believe that the culture will survive. Says Ludvik Vaculik: "The history of literature is different from the territory under any government. The history of Czech literature measures a thousand years on the map of Europe. Although transitory governments of all sorts have cut their capers, the government of Czech thought and word persists implacably."[7] However, Vaclav Havel, asks: "What profound intellectual and moral impotence will the nation suffer tomorrow, following the castration of its culture today?...I am speaking of that open warrant for the arrest of anything inwardly, and therefore in the deepest sense, 'cultural.' I am speaking of the warrant of the arrest of culture, issued by the government."[8] Havel wrote these words in a letter sent to the president of Czechoslovakia in 1976. That was at the time when the destruction of Czech culture had reached its peak. Charter 77 came into existence a year later, and with it, a slightly different perception of the possibilities to create independently of the regime and keep the culture alive. Lenka Prochazkova wrote: "I believe that the fate of Czech culture at home is not as dismal as it appears to many friends abroad. I certainly do not feel as if I was on a leaking ship which, while it has not yet sunk, can be expected to sink any minute. Our ship is not leaking, only its sails are torn."[9]

Literature under totalitarianism

The fate of culture in totalitarian regimes has even become a subject of international debate. Philip Roth, the American novelist, in an interview published in the *Paris Review*, said: "When I was first in Czechoslovakia, it occurred to me that I work in a society where, for writers, everything goes and nothing matters, while for the Czech writers I met in Prague, nothing goes and everything matters."[10] However, after his seemingly flattering comment, Roth continues: "I did not envy them their persecution and the way in which it heightens their social importance. I did not even envy them their seemingly more valuable and serious themes...A literature that has the misfortune of remaining isolated underground for too long will inevitably become provincial, backward and even naïve, despite the fund of dark experience that may inspire it."

Czech writer Ivan Klima responded: "I cannot in all conscience accept your assertion that the literature which originates in these countries and does not enjoy official favor...is doomed to remain provincial, backward and naïve...I am sure you will agree with me that one of the finest literatures of the nineteenth century came from the most unfree empire of its time—Russia...By this I don't mean to say that you need unfreedom to create a great literature...There can be no argument but that the conditions of unfreedom have silenced, broken or destroyed a large number of talented writers, but to say that because of this no genuinely great work of art can come out of this entire huge part of the word seems to me no more justified than to say that it cannot be created in conditions of freedom because writers who are free lack suffering and thus have no great topics to write about, that they are demoralized by their comfortable life and corrupted by their fame and earnings. Surely every genuine work of art is the result of creative activity. Only a free human being can create genuine art, but perhaps you will agree that one can be free even while living in conditions of unfreedom. The creative act is only partly dependent on outside circumstances."[11] Milan Kundera explains the boom of the Czech literature in the last twenty years as a result of the reaction of major literary talents produced by the relative freedom of the 1960s to the current oppression. But, Kundera thinks that in the end the destructive effects of totalitarianism will prevail. However, some recent events prove Kundera and Roth partly wrong. There are now promising writers in Czechoslovakia who are too young to have been established writers in 1968. They grew up under communism, yet it does not seem to have destroyed their creativity. Some of the new *samizdat* editions have been founded by young writers.

The literature produced by these writers shows a certain bias toward dealing predominantly with oppression, absolute power vs. individual themes, and the essence of totalitarianism. Some of them try to avoid that bias, but oppression is, unfortunately, the reality that surrounds them and which they *have to* reflect on. They often write under extremely difficult conditions. Writes Vaclav Havel: "You live in fear for your manuscript. Until such a time as the text which means so much to you is safely stowed somewhere, or distributed in several copies among other people, you live in a state of constant suspense, and uncertainty—and as the years go by, surprisingly enough, this does not get easier, but on the contrary, the fear tends to grow into pathological obsession...As long as the papers are spread over my desk in almost illegible manuscript, I tremble with apprehension. Not only for the play, you understand, but for myself, that is, for that piece of my identity which would be torn from me were I to lose the manuscript."[12] Ludvik Vaculik describes this fear in one of his *feuilletons:* "Someone rings my doorbell, so I quickly remove the paper from my typewriter and hide it before going to open the door. It was the rent collector. What a pleasant surprise!"[13]

A writer's fear in totalitarian Czechoslovakia concerns things that are mostly intangible. The police do not kill as they did in the 1950s, the era of Stalinist terror. With exceptions, they do not physically mistreat their ideological opponents. They intimidate. They let the writers know that they are watching them and may strike at any moment. The police bug writers' apartments, disconnect telephones, take away their driving licences or passports, and openly follow their victims everywhere they go. From time to time the writers are taken for interrogation; sometimes they are jailed. Yet, "this is no *Darkness at Noon* or *Nineteen Eighty-Four*,"[14] observes Walter Goodman in his *New York Times* review of Vaculik's *A Cup of Coffee With My Interrogator*. Indeed it is not a *Darkness at Noon*. Totalitarian regimes have matured. Their methods have become more sophisticated. These systems are not dictatorships in the true sense of the word. They do not use brutality as their most important means. Rather, they are, as Havel asserts in his essay *Power of the Powerless*, post-totalitarian societies where the blame for social malady cannot be traced anymore to any particular culprit. Every person who does not guard his or her authenticity against the depersonalizing power of such a system is its inherent part. Society and the state are one entity. Totalitarianism permeates everyone who is not on constant guard.

How do the writers deal with such a situation? Again and again, they seem to emphasize civil courage and authenticity. "The independent activity in a totalitarian system," writes Eva Kanturkova, "puts sense against senselessness, creativity against destruction, contents against vacuum ...Although we live in constant fear of prison, we are trying to create democracy by what we are. Nothing can be given to us. In that notion is the source of independent activities."[15] Most of the writers are trying to live as if they were free. In their lives, they are trying to ignore the conditions that surround them. It is, however, very difficult to do the same in their works.

Havel and Hrabal

Among contemporary Czech writers who live in Czechoslovakia, two personalities tower over the rest, each reflecting the conditions in the totalitarian state in his own way. They are Vaclav Havel and Bohumil Hrabal. Havel is a playwright and a political thinker, for whom the political situation in his own country is inseparable from his artistic work. His early works were basically absurd visions of modern society, with its bureaucratization, regimentation and depersonalization. *Zahradni Slavnost (The Garden Party)*, published in the mid-sixties, deals with topics that Havel pursues today. Havel's personal life may serve as a permanent testing laboratory for his thoughts. He was born into a bourgeois family, and after the Communist putsch deprived of the possibility of receiving a university education. He is a self-made, self-educated, man who has never compromised with authorities and the system he dislikes. All of his latest writing reflects, in one way or another, the cancer of totalitarianism which he sees as the cancer of the modern world in general. In his letters from prison addressed to his wife, (published under the name *Letters to Olga*) he repeatedly talks about the lack of responsibility accompanying our age. He sees his jailers not only as products of specific Czechoslovak conditions but also as the products of larger deficiencies that plague modern civilization. *Largo Desolato*, a play that two years ago swept through world theaters, deals with the personal situation of a dissident philosopher, Kopriva, who, although admired by his fellow dissidents and the nation, lives in constant fear of arrest, in terror of another interrogation, knocking on the door.

In *Pokuseni (Temptation)*, Havel's last play, he returns to what he calls "structures," meaning society outside the dissident ghetto. The play was conceived in the prison in which Havel spent several years for his human rights activities.

> Ever since 1977, when I landed in jail for the first time, I was vaguely haunted by the theme of Dr. Faust. Although I only was imprisoned for a relatively short time on that first occasion, for various reasons I found it extremely hard to bear. I realized that they (the interrogators) were preparing a trap for me: they intended politically to misuse something I had said in one of my appeals against my detention, something that I had said in all innocence, but which was now to be distorted and twisted in order to discredit me. I had strange dreams and strange ideas. I felt I was being tempted by the Devil. I realized that I somehow got tangled up with him. The fact that something I had written, something I had really thought was true, could be misused in this way brought it home to me yet again that the truth is not only that which one thinks, but also under what circumstances, to whom, why and how one says it. And that became one of the themes of my latest play, *Temptation*. It was then, in prison, that I conceived the idea of doing my own version of the Faust theme.[16]

In *Temptation* the devil, who brings new ideas to a scientist, Dr. Foustka, turns out to be a police informer, his "devilish" tricks a mere set-up. The devilishness of the totalitarian system touches even the supernatural.

"Totalitarian systems," writes Havel in his excellent political essay, *Politika a svedomi (Politics and Conscience)* "warn of something far more serious than Western rationalism is willing to admit. They are, most of all, a convex mirror of the inevitable consequences of rationalism, a grotesquely magnified image of its own deep tendencies, an extremist offshoot of its own development and an ominous product of its own expansion...They are the avant-garde of a global crisis of this civilization, first European, then Euro-American, and ultimately global."[17] How did totalitarianism come about? Havel says:

It is paradoxical: people in the age of science and technology live in the conviction that they can improve their lives because they are able to grasp and exploit the complexity of nature and the general laws of its functioning. Yet it is precisely these laws which, in the end, tragically catch up on them and get the better of them. The fault is not one of science as such but of the arrogance of man in the age of science. Man simply is not God, and playing God has cruel consequences. Man has abolished the absolute horizon of his relations, denied his personal "pre-objective" experience of the lived world, while relegating personal conscience and consciousness to the bathroom, as something so private that it is no one's business. Man rejected his responsibility as a "subjective illusion"—and in place of it installed what is now proving to be the most dangerous illusion of all: the fiction of objectivity stripped of all that is concretely human, of rational understanding of the cosmos, and of abstract schema of putative "historical necessity." At the apex of it all, man has constructed a vision of a purely scientifically calculable and technologically achievable "universal welfare," demanding no more than experimental institutes invent it while industrial and bureaucratic factories turn it into reality. That millions of people will be sacrificed to this illusion in scientifically directed concentration camps is not something that concerns our "modern man" unless by chance he himself lands behind barbed wire and is thrown drastically back upon its natural world.[18]

What accompanies the emergence of planned societies, these rationalist monsters, says Havel, is the depersonalization of power and its reduction to a mere technology of rule and manipulation. In Havel's opinion, this is a universal trend. "It is the essential trait of all modern civilization, growing directly from its spiritual structure, rooted in it by a thousand tangled tendrils and inseparable even in thought from its technological nature, its mass characteristics and its consumer orientation."[19] Politicians everywhere, less so in free societies, more so in totalitarian ones, says Havel, are mere power technicians.

System, ideology, and aparat have deprived humans—rulers as well as ruled—of their conscience, of their common sense and natural speech and thereby, of their actual humanity. States grow ever more machine-like, men are transformed into statistical choruses of voters, producers, consumers, patients, tourists or soldiers. In politics, good and evil, categories of the natural world and therefore obsolete remnants of the past, lose all absolute meaning; the sole method of politics is quantifiable success. Power is *a priori* innocent because it does not grow from a world in which words like guilt and innocence retain their meaning. This impersonal power has achieved what is its most complete expression in the totalitarian systems.[20]

How does a writer, or any dissident, whose obligation it is truthfully to reflect the world around him, deal with a totalitarian system? Havel says: "The task is one of resisting vigilantly, thoughtfully and attentively, but at the same time with total dedication, at every step and everywhere, the rational momentum of anonymous, impersonal and inhuman power—of the Ideologies, Systems, Aparat, Bureaucracy, Artificial languages and Political slogans...I am convinced that what is called 'dissident' in the Soviet bloc is a specific modern experience of life at the very ramparts of dehumanized power."[21]

Bohumil Hrabal's answer to the totalitarian state and power is slightly different from that of Havel. Hrabal is only partially a member of the community of dissident writers. For years, his works have been published simultaneously in *samizdat*, in emigre publishing houses and in official publishing houses in Czechoslovakia. Hrabal sees himself as an apolitical man whose objective is to reflect the world around him not abstractly through philosophical concepts but on the most earthy level. Although he obviously shares some of Havel's philosophical premises, totalitarianism almost does not penetrate into the world he describes, the world of pubs, simple people, the world of his childhood. Yet, from these simple things he has managed to create a most complex picture of Czech society and humanity in general. Although he has also experienced persecution, and for a period of time his books were banned, his political reflections come only indirectly in some of his works, such as *Prilis hlucna samota (My Brilliant Solitude)* and lately also in his memoirs. In *My Brilliant Solitude* the hero is an operator of a paper press whose purpose is to destroy old paper. This "old paper" often includes books that the regime considers undesirable. In his memoirs, *Proluky (The Building Sites*; two more parts now circulate in Prague *samizdat* and are to be soon published by emigre publishing houses), Hrabal does not avoid political reflections. For example, he describes how he strolled through Prague with Heinrich Boll shortly after the Soviet invasion, and they stopped at the building belonging to the Union of Czechoslovak writers, only to see a cannon aimed at the windows of the building. "The cannon is still there," remarks Hrabal bitterly.

Authorities allowed Hrabal to publish his books officially only after he recanted the "errors" he made in ·1968. Recently, he was even re-admitted into the Union of Czechoslovak Writers. It seems that the nation understood his gesture as a Schweikian one, a gesture meaningful only for the authorities. Hrabal describes himself in his memoirs as a person unable to take everyday persecution. He cannot exist in a ghetto. His material is the people. In an interview for the *New York Times*, given to Olga Carlise in a Prague pub, Hrabal says: "The people in this room are my friends. You may not believe it, but modern art, real art, real writing has survived in this city, which many people have deserted— but *the* people have not deserted it!"

Milan Kundera describes Hrabal as the best Czech writer. Says Ivan Klima: "The greatest living Czech prose writer (although not too well known in the West because he is difficult to translate and impossible to interpret in politicals terms) is, in my view, Bohumil Hrabal. Timid and shy, he is perhaps the exact opposite of Solzhenitsyn. He was persecuted for many a year. His is the work of an extraordinary imagination, full of humor, poetry and paradox, absurdity, as well as fascinating insight into individual human beings and life in general. I have no doubt that if Hrabal wrote in English, French or Spanish, his books would have long ago received the most prestigious literary prize."[22] Over all, Hrabal has published over a dozen books, all of them tremendously popular in Czechoslovakia. Czech people love Hrabal not only because of his works in which they find themselves, but because of his weakness. It is easier for many of them to identify with Hrabal than with the heroic attitude of writers who live in the ghetto.

The future of literature

Other Czech writers respond to the situation of totalitarian everydayness in Havel's way. Ludvik Vaculik, who published two important novels, *Sekyra (The Ax)* and *Morce (Guinea Pig)* has during the last ten years written a large number of so-called *feuilletons*, short personally flavored essays, reflecting the reality of contemporary Czechoslovakia. Vaculik's diary, *Cesky snar (A Czech Dream Book)*, is a day-by-day account of a life in a dissident ghetto. Eva Kanturkova has been writing essays and is now working on a historical novel. Her latest published book, *Pritelkyne z domu smutku (My Companions from the Bleak House)* depicts the fate of female prisoners in one of the Czechoslovak prisons in which Kanturkova was jailed. Ivan Klima described a writer's life in present Czechoslovakia in a collection of short-stories, *Vesela jitra (My Merry Mornings)*. *Me prvni lasky (My first Loves)*, another collection of short stories, has recently been published in English. His latest novel is entitled *Soudce z milosti (Judge On Sufferance)* and it is based on his earlier novel *Stoji, stoji sibenicka (There Stands a Gallows)*. Lenka Prochazkova published two books in *samizdat, Prijd ochutnat (Come and Taste)* and *Strazce holubu (The Guard of Pigeons).* Several other promising young writers have emigrated, most notably, Jan Pelc, whose realistic description of the demoralization of youth in Northern Bohemia, *Deti raje (The Children of Paradise)* has made it the most discussed book among the Czech literary public in recent years.

While Czech writers have been able to create their own ghetto, Slovak dissident writers have been virtually eliminated. Dominik Tatarka, the most popular of them, writes: "The community of Slovak writers has been broken, both morally and materially. Ever since the invasion I have been living in the prison of so-called administrative measures. Everything has been taken away from us: our publishing house, magazine, fund, and summer retreat."[23] The situation has been made even more difficult by the constant obstruction of contacts between Czech and Slovak writers by the police. Tatarka has, however, written several excellent books. His *Pisacky* received awards that are given by Czech emigre writers and organizations to the best literary products coming out of Czechoslovakia. Another book, *Sam proti noci (Alone Against the Night),* is a personal account of the life of a dissident writer in Slovakia, that writer being Tatarka.

So, what is the future of Czech literature? "I don't know what will happen in the culture of the years to come," writes Vaclav Havel, "I do know, though, what will decide it, if not entirely, then to a great extent —the future development of the confrontation between the graveyard intentions of the powers that be and this irrepressible cultural hunger of the community's living organism, or perhaps that sector which has not yet given up on everything."[24] As for the short term prospects, concretely those for glasnost, Havel is pessimistic: "I don't think history can just stop and turn around. I've lived through so many regimes in my life— the Democrats, then the Nazis, then the Communists, then the Prague Spring, and all the dreams that went with it. Some incongruous hopes have come to the surface recently—that Gorbachev is a savior who will bring us freedom. Our political leaders give lip service to glasnost. They keep repeating that it is necessary to install new democratic policies, but it's easy to see they don't really want to change anything. The present regime has been fiercely persecuting reformers for twenty years and it is not likely they will voluntarily stop."[25] As for long term prospects of the struggle between power and culture, Havel says: "Life can be raped, flattened or deadened for a long time, but it cannot be stopped completely —it will always find a way back to itself, it will survive the power that tried to rape it."[26]

It Was You Who Did It!

Antonin J. Liehm

AT THE BEGINNING of 1988—on the occasion of the 20th anniversary of the beginning of the Prague Spring—the Communist party of Czechoslovakia took notice of the occasion—negatively. It declared in its daily, *Rude pravo,* that the process of democratizing the economic and political system in Czechoslovakia (which the Communist party is prepared to initiate after twenty years of so-called normalization) will have nothing in common with the process that occurred in Czechoslovakia during the first eight months of 1968. *Rude pravo* also declared that Gorbachev's reforms in the Soviet Union have little in common with the 1968 Czechoslovak process.

Several days later, an extensive interview with Alexander Dubcek appeared in *l'Unita,* the most important press organ of the Italian Communist party. In that interview, the general secretary of the Czechoslovak Communist party at the time of the Prague Spring points to a remarkable similarity between the basic tendencies and objectives of "Gorbachevism" and the tendencies of the Prague Spring. Dubcek pleads for the rehabilitation of 1968 and a return to its ideas and practices.

After the twenty years that have elapsed since 1968, it is possible to reflect on the current Czechoslovak reality as more than debris and burned-out land left behind by the Soviet invasion.

Opening the doors for Stalin—1938

The history of 1968 and of modern Czechoslovakia began with the final disintegration of the Peace of Versailles in Munich in September 1938. At the time, a well-armed and modestly fortified country was ready—in full armor and with the enthusiasm of its populace—to defend its borders. It was only half a year after its strategic siege had been basically completed by the "anchluss" of Austria. Czechoslovakia was ready, with the help of allies, not only to call Hitler's bluff, but also, if necessary, to take up the unequal fight, a fight which it most probably would have lost at great expense. But such a fight would have determined quite a different course for the coming conflict—by sacrificing Czechoslovakia and Europe as they existed after World War I, it would have postponed the ensuing war by at least a year.

It was in 1938—and not at Yalta or in 1948—that the doors to the heart of Europe were opened for Stalin, and the first chapter of Europe's division was written. Foundations of the future world divided between two superpowers were laid. As an ultimate result of that process, Central and Eastern Europe came under Soviet bondage and became a part of the Soviet empire. Especially when the course of the war and the situation on the war fronts are taken into account it becomes clear that nothing could have been changed about that fact by Yalta or various episodes in later developments. The map of Europe and the ratio of forces were determined for a long historical period when Stalin's armies— as a result of the policy of appeasement and Munich—finally stood in Berlin, Warsaw, Prague, Budapest and Vienna. Today, everyone realizes that a basic change in this situation could be brought about only through developments inside the blocs themselves and not through outside intervention.

The significance of the Prague Spring, and of its crushing by Soviet tanks, must be understood from this perspective. The Czechoslovak attempt to reform "real socialism" was an attempt at a constructive answer to the collapse of the Stalinist system in its entirety. It was an attempt to create a model of a renewed, permanently self-reforming civil society. This attempt could have eventually amounted to a gradual transformation of the Soviet empire into a commonwealth of nations, one that would have been based on mutual advantages, especially economic, for example, a huge market, and not on military and police coercion. In the aftermath of World War II, such an attempt could have been realized first only in a country with a deep, more than one-hundred-year-old tradition of civil society, and with an equally long tradition of democratic socialism. And it could have had happened only in a country that—despite the difficult experience of the post-war developments—was spared by history from direct contact with Russian imperialism; in a nation where there was still a desire for friendship and sincere cooperation with the biggest Slavic nation. And the reform was possible only in a country that belonged, before World War II, among the most advanced industrial coun-

tries in Europe, a country with a deep tradition of technological skill
and industrial organization, and a high level of general education and
culture. It could have happened only in a country that, on the one hand,
was deeply Western, and, on the other hand, without historically caused
prejudice against the European East and its superpower.

The entire course of the first eight months of 1968 showed that the
possibility for real reform did actually exist. Despite the great openness
that accompanied this period, and despite the absolute disappearance of
the official censorship—indeed amidst a real practical self-management
of the news media—the entire process of the social reform unfolded in
a calm and orderly manner, with increasing participation of the citizenry.
There was real hope that the period of social and economic stagnation
would end, and that—without changes in the geopolitical situation in Europe—a process of gradual recovery of the whole eastern part of Europe
would begin. Such a process could be accompanied by a recovery of
good mutual relations between the countries of this region, and perhaps
even between the two parts of the divided Europe and the world. This
possibility—without being given a real chance—was destroyed by the Soviet
tanks during the night of 21 August 1968. I am deeply convinced that
this night was a tragedy not only for Czechoslovakia but, above all, for
the *Soviet Union*. The Soviet Union eliminated the possibility of creating a reform model that would have been constructed on foundations
much more suitable for reforms than those that could have been provided by Soviet society—then or today. The possibility for reform was
eliminated in the only advanced country of the Soviet bloc, a country
that was not hostile to the Soviet Union.

"Dubcekism" and "Gorbachevism"

In contrast to the January 1988 analysis in *Rude pravo*, I would say that
there is a deep similarity between the philosophies of "Dubcekism" and
"Gorbachevism." However, there is also a big difference: in Czechoslovakia
this philosophy was applied to a society that, despite the thirty years
since September of 1938, immediately began to behave as a mature, orderly
and active civil society, fully aware of its possibilities and limitations.
The Soviet Union does not have such a tradition. The basic difference
between Gorbachevism and Dubcekism therefore is that Gorbachevism
does not and cannot depend on the civil society. It relies above all on
reforms ordered and enforced from above, reforms that are stimulated
and controlled by the bureaucracies and the police. The current leadership
of the Communist party of Czechoslovakia envisions the reforms—should
it actually be forced to initiate them—in the same way. Unfortunately,

173

what may amount to a degree of progress and enlightened rule in Russia will become mere "steel lungs" in Czechoslovakia, "lungs" that will prolong a dangerous and explosive situation that was begun in the August of 1968.

Unfortunately, not even Dubcek's *l'Unita* analysis is quite correct. The process of liquidation of the once advanced and prosperous democratic Czechoslovak society, which was slowed gradually in the 1960s and disrupted in 1968, has continued for the last twenty years in a most primitive and brutal fashion. Although the standard of living in Czechoslovakia is still higher than that in the USSR and other Communist countries, with the exception of the GDR, Czechoslovak workers are worse off than workers in all the European countries whose standard of living in 1938 was comparable to that of Czechoslovakia. The middle class is even worse off. Only farmers are relatively prosperous. Even so their production cannot match the agricultural production of the West.

As a result of shortages in the economy and the rule of unchecked police and bureaucratic despotism, corruption has spread to a degree never previously seen in Czechoslovak society. Citizens show no interest in public matters. Society has been fully atomized. Ties between individuals and society have disappeared. The level of education has fallen sharply. Twenty years of the cultural policy of "burned land" have transformed one of the main traditional European cultural centers into a cultural wasteland, where only few oases are kept alive—with incredible difficulties. Not only have civil and socialist traditions been forgotten, but the younger generation has never learned them. A balanced and, on the whole, friendly relationship with Russia and then with the USSR has changed into one of distaste, resistance and, often, open hatred.

The idea that it is possible to return to the concepts of 1968 under such circumstances seems to me illusory. A certain autonomy of the civil society, the source of its self-discipline, which Czechoslovakia reestablished during the 1960s, has been destroyed. And unless the autonomy of the civil society is renewed, no attempt at reform stands a chance.

Unfortunately, today an exhausted, tired and apathetic Czechoslovak society does not have the energy for such a renewal. Since it is the Soviet Union that bears the full responsibility for this situation, it is necessary to turn toward Moscow, toward the new Soviet leadership, and all those in the Soviet Union who support the leadership's attempts at a new policy, and ask them: "What have you done and what will you do to correct, at least partially, the crime committed in your name in August 1968?"

"It was you who did it," a Spanish philosopher said to general Franco, looking over the terrible destruction of his country. "It was you who did it," should be repeated again and again to those who speak from Moscow of a new approach to the world and its problems. It was you who did it, and not the Czechoslovak government put in power by you, a government that—because of its policies—has never achieved legitimacy, not even the degree of legitimacy attained by Janos Kadar in the years that followed the Hungarian uprising of 1956. It was you who did it, and the situation in today's Czechoslovakia is the direct result of your work. Until you remedy—step by step—what you committed, the world will look at the debris of Czechoslovakia and will not believe anything that you today declare and promise.

Every reasonable person in Czechoslovakia supports Gorbachev's policy today because its success could mean a new future for the nations of the Soviet empire. Nobody demands that the USSR again "clean up house" in Czechoslovakia; such an act would amount to the repetition of the old policy, only played to a new tune. However, until Moscow distances itself from what happened on 21 August 1968; until the books banned in Czechoslovakia are published at least in Moscow; until the films banned in Czechoslovakia are played there; until they write in Moscow that the inspiration for the Soviet perestroika comes from the economists of the Prague Spring; until it is said publicly that the Czechoslovak attempt at the renewal of civil society was the only possible direction for reform, and that accusations leveled against that experiment remain a lie, until then it will be necessary to repeat to those in Moscow: "It was you who did it!"

The Premature Perestroika

Ivan Svitak

THE PRAGUE SPRING of 1968 was a confirmation of Max Eastman's assertion that critical truth speaking is an element of the struggle for socialism that is essential for its success. The Czech *nomenklatura* realized that the Soviet economic model was not working and that it was in the interest of the power elite to start a restructuring, which today we might call a premature and untimely *perestroika*. The politburo was divided between reformists and conservatives, but this division was not due to different notions about the necessity of economic reforms; rather it was due to differences of a political and personal nature. The leadership was faced with an important, yet very simple choice: Should the economic performance be improved by democratization of an oppressive system, or should the Czechs follow the example of Walter Ulbricht in the GDR, where substantial improvements had been achieved without political concessions to the masses? The reform-minded group among Czech leaders chose the first alternative. That gave the creeps to both Ulbricht and Brezhnev—even though both factions in the Czech leadership tendered unquestioned faithfulness to Moscow.

When, in April, the reformists announced their Action Program (it was a bad April Fool's joke indeed), they were surprised that the dire predictions of the conservative faction came true. Criticism suddenly came from everywhere, and the critical voices were not only those of intellectuals! Despite twenty years of systematic brainwashing, an unorganized opposition suddenly came out of the blue, and people—students, miners, Slovaks, artists, political prisoners, militias, journalists—began to express their opinions without asking for permission. People, yes, the people— *puer robustus sed malitiousus*—a strong but vicious boy in the minds of every power elite. The Prague Spring started to roll in 1968 because the Czech bureaucratic dictatorship was unable any longer to secure two vital functions—economic growth and/or the undivided monopoly of power. Democratization became the inevitable choice for the survival of bureaucratic dictatorship itself and for its power elite. This built-in paradox of democratization was a fatal flaw, one that eventually brought about tragedy, and buried the perestroika with the same necessity which will lead to a similar collapse in Moscow. Gorbachev is simply a Dubcek, but he does not know it yet.

From the beginning of the Prague Spring until its bitter end, I considered the policy of the Communist party to be a Gomulka-type fraud, or a Chinese policy of the one hundred flowers that were encouraged to bloom—only to be cut down later. Nevertheless, even a mild improvement was better than nothing. But, I had no confidence in the reformist group, mainly because I knew some of them too well. So I started to test the validity of the new freedom declared by the reformists. I deliberately questioned their promises, formulating exactly those problems which transcended the limits of the newly declared policy and which were expressed in my slogan that later became: "We do not need democratization, we need democracy." From this point of view, the main abysses between the Party and the people, between the Communists and non-Communists, between the *apparatchiki* and the intellectuals, were immediately visible. Today, the same abysses are equally unbridgeable and the slogan is more valid than before. I expected that the Party would stop the democratization game pretty soon, and I was surprised that they did not; the process continued. In this temporary interlude, I formulated my comments without tactical considerations, testing simply the possibility of speaking the truth. The impact was deep and dramatic, because I was addressing my public speeches to students in Prague, to miners in the industrial Ostrava region, to artists and to new political clubs (KAN). I wrote open letters to the prosecutor general and to members of the politburo—without any respect to the new Party line.

To fight for democratic freedoms in bureaucratic dictatorships is certainly an extremism. On the other hand, to reach for the impossible is the privilege of the human species and a noble role of a thinker. To express a truthful idea is a relevant act, lasting longer in history than the individual himself. I was expressing the truth about the Prague Spring and its paradoxes at the time they took place and not with a delay of ten years, as was the case with my Chartist and reformist friends, who recognized their blunders too late. My main contribution to the Prague Spring was not the shock of truth that people suddenly felt when reading the open letter regarding the death of Jan Masaryk or essays about politics. The main issue was the challenge to the leading role of the Communist party, the disregard for the sacred cow itself.

The most important thing I did during the Prague Spring was to formulate openly strategic goals for independent organizations—practically illegal—which escaped the control of the Communist party and *eo ipso* challenged the power elite as a budding opposition. I promoted the idea of an act of unity between workers and intellectuals—an idea of independent force—since neither faction in the Communist leadership represented an alternative to a democratic development. This independent democratic line, the emancipation from the rotten idea of the National Front policy based on the leading role of the Communist party, is still controversial, even among the best minds in Czechoslovakia. However, the chances today for an authentic democratic movement are much better than twenty years ago. Totalitarian systems are in decline everywhere in the world and a *democratic revolution*—yes, friends, democratic revolution, you hear well—is waiting for future generations. The debts to the growth of freedom and human rights are never repaid.

Democratic revolution

In comparison to the past Hungarian, Polish and German experiences, the Prague Spring contained certain particular elements. The first element was the sudden explosion of truth, an intellectual revolt ensuing in a series of nonviolent challenges to a repressive system. The media started to reveal the truth about the reality and, thereby, the monopoly of the official "truth"—that is, the lies of the Communist party—was seriously undermined. Any monopoly of truth is a coffin of truth. It is just a warranty for liars so that nobody can question them. However, if the truth starts to crawl out of the grave of a bureaucratic dictatorship, the elite is understandably horrified, because the ghosts of murdered persons and suppressed problems begin to haunt the living. Every bureaucratic dictatorship collapses as a whole whenever any part of the system ceases to function in a repressive way—economics, politics or the media. This is also the reason why in a bureaucratic dictatorship it is impossible just to add constitutional freedoms, human rights or a prosperous economy to the existing dominant function of repression. The system functions as a whole and collapses as a whole. Squaring the circle is an impossible task, and democratizing a dictatorship is an impossibility, irrespective of noble motives. Brezhnev knew that truth in the media is a ticking bomb, which the elite must deal with or become a victim. He did not wait.

The second revolutionary element was unauthorized democratic practice. In the spring of 1968, it was not clear if the democratization program was only a trap door for radical intellectuals and conservative *apparatchiki* or whether it was meant as a broader policy that would survive the replacement of the Party leadership. If the second alternative were correct, then it should have been impossible to refuse legal status to the newly emerging independent organizations outside the existing National Front—that is to the Social Democratic party and political clubs such as KAN, K231. The activities of these organizations, despite their illegal status, were *ipso facto* questioning the leading role of the Party and, therefore, were instantly branded as counterrevolutionary antisocialist forces.

Such demagogic characteristics are of course valid only within the fraudulent framework of Communist propaganda, where the elementary rule of the democratic game—the will of the people—is permanently vetoed by the privileged status of the Party bureaucracy, which does not share power with anybody. On the other hand, the label of antisocialist counterrevolution is *de facto* a flattering statement, acknowledging the unexpected phenomenon, namely that these organizations were able to cast some doubt on the despotic power and challenge the self-appointed elite. How could the Communists talk about democratization if they were not willing to respect working class leaders of a Social Democratic Party, which had existed fifty years before the Communist one? Was freedom of assembly respected if leading reformers like Cisar, Smrkovsky or Mlynar were openly declaring their readiness to repress the Social Democrats by violent means? These freshly baked democratizing "pluralists" branded as counterrevolutionary everything that transcended the narrow space of their Stalinist thinking.

The best example was the scandal surrounding the *Two Thousand Words* manifesto. Less known are the problems of the earlier *KAN Manifesto,* of which I was the author, but which was suppressed. In critical situations, the reform Communists had to defect from their own program, and betray their own promises, not because they would not take their own reforms seriously, but because they ran into unforeseen troubles which were threatening their monopoly of power. Fortunately for us, the reformists never understood that their reforms were endangering their own power.

The third element of the Prague Spring was the failure of the Communist party to defend national interests, the state sovereignty and Czech cultural traditions against aggressive Sovietization. The Communist party is fully responsible for the disastrous consequences of their mishandled reforms. The reformists tried later, without success, to pass the responsibility for their own failure to Western espionage and to antisocialist elements. The Communists—reformed or unrepentant Stalinists—have never accepted the will of the people as superior to their own totalitarian doctrine. The basic democratic principle, to ask for the approval of the governed, is for them a meaningless and ridiculous eccentricity. As all revolutionary elitists, they have a cordial contempt for the actual opinions of the people for whom they want to speak exclusively. The Communists do not conceal that the democratic process is repulsive to them and that all elections must simply confirm the existing power structure. The question of who should rule and for what purposes he should exercise power is not even permitted to be asked. Prague Spring revealed this ambivalent attitude of all brands of communism to the masses, who realized that with the Communist party no future reform was possible.

Today communism has lost all credibility. It is correctly seen as an unreformable system of oppression, as a barbaric challenge to Europe, and as a system which will succumb only to democratic structural changes. The only people who want to reform communism are the Communists themselves—*not* the masses who know from experience that communism is doomed and that it has no future. This good news concerns exactly those countries where people have had experience with communism.

International consequences

Among the international consequences of the Soviet invasion of Czechoslovakia was the hypocritical rhetoric of Western liberals, who did not move a finger in the critical situation, because they were fascinated by a bridge-building policy toward the Soviet Union. A more lasting consequence was a possible decline of Soviet prestige in the Third World, but in most countries Soviet army supplies are more important than the violated sovereignty of a small European country. Another, and the worst, consequence was the detente policy which rewarded Soviet aggressive postures with far-reaching concessions.

The Soviet intervention worked in the short run, and history again seemed to confirm that the West has written off the Czechs and the other Central Europeans behind the Iron Curtain. In the long run, the results of the Soviet intervention are much more problematic, because the Western left, including Eurocommunists, ceased to see the Soviet Union as a model for emulation. The European power elite had to face the fact that the Soviet imperialist aggression offers no rational alternative to the continuity of NATO. The fate of the Czechs and the Poles offered a horrifying warning to those who take the Soviet threat lightly.

The subsequent policy of (abnormal) normalization, that is, the pacification of local Central European reformists by the Red army, has ruined the possibility of systemic reform through the existing Communist parties. The Czechs and the Poles are now slowly sinking to the level of the Soviets, to the level of Third World countries—despite huge capital investments from the West! That is also the reason why the Prague Spring cannot be repeated and why, on the other hand, the perspective of human rights, of neutrality and democracy has gained beyond all expectations. Ludvik Vaculik, the author of the *Two Thousand Words* manifesto and the cleverest Czech political thinker, has recently observed that the Soviet reformers are simply rummaging in the intellectual luggage of the Prague Spring. He did not mind; it was the Soviets' luggage. How true!

For the Soviet Union, the suppression of the Prague Spring signaled the return to Stalinism. The Prague Spring tested an imperialist policy which solves differences of interests between a small nation and a superpower by a military method of colonial expansion. The Soviets had been ready for a military intervention in advance. They were determined to place Soviet military units on the Czechoslovak territory under any pretext. Their actions were not determined by what actually happened in Prague. Military intervention was completely unnecessary, because the new Communist leadership would have stopped the democratization very quickly. Dubcek would just have played the shameful role of a Czech Gomulka. Gustav Husak allegedly said that the invasion could have been prevented by neutralizing Vasil Bilak and locking up Svitak. (I would prefer to lock up both of them in one cell.) Brezhnev was afraid that the democratic infection would spread to Soviet Union. The reformists were unable to grasp the consequences of their own policy in the international context, and they failed to see that they unintentionally generated destabilizing pressures within the Soviet bloc, pressures which were unacceptable to Brezhnev. The Czech reformists were not losing political power in the country—on the contrary, they became more popular—but their attack on Stalinism was a mortal sin. The same lesson is waiting for Gorbachev.

Yet another lesson is a bitter one for the victims. The Czechs should have defended themselves by all means, including the military, because truth, freedom and democracy are worth the sacrifices. A young student, Jan Palach, knew of this old wisdom and so his message is still alive. A skilled apparatchik, Alexander Dubcek, has not learned that wisdom, not even two decades later, and so his January 1988 message to Moscow is as dead as the Prague Spring. The Czechs should have defended themselves, because values cannot be defended otherwise. Czech history in this century has proved several times that capitulations before bureaucratic dictatorships do not pay off.

On the other hand, it may be a blessing in disguise that the Communist party was unable to leave behind some heroic symbols, some models of virtue, a memory of resisting the occupation. The only symbol of the inept leadership is still Alexander Dubcek, crying on national TV—the same man who now has the guts to congratulate the new Soviet leader whose armies still occupy Dubcek's country. It is almost as if Dubcek would like to confirm that the Communist party has been the backbone of internal repression and a criminal institution which has betrayed the democratic character of the Czech state and of national culture. Despite the arrogant assumption that the reformists themselves should be the judges of the Czech history, the real value of the Prague Spring is the recognition that, after twenty years of abnormalization, everybody knows that the Communist bureaucratic dictatorship must go. The Czech national future is a radical departure from the Communist capitulators, from the rotten tradition of coalitions with Communists, and in a return to Europe—to democratic and humanist values. This emerging knowledge is the precious lesson of the Prague Spring: the Czechs and the Poles know from their own experience that any reformist program of the Communist party, any future glasnost, perestroika and democratization are only fraudulent maneuvers. It is not in their interest to support the new wave of Sovietization. The nations need a neutral state, a democratic republic, a humanist culture.

Democratization? No. Democracy, yes, yes.

Consequences for Soviet communism

The Soviet invasion of Czechoslovakia is proof of the impossibility of reforming communism—the most conservative, most backward and most dangerous system of modern slavery and imperialist oppression. This system was introduced into Central European countries under a mask of socialism and under a flag of defense of national interests against Nazism. Otherwise, the free countries would not have accepted the Soviet program of gradual colonization, hidden behind slogans about social justice and material progress. The transformation of democratic states into Russian gubernias was hidden behind the mask of ambitious promises to overtake America, while the actual results consisted in sinking slowly to the level of the underdeveloped countries. The Soviet system is beyond the possibility of reform because it is not just passing through a temporary, evolutionary stage. It is a fully developed system of modern despotism, totally incompatible with Western civilization. The Soviet Union is a product of the rebarbarization of industrial society. It has perfected the imperialist methods of colonial oppression exactly at the time former empires ceased to exist. Stalin succeeded where Hitler failed.

Recent European history is dominated by ideas of human rights, constitutional freedom, and respect for uniqueness in culture, ideas which are reflected in legal norms and in humanist traditions. The Soviet Communists despise these values, and every decade or so they drive their tank divisions over the remnants of European culture in the Central part of the continent. The only possible "reform" of Soviet communism would be the deliberate destruction of the current system of oppression—nothing else. The Communist system can and will collapse, but it cannot be democratized. Any policy based on a belief in Communist reforms is as fatefully wrong as the policy of Czech reformers twenty years ago.

Leszek Kolakowski once said that after the Prague Spring, Soviet Marxism ceased to be an intellectual problem and became—for Central Europe —just a question of naked power. Correct, but the contemporary paradox reaches a new level of absurdity when the reformed Czech Communists present their own failure as an attractive future for the Soviet Union and try to convince us that they initiated a promising movement toward "pluralism." (The Devil only knows what that means in the context of communism.) Today, the defeated revisionists are openly falsifying the historical evidence. All that was valuable in the short period of national rebirth was the result of forces that were challenging the Communist politbureau, the reformists' empty promises, and the deceptive "opponentura," which was supposed to tame the national will to freedom. The reformists are grossly distorting the meaning of the fateful year 1968 if they see the events as confirmation of the triumph of a future "Moscow Spring."

The sad historical reality of Central Europe does not justify such optimism, because all previous revisionist/reformist Communists have failed, and the only realistic expectation is to wait for the failure of reformism in the USSR. The last seven decades show beyond any doubt that the Soviet Communist leadership has always prevented all attempts at structural changes by violent means—the system made its own reform impossible. The power elite always postpones the changes and stabilizes the system at a new level of decay, reached after a failed reform. No democratization emulating the Prague Spring is ready for the Soviet future. A normalization, with the Polish type of internal repression, is waiting for new protagonists of Soviet reforms.

The relevance of the Prague Spring for Soviet communism lies in the successful initiatives of independent organizations which were pushing the ideas of democracy and humanism, but not in reform communism. These organizations (KAN, Social Democracy, K 231) have provided the stimuli for the future, which will emerge again in a future crisis. All organizations are as mortal as humans are, but we have good reasons for optimism, for the ideas of freedom are surviving both institutions and human beings. The reality of Soviet communism—this export of barbarism to the West—is providing Central European nations again and again with new impulses for a struggle against despotic dictatorships and for democratic institutions in open societies. Look at the evidence: the Hungarian Petofi circle, the Czech independents (KAN, Social Democrats, K 231) and Polish Solidarity are all organizational and intellectual centers, through which young intellectuals and dissatisfied workers have created an explosive atmosphere and a climate of freedom precisely because they were able to escape the control of the Communist party. True, the Hungarian example lasted only weeks, the Czech a few months, the Polish a few years, but the impact of democratic ideas has grown immensely, despite defeats, perhaps because of them. The bureaucratic dictatorships are running out of steam and a new generation will dance on their tomb.

Conclusions

1. The Prague Spring was an important historical initiative, a chance for the Czech reform Communists to influence European development and de-Stalinize socialism. The democratization program was a possible and realistic alternative in Prague, but it has failed. A reasonable, viable attempt at a Czech return to Europe has been reduced to a mere marginal note in the book of history. In the global approach, the Prague Spring appears only as an ill-timed effort of local nomenklatura against the Kremlin. It was one more failed rebellion against Sovietization in favor of "national communism." What follows from these Central European repeated failures to emancipate the nations from the comradely Russian embrace is only the certainty that the Soviet leadership is not willing to share power in the imperial provinces with the national Communist parties and will not grant larger elbow room, even in minor economic matters.

2. In the Czech national context the Prague Spring remains a source of positive traditions, and is still seen as a noble effort at national independence, a democratic state and as an effort at Europeanization of a Sovietized Russian gubernia. However, it is clear that the Communist party has become unable to lead the nation toward such goals, because

the era of abnormal normalization has disqualified this institution from future claims of leadership. The Communist party has always been a criminal institution betraying national and state interests, but that role was not obvious to most Czechs, including democrats, humanists and liberals. Now, emancipation from the Communist myth is complete, and the future belongs to the groups which will follow in the footsteps of the independent clubs (KAN), of Social Democracy, and the Polish Solidarity movement. The future development of the Czech state will inherit the same problems which the Soviet intervention interrupted: the need for democratic, not just democratizing procedures; the vital importance of demilitarization of state territory by some kind of neutrality, and the absolute necessity to stop Sovietization—and not just replace it with a more liberal one. The Prague Spring is dead—long live the Prague Spring!

3. In Prague, the reformist program has no future. An attempt to repeat it by following Gorbachev would be a farce. With the invasion in 1968, the Soviets performed a disgusting abortion on a nascent democracy that was ready to emerge from the womb of a national body. They have committed a crime which will not be forgotten even if "Doctor" Gorbachev would offer himself as a benevolent father willing to conceive a new life. The Communists, Czech or Russian, reformed or not, Stalinists or de-Stalinized, are no more capable of conceiving life; they are only routine killers of the innocent and defenseless fetuses of democratic movements. In Prague, and in Moscow as well, the reformists can only exhume the corpses of their abortions. They can produce their new illusions, but they cannot find the strength which would generate historical relevance for a program of reform communism. The Prague Spring is as dead as the project of reforming communism in Moscow, which will be aborted sooner than we might expect. Why? Because the newly appointed historical committees which are supposed to reevaluate the Soviet attitude toward the invasion of Czechoslovakia will follow Gorbachev's Party line, and not the truth, when they start rummaging in the old luggage of the Prague Spring. Perhaps it might help them discover what Max Eastman, an American representative at the Third International, said more than half a century ago:

"I am on the side of the Soviets and the proletarian class struggle. But I think that critical truth speaking is an element of that struggle essential for its success."

A Brief History
of Czechoslovakia

A Brief History of Czechoslovakia

400 B.C.
The territory of today's Czechoslovakia is settled by Celts—the first people whose name is known among many that had inhabited the region since the stone age. *Boii*—the Latin name of a Celtic tribe residing in the region—gives the name to Bohemia.

1st century A.D.
Germanic tribes move to the territory. The Romans build a string of forts in Southern Slovakia and Moravia to defend their territories against Germans.

4th to 6th centuries
First Slavic tribes move to Central Europe from their original settlements in Northeastern Europe. Bohemia belongs among the Westernmost Slavic settlements.

623
Western Slavs are united under the leadership of Samo who leads them in victorious battles against Avar invaders and later against the Franks.

8th and 9th centuries
Slavic tribes on the territory of Bohemia and Moravia are Christianized by missionaries. In the 9th century, Bohemia, Moravia and Slovakia are united in the Great Moravian Empire.

863
Cyril and Methodius, the Greek missionaries, come to Moravia at the invitation of the ruler of the Great Moravian Empire and give the Western Slavs their alphabet.

10th century
After the disintegration of the Great Moravian Empire, Slovakia is overrun by Magyars; Bohemia and Moravia are incorporated into the Holy Roman Empire. St. Wenceslaus, the first great Bohemian ruler, acknowledges himself the vassal of the Holy Roman Empire.

1198
Premysl Ottocar I is crowned king of Bohemia and the royal title becomes permanently attached to the crown.

1253-78
Premysl Ottocar II extends the territory of Bohemia through conquest to the Oder River in the North and to the Adriatic Sea in the South.

1310
John of Luxembourg is elected king of Bohemia.

1346-1378
The rule of Charles IV, emperor of the Holy Roman Empire, marks the golden age of Bohemia. Charles rules from Prague, transforming Prague into a major European cultural center.

1348
Charles University, the oldest university in Central Europe, is founded in Prague.

1356
Charles's Golden Bull permanently establishes the kings of Bohemia as electors of the emperor.

1415
At the end of the reign of Wenceslaus IV, Charles's incompetent son who has been stripped of the emperor's crown by electors, Bohemia finds itself in the middle of a major economic, political and religious crisis. John Huss, a religious reformer who is strongly influenced by the teaching of Wycliffe and who has a large following in Bohemia, is tried as a heretic at the Council of Constance and is burned at the stake.

1415-1436
Bohemia becomes the center of the Hussite movement that seeks to reform the Catholic church. The Hussite wars—partly civil and partly against

invaders—ravage the country. In 1434, a decisive clash between two major branches of the reform movement—radical Taborites and moderate Utraquists—takes place, and the Taborites are defeated. The Utraquists return to the communion with the Roman Catholic church and establish Utraquism as the national religion in Bohemia.

1436-1526

Emperor Zigmund, king of Hungary, is crowned Czech king in 1436. Jiri of Podebrad, a Czech noble, is Czech king from 1458 to 1471. The Polish king, Ladislaus II Jagiello rules in Bohemia from 1471 to 1526. The period is marked by disorders. In 1487, nobles secure for themselves vast privileges and, in fact, institute serfdom.

1526

The accession of Archduke Ferdinand (later Emperor Ferdinand I) marks the beginning of the Hapsburg domination of Bohemia that will end in 1918. Ferdinand introduces Jesuits into Bohemia, further deepening the unstable religious situation.

1567

The Bohemian Brethren, a Czech Protestant movement, along with the Lutherans, win from Maxmillian II equality with the Utraquists.

1583-1612

Rudolf II, who became emperor in 1576, rules from Prague.

1609

Rudolf II is forced to grant freedom of religion by issuing the so-called Letter of Majesty.

1618

Emperor Mathias disregards the Letter of Majesty, and his action starts a revolt by Protestants. Two imperial councilors are thrown out of the window of Prague Castle (Defenestration of Prague, 23 May 1618). Mathias's son Ferdinand II is declared deposed and Frederick the Winter King is elected king of Bohemia. The revolt is a signal for the beginning of the Thirty Years War.

1620

Frederick and Protestant nobles are crushed in the battle of the White Mountain by the Catholic armies of Ferdinand II. Protestants in Bohemia become the target of severe persecution. Their leaders are executed, and many flee into exile. The Thirty Years War lays Bohemia waste. Its population is greatly reduced. Forced re-Catholicization begins.

1648
The Peace of Westphalia ends the Thirty Years War. A number of measures are enacted that start forcible Germanization and institute further economic plundering in Bohemia.

1749
Empress Maria Theresa (1740-1780) introduces German as the sole official language of Czechoslovakia and suppresses the separate chancellery at Prague. Her son Joseph II (1780-1790) continues the campaign of Germanization.

1781
Serfdom is abolished in Bohemia. Joseph II issues The Patent of Tolerance which provides for extensive freedom of religion.

1785
Serfdom is abolished in Slovakia.

Late 18th century
The revival of Czech nationalism begins. The Czech language is resurrected and slowly returns to towns and cities. A similar process occurs in Slovakia.

1848
Czechs participate in the 1848 revolution, voicing nationalist and autonomist demands. Frantisek Palacky, a Czech historian and politician, leads the Czech delegation at a Slavic Congress in Prague during the revolution. In June 1848, an uprising in Prague is suppressed by the Hapsburg army.

1849-1853
Prague is kept in a state of siege which is declared in 1849 after an unsuccessful uprising.

1867
The Austro-Hungarian Monarchy is established. Czechs are excluded, their autonomist aspirations ignored.

1879

Vienna makes concessions to the Czechs. Czech delegates enter the parliament in Vienna.

1918

At the end of World War I, under the guidance of Tomas G. Masaryk, and with the help of American President Woodrow Wilson, Czechoslovakia is established as an independent state. The new democratic republic is composed of Czechs, Slovaks (who gain independence from Hungary) and large ethnic minorities, among them over 3 million Germans. Masaryk becomes president of Czechoslovakia.

1918-1938

Czechoslovakia is a democratic country whose standard of living is among the highest in the world. In foreign policy, the country's primary ally is France. Czechoslovakia also signs the so-called Little Entente, a defense pact with Yugoslavia and Romania. In the 1930s, Czechoslovakia becomes a temporary haven for refugees from Naziism.

30 September 1938

Without Czechoslovakia being invited, Adolf Hitler succeeds in Munich in extorting from France and Great Britain an agreement to the secession of so-called Sudetenland—areas in Czechoslovakia inhabited predominantly by Germans. The Munich agreement is intended to appease Hitler who has complained of the ethnic oppression of Germans by Czechs. Sudetenland is occupied on 1-2 October.

15 March 1939

Hitler occupies the rest of Bohemia, creating the so-called protectorates of Bohemia and Moravia. He grants autonomy to Slovakia, which is proclaimed independent on 14 March.

9 May 1945

Prague is liberated by Soviet troops while Americans, who had arrived in Western Bohemia at the beginning of May, wait at Pilsen—adhering to earlier agreements between Stalin and Western leaders.

May 1946

Communists, boosted by the Soviet liberation of Czechoslovakia, win 38 percent of the vote. President Benes accepts Klement Gottwald, a Communist, as prime minister. Communists also get several other key ministries. A network of Soviet agents in the country becomes extensive.

25 February 1948

Communists seize power shortly before scheduled elections that they seem certain to lose. They eliminate the opposition and become the sole rulers in the country. The economy is nationalized. Gottwald becomes president following Benes's death.

1949-1956

The period of Stalinism is marked by political trials and harsh oppression in Czechoslovakia. A number of people are executed, thousands are sent to prison. (The exact number of victims of the terror is still unknown.)

1953

Workers revolt in Pilsen.

1956

Following Khrushchev's speech at the XXth Congress of the Soviet Communist Party, a gradual thaw follows in Czechoslovakia.

1965

Economic reform is accepted by the Communist leadership after the failure of a five-year economic plan.

1967

The economic reform is enlarged. Several speakers at the Congress of Writers' Union voice radical demands for the end of censorship and criticize the past. In the fall, students march in Prague, demanding changes.

The Chronology of 1968 Events

JANUARY

5 January

Alexander Dubcek replaces Antonin Novotny as Party leader and expresses the intention of the leadership to go ahead with extensive reforms.

24 January

Eduard Goldstuecker becomes chairman of the Writers' Union. His appointment is the confirmation of the Union's nonconformist course started in 1967. *Literarni noviny,* the newspaper of the Union banned in 1967, is relaunched.

29-30 January

Dubcek travels to Moscow to discuss his new course with Leonid Brezhnev, the Soviet leader.

FEBRUARY

The leadership of the Communist party gives a green light to the enlargement of the economic reforms of 1967.

Journalists, students and writers appeal for an amendment to the Press Law of 1966 with the aim of terminating censorship.

MARCH

Public rallies are held in Prague and other cities and towns in support of reform policy.

A number of independent organizations and groups are established and reestablished, such as the Club of Former Political Prisoners (K-231), the Group for the Resumption of Activity by the Social Democratic Party, and the Boy Scouts.

Demands are raised to rehabilitate the victims of the illegalities of the previous era, especially of the 1950s.

Censorship crumbles as it is ignored first by *Prace*, then by a number of other publications.

22 March

Novotny resigns as president. A number of officials connected to the previous era resign or are recalled.

23 March

The Communist leadership participates in a meeting of Communist parties in Dresden where the new Czechoslovak course is severely criticized.

30 March
General Ludvik Svoboda is elected president of Czechoslovakia.

APRIL

The Czechoslovak Socialist Youth (CSM) organization begins to fall apart, and a number of independent youth associations come into existence.

The Federation of Engine Crews forms an independent union.

Regional CPCS conferences demand that an extraordinary Party Congress be held.

5 April
The Action Program of the Communist party is published. It outlines the scope and pace of change to be followed and calls for extensive "democratization" of the political and economic system.

18 April
A new government is formed under Oldrich Cernik.

26 April
A group of workers from Ostrava issues an appeal for the creation of Workers' Committees for the Defense of the Freedom of the Press.

MAY

A number of new independent groups come into existence, among them the Club of Committed Non-Partisans (KAN) and the Society for Human Rights.

An extraordinary Party Congress is scheduled for 9 September.

The element of "self-management" councils in enterprises is added to the reform.

1 May
The May Day celebrations show huge support for the new cause.

4-5 May
The Czechoslovak leaders embark on a to visit Moscow, where the

Soviet leadership expresses its dissatisfaction with developments in Czechoslovakia.

29 May
A number of high Soviet military officials visit Czechoslovakia to lay the groundwork for Soviet military exercises. The next day, a first contingent of Soviet soldiers arrives in Czechoslovakia.

JUNE

18 June
Changes in Party statutes are discussed.

20-30 June
A Soviet military exercise is held, and the Soviet troops remain on Czechoslovak territory after its completion.

26 June
Censorship is officially abolished.

27 June
Two Thousand Words manifesto is published. It demands thorough democratization, removal of dogmatics and the reestablishment of the Social Democratic Party. The political leadership rejects the manifesto. Conservatives in the Party proclaim the manifesto counterrevolutionary.

JULY

4-6 July
Letters containing warnings are sent to the Czechoslovak Communist party by the Hungarian, German, Polish, Bulgarian and Soviet leaderships.

15 July
The Soviet Union, Hungary, Poland, the GDR and Bulgaria meet in Warsaw. Dubcek's leadership refuses to attend, but the Czechoslovak leadership does offer to meet with the leaders of the five countries in Czechoslovakia.

29 July-1 August
Negotiations are held between the Presidiums of the Czechoslovak Communist party and the Soviet Communist party in Cierna nad Tisou.

31 July
East Germany, Poland, Hungary and the Soviet Union announce that their troops will hold military exercises near the Czechoslovak border.

AUGUST

In a series of meetings, Czech leaders meet with Walter Ulbricht, Janos Kadar, Josif Broz Tito and Nicolae Ceascescu. Kadar warns Dubcek of the danger of an invasion.

3 August
The Warsaw Pact summit meeting (without Romania) is held in Bratislava. The meeting brings about a seeming "reconciliation."

20-31 August
Czechoslovakia is invaded by the armies of five Warsaw Pact members during the night of 21 August. Dubcek and other leaders are taken to Moscow and forced to sign a document in which they renounce parts of the reform program and agree to the presence of Soviet troops in Czechoslovakia. The invasion is defined as "fraternal help" against the forces of "counterrevolution." An extraordinary Party Congress is held in Vysocany, voicing support for reforms and abducted leaders. On 31 August, the Central Committee of the Communist party accepts Soviet diktat.

After the Prague Spring

18 October 1968
The National Assembly formally legalizes the intervention. The Soviet troops are to remain stationed "temporarily" on the territory of Czechoslovakia.

28 October
Czechoslovakia is formally federalized. The country now has two federal republics Slovakia and Bohemia (Czech lands).

16 January
Jan Palach, a Charles University student, sets himself on fire in protest against the occupation and the gradual abandonment of the reform course. His death sparks huge demonstrations.

17 April 1969
Dubcek resigns under pressure and is succeeded by Gustav Husak. Husak's appointment begins the era of "normalization," at the beginning of which censorship is revived, and progressive magazines and theaters closed. A number of books soon to be published are destroyed. Borders are closed.

January 1970
Premier Cernik is ousted.

December 1970
Purges of the Communist party cost 400,000 people their Party cards and in most cases their jobs too. More than 150,000 have left the country since the invasion.

1972
More than forty people who were prominent during 1968 are jailed on subversion charges.

January 1977
Over 200 people sign a manifesto called Charter 77 in which they demand that the Czechoslovak leadership observe international human rights agreements to which it is a signatory, and restore legality in the country. (Since 1977, Charter 77 has issued hundreds of documents and the number of its signatories has grown to almost 2,000.)

1979
Several leaders of Charter 77, and of Charter's offshoot, the Committee for the Defense of Unjustly Prosecuted, including dramatist Vaclav Havel, are sentenced to long prison terms.

1987
Several leaders of the Jazz Section of the Czechoslovak Union of Musicians are jailed. The Section, publishing uncensored materials, is suppressed. A group of workers from Moravia writes to President Husak asking him to step down. Democratic Initiative, an independent movement, is founded.

December 1987
Milos Jakes replaces Gustav Husak in the position of the general secretary of the Communist party, and the Central Committee of CC ap-

proves economic reform in the form of a new Law on Socialist Enterprises.

January 1988
Over 300,000 Czechoslovak Catholics and sympathizers sign a petition in which they demand more religious freedom.

March 1988
Catholics organize demonstrations in Prague and Bratislava.

Biographies

Jiri Hochman

Born in Plzen in 1926, Jiri Hochman was one of the best known Czechoslovak political journalists during the 1960s and especially during the Prague Spring. From 1950 to 54 Hochman was a correspondent for *Obrana lidu,* and from 1955 until 1969 a correspondent and commentator for another daily, *Rude pravo.* As a foreign correspondent he was stationed in Cuba, Switzerland, France, the U.S. and China. He has interviewed Mao, Khrushchev, Nasser, Nehru, Ben Bella, Boumedienne, Che Guevarra, Castro and many other world figures. In 1968-69, Hochman was an editor of *Reporter,* a weekly eventually banned by the authorities. At the beginning of the period of "normalization" Hochman worked as a manual laborer and was later imprisoned. In 1974 he emigrated to the United States and earned a Ph.D. in history. He currently teaches at the Ohio State University School of Journalism in Columbus. He is the author of several books of interviews and travel, and of novels. His latest books include *Jeleni brod (A Deer Ford,* Koln, 1971); *Cesky happening (The Czech Happening,* Toronto, 1978); and *Vsechno bylo jinak, vsechno je jinak, vsechno bude jinak (Everything Was Otherwise, Everything Is Otherwise, Everything Will Be Otherwise,* Zurich, 1979).

Frantisek Janouch

Born in Lysa, Czechoslovakia, 1931, Frantisek Janouch graduated from the University of Leningrad with a degree in theoretical physics, and later received a Ph.D. from the University of Moscow and Charles University in Prague. Until 1970 he was head of the Department of Theoretical Nuclear Physics at the Institute of Nuclear Physics of the Czechoslovak Academy of Sciences in Prague and assistant professor at Charles University. He was a member of the European Physics Society's Executive Committee. In 1970 Janouch was dismissed from his positions and forbid from publishing in Czechoslovakia. In 1974 he left the country at the invitation of the Swedish Royal Academy of Sciences in Stockholm. He was a professor at the Niels Bohr Institute in Copenhagen, and is presently active at the Research Institute of Physics in Stockholm. Professor Janouch is the author of numerous articles and studies in nuclear theory, weak interactions, nuclear reactions, and radioactivity. He has lectured in Europe, the U.S. and Asia and has been a visiting professor at several universities. He has published a number of popular and political articles as well as several books, among them *Letters from Czechoslovakia; No, I Don't Complain;* and *Dialogues with Arnost Kolman.* He is a member of the Swedish PEN Club and the Swedish Writers' Union. Professor Janouch is the founder of the Charter 77 Foundation in Stockholm. In 1983 he was awarded the U.S. Open Society Prize.

Eva Kanturkova

Born in Prague in 1930, Eva Kanturkova lives in Czechoslovakia where she is known as one of the most prominent dissident writers and human rights activists. In 1949-1950 Kanturkova worked as an editor of *Mlada fronta,* a newspaper of the Union of Czechoslovak Youth, and later in the aparat of the Union. In 1956 she graduated from the School of Philosophy and History at Charles University in Prague. In 1966-67 she worked for the directorate of the Czechoslovak Book Culture organization. Since 1967 she has devoted herself to writing. In 1977, Kanturkova signed Charter 77 and eventually served as one of the Charter's spokesmen. In 1980 Kanturkova was accused of sedition and detained in Ruzyne prison for eleven months. She was eventually released for lack of evidence. She is the author of numerous articles, essays and books, among them *Smutecni slavnost (The Funeral Celebration,* Prague, 1967), *Pozustalost pana Abela (The Inheritance of Mr. Abel,* Prague, 1971-destroyed; Koln, 1977); *Cerna hvezda (The Black Star,* Prague *samizdat,* 1974); *Pan veze (The Master of the Tower,* Prague, *samizdat,* 1978). Her book based on her prison experience, *My Companions From the Bleak House,* was published by Overlook Press, New York, in 1987. She is also the author of two film scripts, one of which, *The Funeral Celebration,* was made into a film in 1968-69 but never officially released.

Jan Kavan

Born in London in 1946, Jan Kavan is a son of a Czechoslovak diplomat and an English teacher. His family moved to Czechoslovakia in 1950. In political trials at the beginning of the 1950s, Kavan's father was sentenced to twenty-five years imprisonment. From 1964 to 1968 Kavan was a student at the School of Journalism of Charles University in Prague. At the same time he became a member of a group known as "the Prague Radicals" and became known as one of the most prominent student leaders. From 1966 to 1968 he held high positions in the Union of Czechoslovak Youth, and in 1968-1969 was vice-president for International Affairs of the National Union of Students of Bohemia and Moravia. The organization was banned in 1969. In 1969, while studying in Oxford, England, Kavan decided to stay abroad. From 1970 to 1974 he was a student of International Relations at the London School of Economics. In 1975 Kavan founded Palach Press agency and became the editor of *Palach Press Bulletin.* In 1985 he was elected vice-president of the East European Cultural Foundation and became an editor of the *East European Reporter.* Kavan has written a number of articles and essays for magazines and newspapers in the United States, the U.K. and Czechoslovakia. He has lectured extensively in Europe and the United States and is the author of *Socialist Opposition in Czechoslovakia* (London, 1976), and co-editor of *Voices of Czechoslovak Socialists* (Merlin Press, 1977), and *Voices from Prague* (London, 1983).

Antonin J. Liehm

Born in 1924 in Prague, Antonin Liehm was educated at Charles University in Prague. In 1945 he founded a Czech cultural weekly, *Politics of Culture.* Later he worked for the Press Section of the Czechoslovak Ministry of Foreign Affairs and for the Czechoslovak Press Agency. In 1961 he became a member of the editorial board and foreign editor of *Literarni noviny,* the weekly journal of the Czechoslovak Writers' Union. In 1968-1969 *Literarni noviny* was one of the most outspoken publications, and Liehm was known as one of the most prominent pro-reform journalists in Czechoslovakia. From the fall of 1968 until the spring 1969, Liehm was a representative of Czechoslovak Film in Paris. In 1969 he organized a show of Czechoslovak films at the International Film Festival in Cannes. In September 1969 Liehm refused to return to Czechoslovakia. He has taught at the Universities of Paris, New York, and Pennsylvania. Currently, Liehm teaches at the Ecole des Hautes Etudes en Sciences Sociales in Paris. He is the editor of the European intellectual journal *Lettre Internationale,* published in Paris, Madrid and Berlin. He is the author of several books. Among his English titles are *Politics of Culture, Closely Watched Films, Milos Forman Stories, The Most*

Important Art (Film in the USSR and in Eastern Europe after 1945).
He edited (with Peter Kussi) *The Writing on the Wall.*

Jiri Loewy

Born in 1930 in Rumburk, Czechoslovakia, Loewy became the editor of
a daily, *Straz severu,* and regional secretary of the Social Democratic
Youth Organization in Liberec, Northern Bohemia in 1947. After the Communist putsch in 1948, Loewy was fired from his job and persecuted.
He was active in the resistance movement as a member of UKM—the
underground committee of Social Democratic Youth. He was arrested in
November 1948 and sentenced to six years imprisonment. For more than
three years he was a forced laborer in the uranium mines of Jachymov.
From 1955 to 1967 Loewy held a variety of jobs in cotton mills in Northern Bohemia. From July 1967 until August 1969 he was a press officer
with the Cotton Industry in Hradec Kralove. During the Prague Spring
he was the editor-in-chief of the bulletin *B-express,* a press organ of the
Cotton Industry. In August 1969 Loewy and his family fled to Austria
and later settled in Wuppertal, West Germany. He has been employed
by Enka, a Dutch-German company, as a copy writer, press officer and
editor. Since 1978 he has been the publisher and editor of the Czech
exile magazine *Pravo lidu.* He holds several positions in the Central Executive Committee of the Czechoslovak Social Democratic Party in exile.

Jiri Pehe

Born in Rokycany, Czechoslovakia in 1955, Pehe defected to the West
in 1981. Educated in Czechoslovakia and the United States, Pehe studied
law and philosophy at Charles University in Prague where he earned
a doctorate in 1980. In 1985 Pehe earned an M.A. degree in International
Affairs from Columbia University in New York. In Czechoslovakia Pehe
worked as an editor of *Kulturni prace* magazine. He also wrote on film
and the theatre, and he published poetry and short stories in magazines
and in *samizdat.* In 1981 his paper on the totalitarian nature of communism
was unofficially distributed in Prague. In 1985 Pehe joined the staff
of Freedom House where he is currently director of East European Studies.
Pehe has written and lectured frequently on East European affairs. His
articles have appeared in the *New York Times,* the *Wall Street Journal,*
the *International Herald Tribune, Freedom at Issue, Pensamiento Centro
Americano* and other publications. Pehe's essay in this book is an adaptation
of a lecture he delivered at the Wilson International Center for Scholars
in Washington, D.C.

Radoslav Selucky

Born in 1930, Selucky studied political economics at the State University in Leningrad in 1949-1952 and completed his studies at the Prague School of Economics in 1953. He earned a doctorate from the same school in 1961. In 1953 Selucky was expelled from the Communist party for his criticism of Stalinism. After 1956 he taught political economics at Prague Technical University. In 1960 he was readmitted to the Communist party. However, for his critical articles on the command economy Selucky was fired from his job and banned from working in his field. From 1964 to 1968 he worked for the Czechoslovak Film Board. From November 1967 until April 1968 he was an advisor to Josef Smrkovsky, one of the chief reformers, and in April-November 1968 he was an advisor to the government. During 1968 he participated in drafting documents for the XIVth Party Congress. Starting in June 1968 he worked as a senior research associate at the Sociological Institute of the Czechoslovak Academy of Sciences in Prague. In 1969 Selucky was a fellow of the Ford Foundation in New York, and in 1970 visiting professor at the University of South Carolina. Since September 1970 he has been professor of political science at Carleton University in Ottawa, Canada. He is the author of a number of books, studies and essays published in Czech, English, Italian and German, among them *Czechoslovakia: The Plan That Failed* (London, 1972), *Economic Reforms in Eastern Europe* (New York, 1972) *Marxism, Socialism, Freedom* (London and New York, 1979), and *East is East* (Cologne, 1972).

Vladimir Skutina

Born in 1931 in Prague, Vladimir Skutina graduated from the Film and Television Institute of the Academy of Arts in Prague and from the School of Psychology at Charles University. Prior to 1969 he had published fifteen books of humor and written scripts for 150 television programs. In 1968-69 Skutina was one of the most outspoken and popular TV personalities in Czechoslovakia. At the beginning of the era of "normalization" that followed the Soviet invasion of Czechoslovakia, Skutina became the first political prisoner; he was sentenced to four and a half years imprisonment. In 1977 he signed Charter 77. Since 1979 he has been living with his family in Zurich, Switzerland. He was awarded the Mark Twain Prize for Humor and is the recipient of the Olympic Gold Medal for Literature. Two of his television comedies have received the Golden Rose Award at Montreaux. *The Driver and Death*, a film based on his novel, won the Grand prize at the International Film Festival at Carlsbad. Skutina is particularly well-known in Western Europe as the author of a fifty-two-part TV series "The Criminal Laboratory." He is a member of the German-Swiss PEN Center. Skutina's essay in this book is a translated excerpt from a special issue of *Reporter*, a Czech emigre magazine which is published by Skutina in Switzerland.

Josef Skvorecky

Born in Nachod, Czechoslovakia in 1924, Josef Skvorecky is an internationally renowned writer. From 1943 to 1945 Skvorecky worked as a forced laborer in a German-controlled factory. From 1945 to 1949 he was first a student at the School of Medicine at Charles University in Prague and later a student of English and Philosophy at the same university. After his graduation Skvorecky taught at a high school. In 1951 he earned a Ph.D writing his dissertation on Thomas Paine. From 1953 until 1963 he was an editor at Odeon, a publishing house in Prague. In 1956-58 he was also an editor of *Svetova literatura*, a literary bimonthly. From 1963 until his departure from Czechoslovakia in 1969, Skvorecky was a freelance writer. He was one of the most outspoken writers during the period of cultural thaw that preceded the Prague Spring and during the Prague Spring itself. The publication of his book *Zbabelci (The Cowards)* in 1964 was not only a source of great irritation to the authorities but marked the first real breakdown in the system of Stalinist censorship. Since 1969 Skvorecky and his writer-wife Zdena Salivarova have lived in Toronto, Canada, where they founded and run a Czechoslovak emigre publishing house, Sixty-Eight Publishers, Corp. Since 1969 Skvorecky has taught at the University of Toronto. Skvorecky is the author of numerous articles, essays and books. His novels include *Legenda Emoke (The Legend Emoke*, Prague, 1963); *Konec nylonoveho veku (The End of the Nylon Age*, Prague, 1968); *Tankovy prapor, (Tank Corps*, Toronto, 1971); *Mirakl (The Miracle*, Toronto, 1972); *Pribeh inzenyra lidskych dusi (The Engineer of Human Souls*, Toronto, 1977); and *Dvorak in Love* (New York, 1987). Skvorecky's books have been translated into all major languages. Skvorecky is also the author of several film scripts, and of books on film and jazz. He is the recipient of several international literary prizes.

Ivan Svitak

Born in 1925 at Hranice in Moravia, Svitak was a forced laborer during World War II. In 1949 he graduated from the School of Law of Charles University in Prague, and in 1953 from the School of Political and Social Sciences in Prague. Starting in 1954 he lectured in philosophy at Charles University and was a member of the Czechoslovak Academy of Sciences. He became a leading protagonist of Humanist Marxism. In 1964, he was expelled from the Academy for his writings; however, he had been effectively silenced by the authorities five years prior to his expulsion. In 1965-68 Svitak was employed by the Film Institute in Prague. Svitak was one of the leading intellectual forces during the Prague Spring. During that period, he organized the New Democratic Left, independent of reform communism, and published a number of influential articles and essays for which he was attacked by the Russian press. After the Soviet invasion Svitak was deprived of his citizenship and sentenced to eight years imprisonment *in absentia*. In 1968-70 he was a visiting scholar at the School of International Affairs of Columbia University in New York, and since 1970 he has been teaching philosophy at California State University in Chico. Svitak is the author of numerous books, among them *The Czechoslovak Experiment 1968/69* (New York, 1971), *Man and His World* (New York, 1970), *The Dialectics of Common Sense* (Washington, 1970) and *Unwissenschaftliche Anthropologie* (Frankfurt, 1972).

Pavel Tigrid

Born in 1917, Pavel Tigrid studied law in Prague. As a student he founded a theater group in Prague and was an editor of a student magazine. In 1939 he went to London where he worked as a Czech announcer at the BBC and later editor of the radio broadcast of the Czechoslovak government in exile. Also during the war, he published (with Walter Berger) *Kulturni zapisnik* and *Review 42*. After the war Tigrid worked first at the Ministry of Foreign Affairs in Prague and later was the editor (with Ivo Duchacek) of two weeklies, *Obzory* and *Vyvoj*. After the Communist putsch Tigrid remained abroad. He was a contributor to *Neue Zurcher Zeitung* and the *Irish Times*. He founded the Committee for Czechoslovak Refugees and organized the Czechoslovak department of Radio Free Europe. He was a program director of the Czechoslovak department until 1952 when he resigned and went to the United States where he studied at Columbia University. He has lectured on Eastern Europe in a number of U.S. cities. In 1956 Tigrid founded *Svedectvi*, a quarterly which eventually became the most influential Czech emigre magazine. Through *Svedectvi* and other media, Tigrid became one the most influential intellectual figures in Czechoslovakia whose democratic ideas and analyses of totalitarianism influenced the Czechoslovak intellectuals of the 1950s and 1960s and were a source of irritation for Communist authorities. Tigrid is the author of several books, among them *Marx na Hradcanech (Marx at Hradcany,* New York, 1960); *La chute irrésistible d'Alexander Dubcek* (Paris, 1969); and *Révoltes ouviéres á l'Est* (Brussels, 1981).

Otto Ulc

A lawyer and political scientist by education and profession, Otto Ulc is among the most popular Czech emigre writers. Born in Plzen, Czechoslovakia in 1930, Ulc was an assistant judge from 1953 to 1956, and from 1956-1959 a district judge in Czechoslovakia. He left the country in 1959. After earning a Ph.D. in political science at Columbia University in 1964, he became a professor of political science at the State University of New York at Binghamton, where he specializes in international law and politics; comparative government; Communist systems; and nation building and political development. Ulc served as consultant for the Department of State; Foreign Service Institute; and Frost & Sullivan, World Political Risk Forecasts. In 1978, he was an adviser to the Premier of Cook Islands. He is the author of many books, among them *The Judge in a Communist State* (Columbus, 1972); *Politics in Czechoslovakia* (San Francisco, 1974); *Mala doznani okresniho soudce (Judicial Confessions,* Toronto, 1974); *Nas clovek na Ceylone a v Indii (Our Man in India,* Toronto, 1976); *Antinostalgicum* (Toronto, 1977); and *Bez Cedoku po Pacifiku (Pacific Explorations,* Toronto, 1980). Ulc has written a number of articles for American political science magazines and has contributed to different volumes of edited political science literature. He is also a co-editor of and a regular contributor to *Zapad/The West,* an interdisciplinary Czech bimonthly magazine published in Canada. The data mentioned in his article are excerpted from a survey—part of an ongoing project (a study of new forms of dissent) for which the author received and gratefully acknowledges a research grant from the American Council of Learned Societies.

Jan Vladislav

Born in Hlohovec, Czechoslovakia, 1923, Vladislav studied foreign languages and comparative history of literature at the University of Grenoble in France and at Charles University in Prague. After the Communist putsch in 1948 he was expelled from the university on political grounds and it was not until 1969 that he had the opportunity to complete his studies and be awarded a Ph.D. at Charles University. From 1945 to 1948 Vladislav published three books of poetry and contributed critical essays to different journals. After 1948 he was prevented from publishing his own works and devoted himself to translating. He published translations of classical poetry and, later, when the political conditions permitted, translations of works by modern European poets. In 1968-69 a number of new original works by Vladislav were ready for publication, in particular the poetry books *Soliloquies* and *Sentences*, and the collection of essays *Portraits and Self-Portraits*. After the 1968 occupation, publication of his books was forcibly halted; they were issued in the 1970s as *samizdat*. In the mid-1970s Vladislav founded and ran the *samizdat* series *Kvart* in which he published over one hundred different editions including poetry, essays and novels, by both Czechoslovak authors and foreign authors. He was one of the first signatories of Charter 77. In 1981 he was deprived of his Czechoslovak citizenship and forced to emigrate to France. He currently lectures at the Ecole des Hautes Etudes en Sciences Sociales in Paris. He is the author of numerous essays on literature, art and cultural policy, which have been published in Czech, English and German. He is a member of the editorial board of the journal *L'Autre Europe*.

NOTES

Jiri Hochman, pp. 27-40

1. *Novinar* nos. 11-12; the Protocols of the Fifth Congress of the Union of Journalists, 19-20 October 1967 (not published); also, *Rude pravo*, 21 October 1967, p. 2.

2. Private source.

3. Ibid.

4. Hradecky was removed from his position as chief editor of *Reporter* in March 1968, but remained one of its editors. He supported the liberal line of the weekly sincerely and actively. During the invasion, he edited a special edition, and he reassumed the position of chief editor in October 1968. In the most difficult period between the invasion and April 1969, Hradecky showed courage and perseverance. He was expelled from the Party and from the Union in 1970 and was blacklisted until his retirement.

5. A realistic description of this aspect of the Czech reform movement of 1968 can be found in Zdenek Mlynar, *Ceskoslovensky pokus o reformu* (Czechoslovak attempt at reform of 1968) (Cologne: INDEX, 1975), p. 202.

6. H. Gordon Skilling, *Czechoslovakia's Interrupted Revolution* (Princeton: Princeton University Press, 1976), p. 571.

7. Ibid., p. 191.

8. Drafted by the writer Ludvik Vaculik, the manifesto called for public initiative in defense of the reforms. It was published simultaneously in three Prague dailies and in Vaculik's own weekly, *Literarni listy*, on 27 June 1968. Thousands of people added their signatures. The manifesto was described as a "counterrevolutionary" document by the Russians.

9. Pierre Broue, *Le Printemps des peuples commence a Prague; Essai sur la revolution politique en Europe de l'Est* (Paris: Gerard Bloch, 1970); *Ecrits a Prague sous la censure, aout 1968-juin 1969* (Paris: EDI, 1973).

10. *Listy* no. 2 (1974): pp. 8-12.

11. Ibid.

12. *Novinar* no. 1 (1987): p. 4.

Radoslav Selucky, pp. 41-51

1. J. Pelikan, ed., *The Secret Vysocany Congress* (London: Penguin Press, 1971), pp. 112-115.

2. K. Marx, "Economic and Philosophic Manuscripts of 1844," in Marx-Engels, *Collected Works* (New York: International Publishers, 1975), vol. 3, p. 247.

3. In his letter to Bernstein of 25 October 1881, Engels explains that Marx was the author of the draft program of the French Workers' Party: "Its preamble was dictated (to Guesde) word for word by Marx in the presence of Lafargue and myself right in my room." Engels calls this formulation from which I have quoted

the introductory sentence, "a masterpiece of cogent argumentation rarely encountered and couched in a few words for the masses..." See Marx-Engels, *Selected Correspondence* (Moscow: Progress Publishers, 1965), p. 344.

4. "The Communist Manifesto," in Marx-Engels, *Selected Works in One Volume* (New York: International Publishers, 1970), p. 52.

5. Cf., Karel Kovanda, "Czechoslovak Workers' Councils (1968-1976)," in *Telos* no. 28 (Summer 1976): pp. 48-49.

6. Ibid., p. 51.

Jan Kavan, pp. 103-129

1. For a detailed report on the trial of Rudolf Slansky and others, see *The Czechoslovak Political Trials 1950-54* (London: MacDonald, 1971). For my mother's account of the trial and her life in Czechoslovakia, see Rosemary Kavan, *Love and Freedom* (New York: Farrar, Straus and Giroux, Inc., 1988).

2. Quoted from Jan Kavan, "David a Golias," *Student* no.11 (13 March 1968).

3. The "as if game"—the Party pretends that its ideological terms correspond to reality and the people pretend that they believe it, thus everybody acts as if the ideological facade had some meaning. The system is excellently described by Vaclav Havel in *The Power of the Powerless* (London: Hutchinson, 1985).

4. Quoted from Jan Kavan and Helena Klimova, "Jak ty bylo s temi vysokoskolaky," *Literarni listy* no. 2 (3 July 1968).

5. Quoted from Lubos Holecek, Helena Klimova and Jiri Muller, "Studenti a moc" (Students and power)—manuscript prepared for publication in Prague 1968 but banned shortly after the invasion.

6. Jiri Muller, *Host do domu* vol. 16, no. 8: pp. 20-24, quoted in *Voices of Czechoslovak Socialists* (London: Merlin Press, 1977), p. 5.

7. From speech by Lubos Holecek, quoted in Jan Daniel and Jan Kavan, *Socjalistyczna opozycja w. Czechoslowacji* (London: Polonia Book Fund, 1975), p. 18.

8. "Conversation with Jaroslav Sabata" quoted in an extract to be published in *East European Reporter* vol. 3, no. 3 (1988).

9. From *samizdat* circulated in Prague, June 1969, distributed through the worker-student alliance. See Galia Golan, *Reform Rule in Czechoslovakia* (Cambridge: Cambridge University Press, 1973), p. 290.

10. *Rude pravo*, 19 November 1968.

11. Report on Josef Smrkovsky's speech, prepared and circulated by the student press agency TAISS; also author's private archive.

12. Golan, *Reform Rule in Czechoslovakia*, p. 258.

13. From a report from the student press agency TAISS; also author's private archive.

14. Report prepared immediately after the meeting by SVS Bohemia and Moravia (student union) and made available to student officials. Quoted in Jan Ka-

van, "The Legacy of Jan Palach," *Listy* (1979); also the author's private archive.

15. Ibid.

16. Quoted from Ivan Hartel and Jan Kavan, "The Real Value of Jan Palach's Legacy," *The Times*, 19 January 1978.

17. *Studentské listy* no. 1 (1969); also author's private archive.

18. Ibid.

19. Jan Kavan, "The Legacy of Jan Palach."

20. *Voices of Czechoslovak Socialists* (London: Merlin Press, 1977), p. 7.

21. Quoted from "Pravda Vitezi," special issue of the *Bulletin of the Committee to Defend Czechoslovak Socialists* (August 1973); also author's private archive.

22. Translated from "Provolani ideologicke komise Revolucni Socialisticke Strany (ceskoslovenska)" which appeared in *samizdat* in August 1969. See also *Les Textes de l'opposition révolutionnaire* (Maspero, 1970).

23. One of these organizations is the Jan Palach Information and Research Trust, a U.K.-registered charity. Information available on request from the JPIRT, P.O. Box 222, London WC2H 9RP.

24. Jiri Pelikan, *Socialist Opposition in Eastern Europe, The Czechoslovak Example* (London: Allison and Busby, 1976), pp. 136-137; also author's private archive.

25. "Pravda Vitezi," special issue of the *Bulletin*; also *The Observer* (August 1972), and author's private archive.

26. *Labour Focus on Eastern Europe* vol. 2, no. 6 (January-February 1969): p. 5.

27. For the full text, see G. Skilling, *Charter 77 and Human Rights in Czechoslovakia* (London: George Allen and Unwin, 1981), pp. 209-212; also *Palach Press Bulletin* (1977).

28. Ibid.

29. Tom Stoppard, "Prague: the Story of the Chartists," *New York Review of Books* (4 August 1977).

30. Interview with Vaclav Havel by a Dutch journalist, 1986.

31. For books, I would recommend Gordon Skilling, *Charter 77*, especially for a detailed analysis of the origins and first four years of Charter 77; for articles, my own "The Czechoslovak Opposition," Part II, *Poland Watch* no. 6: pp. 123-144 (describes the main political trends of the first seven years).

32. *Charter 77* document no. 13/86; Letter to the Milan Forum, *Palach Press Bulletin* no. 27 (November 1986); *East European Reporter* vol. 2, no. 1 (1986).

33. The Prague Appeal was signed by 64 Czechs and Slovaks and circulated by Charter 77 as a discussion document (*Charter 77* document no. 5/85). *Palach Press Bulletin* no. 26 (October 1985); *East European Reporter* vol. 1, no. 1 (1985).

34. The Memorandum "Giving Real Life to the Helsinki Accords," published

as a booklet by the European Network for East-West Dialogue and in *East European Reporter* vol. 2, no. 2 (1986).

35. Janos Kis, "Can We Have a Joint Programme?" *East European Reporter* vol. 2, no. 4 (1987).

36. Paul Edwards interviews Vaclav Havel: "Why East and East Must Meet...," *East European Reporter* vol. 3, no. 2 (1988).

37. Ibid.

38. Petr Uhl's letter to a press conference organized by the International Helsinki Federation in Vienna to launch the joint CO Appeal: extracts published in *East European Reporter* vol. 3, no. 2 (1988).

39. Ibid.

40. Vaclav Havel, "Why East and East Must Meet..."

41. *Krytyka* no. 8 (1981).

42. A joint statement by activists of independent movements in Poland and Czechoslovakia—Prague, Warsaw, Wroclaw, Brno, Bratislava, 6 July 1987. English translation available from Palach Press, London.

43. From a joint statement issued at a border meeting and dated 21 August 1987. *Palach Press Bulletin* no. 29 and *East European Reporter* vol. 3, no. 1 (1987).

44. *East European Reporter* vol. 3, no. 1 (1987).

45. "The Hungarian Appeal: A Milestone in Cooperation"—Paul Edwards talks to Ferenc Koszeg and Miklos Haraszti, *East European Reporter* vol. 2, no. 3 (1986).

46. Ibid.

47. Ibid.

48. For the full text of the CO Appeal and a list of signatories, see *East European Reporter* vol. 3, no. 2 (1988); ditto for the text and signatories of the appeal on behalf of GDR activists.

49. *The Guardian*, 22 March 1988.

50. Vaclav Havel, "Why East and East Must Meet..."

51. Ibid.

51. Ibid.

52. Ibid.

54. The EECF depends on voluntary donations and grants. It has been fund-raising primarily in the U.S., partly with the help of its sister organization, the East European Cultural Endowment Ltd., a U.S.-registered charity. Information about the work is available from Jiri Wyatt, EECF (U.S.), P.O. Box 0327, New York, NY 10024.

55. Adam Michnik, "Gorbachev, Glasnost and Perestroika," *East European Reporter* vol. 2, no. 4 (1987).

56. Vaclav Havel, "Why East and East Must Meet..."

Otto Ulc, pp. 143-155

1. Rome-based bimonthly *Listy* (December 1985): pp. 28-32.

2. *Rude pravo*, 26 June 1984.

3. According to *Mlada Fronta*, 29 October 1982, p. 7.

4. *Rude pravo*, 29 September 1983, pp. 1-2.

5. *Rude pravo*, 10 March 1984, p. 3.

6. Bratislava's *Pravda*, 14 March 1984, p. 4.

7. *Tvorba*, 26 May 1982, p. 3.

8. Such are the recommendations of *Socialisticka Skola* (May 1977).

9. *Obrana lidu*, 14 January 1984.

10. According to the state press agency CTK, 28 October 1983.

11. Cf., V.V. Kusin, "How Many Czechs and Slovaks Believe in Socialism?" *Radio Free Europe Situation Report* no. 14 (27 July 1982): pp. 5-7.

12. English text in *Survey* (Summer 1985): pp. 167-190.

13. "Pribeh a totalita," written in April 1987 and published in the Paris-based quarterly *Svedectví* no. 81: pp. 21-43.

Jiri Pehe, pp. 157-169

1. An interview in *Le Monde*, 19 January 1979.

2. *A Besieged Culture* (Stockholm and Vienna: Charter 77 Foundation and International Federation for Human Rights, 1985), p. 133.

3. Ibid., p. 81.

4. Ibid., p. 101.

5. Ibid., p. 81.

6. Ibid., p. 102.

7. Peter Kusi and Antonin J. Liehm, *The Writing on the Wall* (Princeton: Karz-Cohl Publishing, Inc., 1983).

8. From the "Open Letter to Dr. Husak, President of the Republic," *Encounter* (September 1976).

9. *A Besieged Culture*, p. 101.

10. *The Paris Review* (Fall 1984).

11. *A Besieged Culture*, p. 55.

12. *Index on Censorship* (October 1986).

13. *Index on Censorship* (July 1986).

14. *The New York Times*, 27 August 1987.

15. *Listy* (February 1987).

16. *Index on Censorship* (October 1986).

17. *Politics and Conscience* (Stockholm: The Charter 77 Foundation, 1986).
18. Ibid.
19. Ibid.
20. Ibid.
21. Ibid.
22. *A Besieged Culture*, p. 56.
23. Ibid, p. 106.
24. Ibid, p. 136.
25. *The New York Times Magazine*, 23 October 1987.
26. *O Lidskou Identitu* (London: Svedectvi-Edice Rozmluvy, 1984).

Index

Index

FREEDOM HOUSE BOOKS

YEARBOOKS

Freedom in the World: Political Rights and Civil Liberties,
Raymond D. Gastil; annuals for 1978, 1979, 1980, 1981, 1982,
1983-84, 1984-85, 1985-86, 1986-87, 1987-88.

STUDIES IN FREEDOM

1. Strategies for the 1980s: Lessons of Cuba, Vietnam, and Afghanistan,
Philip van Slyck; 1981.
2. Escape to Freedom: The Story of the International Rescue Committee,
Aaron Levenstein; 1983.
3. Forty Years: A Third World Soldier at the UN,
Carlos P. Romulo (with Beth Day Romulo); 1986. *(Romulo: A Third
World Soldier at the UN,* paperback edition, 1987.)
4. Today's American: How Free?
James Finn & Leonard R. Sussman, (Eds.); 1986.
5. Will of the People: Original Democracies in Non-Western Societies,
Raul S. Manglapus; 1987.

PERSPECTIVES ON FREEDOM

General Editor: **James Finn**

1. El Salvador: Peaceful Revolution or Armed Struggle?,
R. Bruce McColm; 1982.
2. Three Years at the East-West Divide,
Max M. Kampelman; (Introductions by Ronald Reagan and Jimmy
Carter; edited by Leonard R. Sussman); 1983.
*3. The Democratic Mask: The Consolidation
of the Sandinista Revolution,*
Douglas W. Payne; 1985.
4. The Heresy of Words in Cuba: Freedom of Expression & Information,
Carlos Ripoll; 1985.
5. Human Rights & the New Realism: Strategic Thinking in a New Age,
Michael Novak; 1986.
6. To License A Journalist?,
Inter-American Court of Human Rights; 1986.
7. The Catholic Church in China,
L. Ladany; 1987.
8. Glasnost: How Open? Soviet & Eastern European Dissidents; 1987
9. Yugoslavia: The Failure of "Democratic" Communism; 1987
10. The Prague Spring: A Mixed Legacy
Edited by Jiri Pehe, 1988

FOCUS ON ISSUES

*1. Big Story: How the American Press and Television Reported and
Interpreted the Crisis of Tet-1968 in Vietnam and Washington,*
Peter Braestrup; Two volumes 1977;
One volume paperback abridged 1978, 1983.
2. Soviet POWs in Afghanistan,
Ludmilla Thorne; 1986.
3. Afghanistan: The Great Game Revisited,
edited by Rossane Klass; 1988
4. Nicaragua's Continuing Struggle: In Search of Democracy,
Arturo J. Cruz; 1988